CLASS IN CULTURE

Series in Critical Narrative
Edited by Donaldo Macedo
University of Massachusetts Boston

Now in print
The Hegemony of English
    by Donaldo Macedo, Bessie Dendrinos, and
    Panayota Gounari (2003)
Letters from Lexington: Reflections on Propaganda
New Updated Edition
    by Noam Chomsky (2004)
Pedogogy of Indignation
    by Paulo Freire (2004)
Howard Zinn on Democratic Education
    by Howard Zinn, with Donaldo Macedo (2005)
How Children Learn: Getting Beyond the Deficit Myth
    by Terese Fayden (2005)
The Globalization of Racism
    edited by Donaldo Macedo and Panayota Gounari (2005)
Daring to Dream: Toward a Pedagogy of the Unfinished
    by Paulo Freire (2007)
Class in Culture
    by Teresa L. Ebert and Mas'ud Zavarzadeh

Forthcoming in the series
Dear Paulo: Letters from Teachers
    by Sonia Nieto

CLASS IN CULTURE

Teresa L. Ebert

Mas'ud Zavarzadeh

Paradigm Publishers
Boulder • London

Paradigm Publishers is committed to preserving our environment. This book was printed on recycled paper with 30% post-consumer waste content, saving trees and avoiding the creation of hundreds of gallons of wastewater, tens of pounds of solid waste, more than a hundred pounds of greenhouse gases, and using hundreds fewer kilowatt hours of electricity than if it had been printed on paper manufactured from all virgin fibers.

All rights reserved. No part of the publication may be transmitted or reproduced in any media or form, including electronic, mechanical, photocopy, recording, or informational storage and retrieval systems, without the express written consent of the publisher.

Copyright © 2008 Paradigm Publishers

Published in the United States by Paradigm Publishers, 3360 Mitchell Lane, Suite E, Boulder, CO 80301 USA.

Paradigm Publishers is the trade name of Birkenkamp & Company, LLC, Dean Birkenkamp, President and Publisher.

Library of Congress Cataloging-in-Publication Data is available

Hardcover ISBN: 978-1-59451-314-5
Paperback ISBN: 978-1-59451-315-2

Printed and bound in the United States of America on acid free paper that meets the standards of the American National Standard for Permanence of Paper for Printed Library Materials.

12 11 10 09 08   1 2 3 4 5

To Collective Work

Jennifer Cotter
Kimberly DeFazio
Robert Faivre
Amrohini Sahay
Julie Torrant
Stephen Tumino
Rob Wilkie

Contents

The Public Theorist (a preface)   ix

Acknowledgments   xxii

Part 1   All That Is Cultural Is Real—All That Is Real Is Cultural

1. Getting Class Out of Culture   3
2. Class Binaries and the Rise of Private Property   47

Part 2   Tracing Class

3. Class Is   89
4. Abu Ghraib and Class Erotics   96
5. Class and 9/11   104
6. Eating Class   110
7. The Class Politics of "Values" and Stem-Cell Funding   114
8. Abortion Is a Class Matter   120
9. E-Education as a Class Technology   126
10. Gender after Class   134
11. The Class Logic of *A Beautiful Mind*   150

Part 3   Class Ecstasies of the Culture of Capital

12. A "Potlatch of Signs"—Burning, Consuming, Wasting   167

Bibliography   195

Index   217

About the Authors   221

The Public Theorist

(a preface)

Class is everywhere and nowhere. It is the most decisive condition of social life: it shapes the economic and, consequently, the social and cultural resources of people. It determines their birth, healthcare, clothing, schooling, eating, love, labor, sleep, aging, and death. Yet it remains invisible in the every day and in practical consciousness because, for the most part, it is dispersed through popular culture, absorbed in cultural difference, obscured by formal equality before the law or explained away by philosophical arguments.

Class in Culture attempts to trace class in different cultural situations and practices to make its routes and effects visible. However, the strategies obscuring class are cunning, complex, and subtle, and are at work in unexpected sites of culture. Consequently, this is not a linear book: it surprises class in the segments, folds, vicinities, points, and divides of culture. It moves, for example, from Abu Ghraib to the post-deconstructive proclamations of Antonio Negri, from stem cell research to labor history, from theoretical debates on binaries to diets. It is also written in a variety of registers and lengths: in the vocabularies of theory, the idioms of description and explanation, as well as in the language of polemics, and in long, short, and shorter chapters. Regardless of the language, the plane of argument, the length of the text, and the immediate subject of our critiques, our purpose has been to tease out from these incongruous moments the critical elements of a basic grammar of class—one that might be useful in reading class in other social sites.

Our text on eating, for example, unpacks two diets that, we argue, reproduce class binaries in the zone of desire. The point here is not only when one eats, one eats class, but also class works in the most unexpected corners of culture. Eating as a sensuous, even sensual corporeality, is seen as the arena of desire which is represented in the cultural imaginary as autonomous from social relations. Desire is thought to be exemplary of the singularity of the individual and her freedom from material conditions. One desires what one desires. Desire is the absolute lack: it is the unrepresentable. We argue, however, that one desires what one can desire; one's desire is always and ultimately determined before one desires it, and it is determined by one's material (class) conditions. Our point is not that individuality and singularity are myths but that they are myths in class societies. Individuality and singularity become reality—not stories that culture tells to divert people from their anonymity in a culture of commodities—only when one is free from necessity beyond which "begins that development of

(a preface)

human energy which is an end in itself' (Marx, *Capital* III, 958-59). Class is the negation of human freedom.

A theory of class (such as the one we articulate) argues that class is the material logic of social life and therefore it determines how people live and think. But this is too austere for many contemporary critics. ("Determinism" is a dirty totalizing word in contemporary social critique.) Most writers who still use the concept of class prefer to talk about it in the more subtle and shaded languages of overdetermination, lifestyle, taste, prestige, and preferences, or in the stratification terms of income, occupation, and even status. These are all significant aspects of social life, but they are *effects* of class and not class.

This brings us to the "simple" question: What is class?

We skip the usual review of theories of class because they never lead to an answer to this question. The genre of review requires, in the name of fairness, "on the one hand, on the other hand" arguments that balance each perspective with its opposite. The purpose of *Class in Culture* is not review but critique—not a pluralism that covers up an uncommitted wandering in texts but an argument in relation to which the reader can take a position leading to change and not simply be more informed.

This is not a book of information; it is a book of critique.

To answer the question (what is class?), we argue—and here lies the austerity of our theory—class is essentially a relation of property, of owning. Class, in short, is a relation to labor because property is the congealed alienated labor of the other. By owning we obviously do not mean owning just anything. Owning a home or a car or fine clothes does not by itself put a person in one or another class. What does, is owning the labor power of others in exchange for wages. Unlike a home or a car, labor (or to be more precise "labor power") is a commodity that produces value when it is consumed. Structures like homes or machines like cars or products such as clothes do not produce value. Labor does. Under capitalism, the producers of value do not own what they produce. The capitalist who has purchased the labor power of the direct producers owns what they produce. Class is this relation of labor-owning. This means wages are symptoms of estranged labor, of the unfreedom of humans, namely the exploitation of humans by humans—which is another way to begin explaining class.

To know class, one has to learn about the labor relations that construct class differences, that enable the subjugation of the many by the few. Under capitalism labor is unfree, it is forced wage-labor that produces "surplus value"—an objectification of a person's labor as commodities that are appropriated by the capitalist for profit. The labor of the worker, therefore, becomes "an object" that "exits *outside him*, independently, as something alien to him, and it becomes a power on its own confronting him" which, among other things, "means that the life which he has conferred on the object confronts him as something hostile and alien" (Marx, *Economic and Philosophic Manuscripts of 1844*, 272). The direct producers' own labor, in other words, negates their freedom because it is used, in part, to produce commodities not for need but for exchange. One, therefore, is made "to exist, first, as a *worker*; and, second as a *physical subject*. The height of this servitude is that it is only as a *worker* that he can maintain himself as a *physical subject*, and that it is only as a *physical subject* that he is a worker" (273). Under wage labor, workers, consequently, relate to their own activities as "an alien activity not belonging to [them]" (275). The estranged relation of people to the object of their labor is not a local matter but includes all spheres of social life. In other words, it is "at the same time the relation to the sensuous external world, to the objects of nature, as an alien world inimically opposed to [them]" (275).

The scope of estrangement in a class society, of human unfreedom caused by wage labor, is not limited to the alienation of the worker from her products. It includes the productive activity itself because what is produced is a "summary of the activity, of production," and therefore it is "manifested not only in the result but in the *act of production*, within the *producing activity* itself" (274). The worker, in the act of production, alienates herself from herself because production activity is "active alienation, the alienation of activity, the activity of alienation" (274)—an activity which does not belong to her. This is another way of saying that the activity of labor—life activity—is turned against the worker and "here we have *self-estrangement*" (275).

In his theory of alienated labor, Marx distinguishes between the "natural life" of eating, drinking, and procreating which humans share with other animals and the "species life" which separates humans from animal. This distinction has significant implications for an emancipatory theory of classless society. "Species life" is the life marked by consciousness, developed senses, and a human understanding himself in history as a historical being because "his own life is an object for him" (276)—humans, as "species beings," are self-reflexive. To be more clear, "conscious life activity distinguishes man immediately from animal life activity" (276). The object of man's labor is the actualization, the "objectification of man's species-life" (277). Alienated labor, however, "in tearing away from man the object of his production, therefore, …tears from him his *species-life*" (277). Consequently, "it changes for him the *life of the species* into a means of individual life…it makes individual life in its abstract form the purpose of life of the species, likewise in the abstract and estranged form" (276). This is another way of saying that the larger questions that enable humans to build their world consciously are marginalized, and sheer biological living ("individual life in the abstract") becomes the goal of life in class society structured by wage labor. "Life itself appears only as a *means to life*" (276). Class turns "species life" into "natural life."

Since society is an extension of the sensuous activities of humans in nature (labor), the alienation of humans from the products of their labor, from the very process of labor, which is their life activity, and from their species-being, leads to the estrangement of humans from humans (277)—the alienation in class societies that is experienced on the individual level as loneliness. In confronting oneself, one confronts others; which is another way of saying that one's alienation from the product of one's labor, from productive activity, and from "species life" is at the same time alienation from other people, their labor, and the objects of their labor. In class societies, work, therefore, becomes the negation of the worker: he "only feels himself outside his work, and in his work feels outside himself" (274).

Ending class structures is a re-obtaining of human freedom. Freedom here is not simply the freedom of individuals as symbolized, for instance, in bourgeois "freedom of speech" but is a world-historical "freedom from necessity" (Marx, *Critique of the Gotha Programme*). Class struggle is the struggle for human emancipation by putting an end to alienated labor (as class relations). Alienated labor is the bondage of humans to production: it is an effect of wage labor (which turns labor into a means of living) and private property (which is congealed labor). Emancipation from alienated labor is, therefore, the emancipation of humans from this bondage because "all relations of servitude," such as class relations, "are but modifications and consequences" of the relation of labor to production (Marx, *Economic and Philosophic Manuscripts of 1844*, 280).

Class, in short, is the effect of property relations that are themselves manifestations of the alienation of labor as wage labor. Wage labor alienates one from one's own product, from oneself, from other humans, and, as Marx put it, "estranges the *species* from man" (276).

Owning labor power or being a person whose labor power is owned divides people into only two classes: workers and owners. Those who live by wages and those who live off the profits made from the labor of those who live by wages. In our chapter "Class Is," we explain why there is no middle in this binary and how the "middle class" is more an ideological illusion than an objective class relation. At the end of the first chapter, we also argue that the views expressed by such writers as Michael Hardt and Antonio Negri (*Multitude*)—in which capitalism is now seen as a knowledge regime in which labor has become immaterial and therefore there are no rigid binaries that separate workers from owners—are themselves a class theory that normalizes the class interests of owners.

So are the theories of Jacques Derrida whose writings have contributed greatly to the disappearing of class in contemporary social and cultural critique. Derrida takes a path different from the social analysis of Hardt and Negri. Through epistemological critique and extensive textual analysis, he attempts to make the materialist theory of class as the binaries dividing owners and workers impossible by rendering the very idea of a "binary" relation (owners/workers) a symptom of a will-to-truth: a residue of the metaphysics presence. In other words, he diverts analytical attention away from the economic (class) to the rhetorical and epistemological. Consequently, discussion of class is transformed into the *possibility* of discussing class, a move that has been joyfully embraced by the global North Left—which seems more concerned about essentialism than exploitation and happily substitutes talk about binaries for analysis of class. As we argue at length in chapter two, binaries do not make class, class makes binaries. Or, to put it more directly, binaries are not effects of some metaphysics of presence but the transformation of production practices and the rise of private property.

Derrida's formally subtle, erudite, and at times (when he is not in a conceptual free fall as, for example, in his *Specters of Marx*) rigorous arguments in the end are mostly ecstatic repetitions of the banalities of capital's cultural imaginary which is structured by in-between-ness and hybridity. His textualizing of class is not limited to the thematics of his writings. Like all formalists, most of his influence on contemporary cultural critique derives from his style of writing. His style is marked by a high-writing that weaves a self-reflexive humor into itself, frames its often dangling assertions in an elegant and verbally entertaining aleatory structure, and is itself a class practice. Like Joyce whom he admires, his is a style that teaches social disengagement through a self-reflexive engagement with writing: it shifts attention away from the "why" (the dialectics) of writing to the "how" (the representational technologies) of writing. It involves the reader in the poetics of textuality rather than the economics of what makes such a poetics possible and necessary at certain historical moments. It is, however, a sign of the stubborn facts of history that in order to make his aesthetics credible, his writing are a mimesis of all the signs of textual activism: *Politics of Friendship, Of Hospitality, Philosophy in a Time of Terror,* and, of course, *Specters of Marx.* His texts remain mostly supple semiotic structures whose signifiers are always in search of signifieds—a search, we might add, that Derrida has already declared to be spectral. His activism is aimed not so much at changing reality but at blurring its boundaries with the virtual and thus again raising the epistemological questions about the spectral, thereby shifting the debate from the real to its textual virtuality—its missing presence. The elegance of his writings conceals the way they are bearers of particular class interests; it has impressed many cultural writers and even more academics and thus influenced social and cultural analysis. We examine his writings in detail in various contexts throughout this book because they are exemplary of the most learned and complex writerly strategies used to obscure class. Reading Derrida carefully is necessary for understanding the blissful ecstasies by which contemporary cultural theorists have so aggressively attacked class and declared its death. Derrida is too subtle to do that himself, but his writings have taught others how to do the dirty work for capital.

We discuss not only Derrida's writings (which we think are key to understanding the disappearance of class from recent cultural critique), but also extensively analyze contemporary theoretical arguments and philosophical debates about culture, language, (in)determinacy, subjectivity, singularity, and representation. We believe that without a serious examination of these issues and the way they have been refigured in recent cultural theory, it would be difficult, if not impossible, to understand why class is obscured in culture and how to regrasp it in everyday social life. Why is knowledge of class so aggressively silenced? What does such class knowledge do to the existing social relations? Equally important, what makes people contribute to its disappearance, distortion, and conversion into cultural values, thus erasing it from everyday social life? Unless one understands why and through what kinds of "arguments" class is declared dead (Pakulski and Waters, *The Death of Class*), its absence from social debates will be seen as a natural part of the advent of what is advertised as knowledge capitalism and the development of immaterial labor. There is, of course, nothing natural about the vanishing of class since it is forced out of sight by the discursive violence of the culture of capital.

Class in Culture is the first book in a trilogy on class; the other two are *Hypohumanities*, which engages class and the transformation of education into "training" in the age of free trade, and *Markets of Affect*. *Class in Culture* attempts to produce a new class critique that moves away from social stratification theories, the cultural studies of class, activist journalism (e.g., the *New York Times's Class Matters*), the textual analysis of class, and other discussions of class that focus on class only to translate it into some of its effects (income, lifestyle, policy, tropes...) and hollow out the materialist sense of class as relations of property and exploitation. Instead of simply offering a theory of class in its own terms, we think it will be more productive to tease out such a theory in terms of existing debates and arguments by critiquing some of the most influential interpretive strategies that are being deployed to obscure class and relating them to the actual history of labor and capital.

At the center of our theory of class is a binary analysis of the two "great hostile camps...two great classes directly facing each other: Bourgeoisie and Proletariat" (Marx and Engels, *Manifesto of the Communist Party* 41). Any discussion of class divisions along a binary line is perhaps the most difficult part of talking about class in the U.S. today because it brings to the surface the dirty secret of the every day, one that everyone knows but no one likes to acknowledge: that is, divisions, distinctions, and discrimination. Talking about class is facing the fact that class societies, such as this one, which make a huge point of representing themselves as democratic, are democratic in name only. Democracy, first and foremost, is not about freedom of speech, equality before the law and human rights but about freedom from necessity—when all people's needs are met and no one is left alone to fight for subsistence. Contemporary democracies, such as the U.S., are unfree: they are class societies founded on fundamental and unbridgeable material divisions through which a small minority subjugates the majority by owning and controlling their labor, their livelihood. The goal of these societies is not providing material conditions under which all people's needs are met, but simply offering people an equal opportunity to earn a living. People are free to work (i.e., to be exploited), but even here there are restrictions because freedom to work is contingent on whether work is available, and the availability of work is determined not by human needs but by profit (what is called the law of supply and demand but has nothing to do with demand because unprofitable demands always go without being supplied). This is another way of saying equality of opportunity, is an ideology for reducing class antagonism by offering everyone a formal and empty opportunity. "Equality of opportunity" actually means equality of being exploited—an opportunity to provide surplus value.

Any writing about class has to take a side on these issues if it is not going to hide behind "neutral scholarship" or does not trivialize class, either by turning it into a list of occupations and an index of income (Esping-Andersen, ed., *Changing Classes: Stratification and Mobility in Post-Industrial Societies*) or by using it to mean such things as "the American status system," as Paul Fussell does in his popular *Class*. In other words, class writing has to go beyond description to explain the existing and increasing divide between people and not take easy refuge in difference, heterogeneity, singularity, equality of opportunity, and other cultural mythologies of capital.

Writing about class is unlike writing about any other cultural and social issue because it involves the writing itself: writing about class is itself a class practice. This is another way of saying that writing about class is always an intervention. He who says he is on no one's side is almost always on the side of the class in dominance, as is he who takes sides opportunistically. The practices of Edward Said are exemplary of both. He confined the global to the workings of the local, and by isolating the question of Palestine, for example, from the international class struggles, reduced it to matters of identity. He never allowed it to be related to the logic of capitalism or even the larger question of the "Middle East," which is itself an effect of the relations of capital, labor, and resources. He not only did not relate the question of Palestine to capitalism in its imperialist stage, but he subtly supported capitalism and its political and economic regime; he simply wanted more inclusion. His reduction of the global to the local and then mapping the local in its narrowest terms were not limited to Palestine. In the classroom he insisted, for example, that literature be taught in the most local aesthetic terms and global issues of class and politics never be introduced:

> I do not advocate, and I am very much against, the teaching of literature as a form of politics. I think there is a distinction between pamphlets and novels. I don't think the classroom should become a place to advocate political ideas. I've never taught political ideas in a classroom. I believe that what I'm there to teach is the interpretation and reading of literary texts. (Said, "The Pen and the Sword: Culture and Imperialism" 65)

Class critique that matters is interventionist: it explains in order to change. Avoiding intervention is avoiding the fact that contemporary society is based on the (unacknowledged) institution of exploitation of humans by humans and becoming a collaborator with that practice. To intervene is, of course, risky because it connects what capital disconnects as a way of clouding the material logic at work in all social practices and representing it as merely an ad hoc local operation. Connecting and intervening put one on a blacklist. As a marked person, one is in many ways like class itself—invisible but well known, to be avoided, denied access to the main social resources, and exiled to the margins of the margins. Although writing on power rather than class, Timothy Brennan, in remembering Edward Said, alludes to some of these issues:

> What struck me very early and has remained with me since was that jovial ease you seemed to have in the company of the privileged and the powerful.... Remember that time...we talked about Aijaz Ahmad's book...? [Ahmad] simply

(a preface)

could not fathom how someone could be feted and flattered and, at the same time, a problem to power.... In fact, throughout your career you embodied this very dilemma: Is it possible to be inside and outside at the same time? There is a nobility to absolute noncompliance that you could never appreciate, I think. So long as they are not of the majority...intractable positions usually lead to ostracism. You, Edward, managed to avoid that reaction, but I was not always clear how you managed it. How did you get away with all those acerbic jabs in conversation, or in some of the more angry confrontations in print with people...? Why didn't these remarks put you in the camp of the untouchables?... I am sure that many quietly wonder whether you didn't cheat a little by managing to live comfortably while playing the iconoclast.... There are also people who wonder whether your improbable middle road was cleared by cutting corners, stroking unsavory friends, keeping silent at opportune times.... ("Resolution" 411-412)

No doubt the fear of marginalization is one of the reasons class is absent in contemporary social critique, and when it does become visible, it appears as such innocuous components of social life as lifestyle: how, for example, the "working class lads," who wear expensive Armani cashmere "jumpers" (sweaters), "resist the demands of a conventional working-class masculinity which insists they renounce the sissy or classy meanings associated with such jumpers" (McRobbie, *Postmodernism and Popular Culture* 34). In the sense that McRobbie uses class (as consuming lifestyle), it is not taboo; it is in fact quite diverting and very popular. It is becoming more and more popular because capitalism is quite flexible in accommodating new forms of masculinities, femininities, races, sexualities, and abilities (Zavarzadeh, "The Pedagogy of Totality"). As capitalism becomes more advanced in its social relations of production, all such identities and cultural differences as age, sex, gender, and race become irrelevant to its continuity. The only thing that capitalism depends on for its existence is cheap labor power, which is another way of repeating what Marx and Engels have already stated, namely that for capitalism all people, regardless of their cultural differences, "are instruments of labor, more or less expensive" (*Manifesto of the Communist Party* 53).

Marx's writing on class and capital is sided scholarship that is structured within a theoretically militant polemic. In our discussion of the role of the CIA in recruiting Left intellectuals in support of free enterprise, we outline how the CIA taught a generation of scholars and academics (who are now the ideological gatekeepers of the academy and publishing houses) how to protect capitalism from dangerous class writings by rejecting them as outdated and polemical (i.e., not relevant to the new times and not real scholarship). That lesson is now the common sense of the academy and culture industry so much so in fact that it has become a self-evident argument: in scholarly conferences and on the editorial boards of journals and publishing houses, it is enough to call a text "polemical" to justify its rejection without further explanation. Polemics is, of course, not the issue—class is (Ebert, "Manifesto as Theory and Theory as Material Force: Toward a Red Polemic"). The same people who dismiss class critique because it is polemical have no problem at all praising as polemic books that support the existing social relations. J. Hillis Miller, G. Ulmer, and other contributors to *Deconstructing Derrida*, for example, have compiled an entire book in praise of "Jacques Derrida's polemic" on the humanities. Confronting the stubborn historical realities of class, the putative sophistication of cultural theory collapses, and it concludes, like all vulgar writing, that class polemic = bad, while polemic on behalf of capital = good.

However, the Left, in order to obtain social credibility and cultural relevance, has found a way around the dangerous class. It substitutes race, gender, sexuality, nationality, and other cultural identities for class and talks, for example, about how class is "experienced" through race (Butler, "Merely Cultural"). But objective historical reality always prevails. With the growing awareness of the material realities of the contemporary, there is an increasing recognition that the analytics of race, sexuality, and nationality cannot explain the existing global reality: intellectuals may leave class alone but class will not leave intellectuals alone. This has led to more interest in class. However, fear of class is at work here too because the idea of class used in recent social and cultural critique is itself heavily culturalized: class is made safe by translating it from an explanatory concept into an indeterminate cultural meaning that is always in play. In her *Class, Self, Culture*, Beverley Skeggs turns class into an effect of value and completes the process that we describe as the substitution of the cultural for the material by arguing that culture is itself a form of property.

The culturing of class is broadly based on the writings of Max Weber whose theory of class evolves around life chances in the market ("Class, Status Party" 180-95). But class, we argue, is a property relation; this means class differences are produced at the point of production where surplus labor is extracted from workers and not in the market. The market does not produce wealth; it simply distributes what is produced elsewhere, and the elsewhere is where labor power produces surplus labor.

Weber's theory of class underlies the views of class in what we call the "cultural turn," which is the discursive apparatus for the evasion and disappearing of class in contemporary social critique. The cultural turn is a structural feature in capitalism (and other class societies) by which the class contradictions of capitalism are dissolved into cultural values, and the economic interests of the owners are represented as the universal cultural values of all classes. Free enterprise itself, for instance, is depicted not as a particular regime of labor with a specific history but as a manifestation of instinctive human yearning for freedom. "Cultural turn," as we use the concept in this book, does not mean what is usually designated by this term: namely the turn to culture that emerged in the late 1960s under the influence of new social movements and a turning away from science, especially scientific methods, toward a culturalist theory of the history of science and cultural interpretations of the social (e.g., Feyerabend, *Against Method: Outline of an Anarchistic Theory of Knowledge* and Kuhn, *The Structure of Scientific Revolutions*). This particular historical symptom of the cultural turn reached the height of its public visibility in the scandals of the mid-1990s caused by the publication of a special issue of *Social Text* on the "science wars" under the editorships of Bruce Robbins and Andrew Ross, two Left writers who represented the anti-science cultural turn as cutting-edge reality (1-13), and afterward went into great detail to justify what had happened not as what it actually was—anti-class culture boosterism—but as a brave activist undertaking (Robbins, "Just Doing Your Job: Some Lessons of the Sokal Affair").

The turn to culture represents culture as an assemblage of para-autonomous practices of "difference" that have to be "read" in their own singularities and not as elements of a totality. Not only is culture no longer perceived as an effect of a materialist base, it is treated as if it is itself productive of social and economic life and a place of agency. In the cultural turn, culture is the new materiality that not only fashions the logic of the sensuous every day but also articulates public life and its networks of power and politics, and shapes the knowledge economy (Castells, *The Rise of the Network Society*). Culture, in the cultural turn, becomes everything, and everything becomes cultural. The cultural turn takes the "cultural logic" (Jameson, "The Cultural Logic of Late Capitalism") and not class as the "logic" of the social. It argues that this logic has been radically transformed through what Derrida calls, "the new realities of techno-scientificocapitalist modernity" ("Marx & Sons" 239), which have put the old concept of class and class struggle in ruins.

Class in Culture goes against these fantasies. It argues that capitalism has not changed and that there is only one logic by which the social, the cultural, the theoretical and the daily are articulated and that is the logic of production, which is also the logic of the social division of labor and thus the logic of class. Capitalism remains the same and will remain the same because any change in its fundamental structure—taking surplus labor from workers' labor power—will put an end to capitalism. What has changed is not the ontology of exploitation, without which capitalism will not survive, but the phenomenology of exploitation: how it does the exploiting and thus makes it feel different to workers according to the worker's historical situation. What was "normal" when Taylorism was the regime of daily work and shaped the experience of workers in the workplace is not normal today. Toyotaism—soft teamwork, just-in-time production—has replaced the hard para-military Taylorism. This change in phenomenology is represented as a transformation of capitalist ontology and an entire theory of social change is woven around it.

Our goal has been to go beyond the phenomenology of capitalism and contribute to a development of class consciousness not by appealing to people's "lived experience" but through a theoretical analysis that demonstrates that "This 'lived experience' is not a given, given by a pure 'reality', but the spontaneous 'lived experience' of ideology in its peculiar relation to the real" (Althusser, *Lenin and Philosophy* 223). The emphasis on "theory" in the book is grounded in the certainty that "without a revolutionary theory there can be no revolutionary movement" (Lenin, *What Is to Be Done?* 369). *Class in Culture*, therefore, is not a descriptive resignification but an explanation—a causal analysis at a time when causal relations are, like class itself, declared dead.

Most contemporary critics—not wanting to be accused of "essentialism" and "foundationalism," of unsubtle readings and vulgar materialism—have retreated from critique and instead have emphasized describing the concrete textures and surfaces of culture. In contrast, we focus our analysis on unpacking the obscured and abstract structures that actually produce the cultural concrete in the every day. We demonstrate that the textures and surfaces, the affective, the sensual and the surprises of desire, which are the main interpretive sites for contemporary cultural critics, are actually highly complex intersections of many abstract social relations. The concrete, we argue, always exceeds itself; it is always an abstract concrete whose logic is not in itself but in the structures of production and commodification [Ebert, *Cultural Critique (with an attitude)*].

To do such critical work requires abandoning the dominant codes and manners of intellectually entertaining writing. Writers on culture today protect themselves against serious thinking and commitment, which might cause the anger of the owning class and its power agents in the culture industry and academy, by writing more and more and saying less and less. Through endless qualifications within qualifications, they find more trivial differences among the familiar codes of interpretations and established habits of thought and produce what is delightful and diverting reading but critically hollow. This pleasurable writing without saying anything has come to be the mark of subtlety. It is actually what we have called "thoughtless thoughtfulness" (Ebert and Zavarzadeh, *Hypohumanities*), which is the stuff of most contemporary cultural theory and social critique.

This thoughtless thoughtfulness is, of course, not the effect of some eccentricity or personal style but the articulation of class interests. What is coded as subtlety and nuance is the self-reflexive space of retreat from the real for the subject of capital: a place where she can escape from taking sides by reproducing the dominant logic in ever more empty writings.

Writing, however, *is* an act of taking sides on social transformation. Thinking for a new and transformative critique needs to move beyond nuance and engage what Walter Benjamin, in his re-reading of Brecht, calls "coarse thinking" (*Reflections*, 193-202). "Coarse thinking" ("plumpen Denken") is a demystification of canonical cultural "subtleties" and an insistence on the coarse "totality." It is, in other words, a resistance against the localization of the social and a fragmenting of those discourses that can grasp the social totality as a world-historical effect. "Coarse thinking" is the analytic of praxis, or as Benjamin puts it, "coarse thoughts have a special place in dialectical thinking because their sole function is to direct theory toward practice" (199).

For the new cultural critique "the main thing," in Brecht's words, "is to learn coarse thinking, that is the thinking of the great" (199). The discourse of "coarse thinking" is polemical. But both "coarse thinking" and "polemic" are taboo practices in an age of the "subtle" and the "hybrid": an age whose social discourses—in the name of being open and thoughtful—do not disturb the existing order and thus let things remain the way they are. Transgression of the nuanced, the witty, and the subtle in order to say something is treated as intemperate—which, it is made clear by the practices of blacklisting, has no place in respectable cultural debates. "Coarse thinking" demonstrates that unless one becomes aware of the roots of social issues, which are almost always hidden, and does not shy away from dealing with the abstract and the conceptual, one will never grasp the social totality. Without a knowledge of social totality, one is condemned to an ephemeral, local activism.

"Coarse thinking," in its serious sense, grounds a complex public theory. However, unlike almost all books that situate themselves in public theory, *Class in Culture* is not written in a populist idiom nor is it a popularization of issues. By "populist" we mean avoiding the conceptual and instead saturating the text with recognizable details and, in the end, confirming widely held, popular convictions about the body, pleasure, singularity (individuality), and the spontaneity of experience. It is not only popular writing (TV, comic books, best-sellers...) that are populist. Cultural theory, in spite of its somewhat abstract language, is also populist writing in this sense. Both the "low populist" of daily writings and media representations and the "high populist" of cultural theory aim at the same ideological effect: the normalization of what Marcuse calls "affirmative culture" (*Negations* 95). Given the conditions of the time, we believe, that populist writing and the popularization of complex issues hurt democracy. They dumb down debates. In the name of offering user-friendly knowledge, empowerment and accessibility, they deprive citizens of the rigorous concepts and sustained arguments that are needed to combat the thinking that constitutes the governing common sense and its political regimes of truth. The populist ("high" and "low") is the reification of the common sense, which is the domain of ideology. *Class in Culture* is a critique of ideology. It is a resistance to the populist which, by jettisoning the abstract and the conceptual, leaves citizens defenseless against "the ideas of the ruling class" which are "in every epoch the ruling ideas" (Marx and Engels, *The German Ideology* 59).

Our critique is aimed at unpacking the social totality rather than simply re-describing local details and regional solutions. Reading such a critique requires some adjustments on the part of readers. The culture of commodities produces impatient consumers who bring their consuming demands to their reading. They learn to demand, before everything else, entertaining writing that makes itself immediately clear and tell the reader in twenty words or less "what" is the main point of the book and "how" it is going to be made.

Class in Culture is not about "what" or "how." It is a book about "why." Why class?

We have sought the "why" not only through immanent critiques of hegemonic arguments, which obscure class, but also, and more importantly, by relating these arguments to their outside and demonstrating that what often passes as an argument is a tissue of ideology—an expression of class interests. It is not enough to read an argument in its own terms or to offer counter-arguments and simply stop there. Such conventions of analysis keep us within the dominant discourse. It is not enough, for example, to critique Negri's argument—that capitalism has changed and imperialism has come to an end—by examining it in its own terms or by showing how the ontology of capitalism remains the same because its fundamental structure, in which the few possess the surplus labor of the many, remains the same. It is not enough to argue that imperialism is a structural feature of capitalism—as the wars in Palestine, Iraq, Afghanistan, Lebanon, and Pakistan demonstrate. Nor is it enough to offer a counter-argument to Zizek's position that classes "qua positive, existing social groups" are impossible because of the eruption of "the real." We do so. But it is more urgent, we believe, to also examine why such arguments, and their numerous variations in the writing of other critics, are received as arguments when their claims are repudiated every single day by the actual living conditions of the many. What cultural imaginary of freedom do they appeal to? How free is that freedom? These questions cannot even be raised by immanent critique, whether as argument or as counter-argument.

This is a book about class and its erasure in contemporary capitalism. But it is also, and at the same time, an ideology critique because class cannot be understood in and of itself—nothing can. Class has to be grasped in relation to the arguments and ideologies that obscure it. The outside of an argument is where the argument loses the discursive protection of the inside and begins to reveal its own class affiliations and the ideology that makes it logic appear to be logical. The critique of ideology is a crucial part of "why."

To be effective, a critique of ideology has to break the lines of common cultural associations congealed in language, especially in its more familiar idioms and structures. Avoiding customary paths, we have drawn different connecting lines. In order to bring back what is repressed by ideology, we have not hesitated to abandon another rule of rhetoric: we have repeated over and over again those subjects excluded by ideology in our efforts to reveal the "why." Why class?

Acknowledgments

Barbara Foley and Peter McLaren as always have given us critique-al and intellectual support in sharpening our arguments against what have been and remain the dominant theoretical and interpretive tendencies of the time. We have also learned from Martha Gimenez's and Leslie Hudson's knowledge, activist wisdom and courage. Lynn Worsham provided us, at a crucial time, with the intellectual space to put forth ideas that others exclude from cultural and social critique.

We would like to thank Dean Birkenkamp for his support of this project. By establishing Paradigm Publishers he has opened up a very different critical space in the U.S. publishing scene and turned publishing from a commodification of ideas to a transformative cultural project unafraid of controversy and supportive of all arguments for social change. We also wish to thank Donaldo Macedo, editor of the "Series in Critical Narrative," for his critical insights and encouragement.

Several chapters of the book are broadly based on essays by the authors that were originally published in earlier forms in various journals: chapters three and eight appeared in *The Red Critique* (No. 7, 2002, and No. 6, 2002, respectively), chapter four in *Against the Current* (March/April 2006), and chapter 6 in *The Los Angeles Times* (September 4, 2000); chapter five draws on part one of Mas'ud Zavarzadeh's "The Pedagogy of Totality" in *JAC: A Quarterly Journal for the Interdisciplinary Study of Rhetoric, Culture, Literacy, and Politics* (23:1, 2003), and chapter ten uses sections of Teresa L. Ebert's "Rematerializing Feminism" in *Science and Society* (69:1, 2005). We are grateful to the editors of these journals.

Teresa L. Ebert   *Mas'ud Zavarzadeh*

Part 1

All That Is Cultural Is Real—
All That Is Real Is Cultural

1
Getting Class Out of Culture

Class, as an explanation of social relations and the dynamics of everyday life, has more or less disappeared from contemporary social analysis, which now considers culture to be the driving force of social life and, therefore, represents society as an assemblage of cultural differences, singularities, and flows of indeterminate meanings. Class, of course, is used by many critics and theorists who readily admit that class is an important aspect of social life. However, what most of them mean by class is something innocuous, something that does not question the existing social relations dividing people into classes and determining how they live: Do they go to good schools? Do they have safe drinking water? Do they have access to health care? Do they have enough to eat? Are they happy? Most treat class divisions, which as Marx writes are among the "requirements" of capitalism, as if they were "self-evident natural laws" (*Capital* I, 899).

In contemporary discussions, class has come to mean such things as lifestyle, taste, accent, income, occupation, status, power, and prestige. These are all important features of social life, but they are effects of class. The cause of class divisions is the process of production through which the labor of some under capitalism is appropriated by others. Since production is the material basis of the social world, class is a material social relation, or to be even more specific, it is a relation of owning. Obviously, it is not owning just anything, but owning what produces more owning. Owning your own home does not make you an owner, but owning labor does because labor is "a commodity" that "possesses the peculiar property of being a source of value" (Marx, *Capital* I, 270). Owning here is a double owning: both buying the living labor of others and possessing the means of production, namely, the labor of the past. In all class societies people are reduced to what they own and, therefore, are divided into only two classes: those who purchase and therefore own the labor of others during the working day and profit from it, and the others who own only their own labor. Under capitalism, they must sell their labor for wages, which then they pay back to the owners in order to buy (depending on where in the world they live) the food, medicine, houses, cars, books, DVD's, Xboxes, etc., that they need to live, educate, and entertain themselves so they are ready and in a fairly good physical and emotional state to go back to work for the owners. Buying and owning the labor of others makes you an owner but owning a home or car or refrigerator or Xbox—which are often mentioned as a sign that nowadays everyone is an owner and there are no classes—does not make you an owner. Using the labor of others brings you profit, owning an Xbox returns your working wages back to the owners. There is no middle between the two: the middle class is an ideological illusion used to cloud class binaries and conceal the fact that under capitalism, society is breaking up more rigidly into two classes whose opposition cannot be dissolved into the hybrid of the playful in-between-ness of the middle class.

Getting class out of culture, which is the environment of everyday life, produces the illusion that there are no classes and everyone lives freely, without any constraints. It produces the myth that "you can achieve anything you want." Making class visible in everyday life, on the other hand, makes people aware that class is the enemy of human freedom because freedom is not simply freedom of speech or association, or freedom before the law, or even freedom from oppression. It is freedom from exploitation, freedom from subordination to the division of labor. This means freedom begins only with freedom from necessity, only after one's needs are met: "the true realm of freedom, the development of human powers as an end in itself, begins beyond it"—beyond "the realm of necessity" (Marx, *Capital* III, 959).

SIX WAYS OF MAKING CLASS DISAPPEAR

Class as Difference, Desire, and Affect

Human freedom, however, is no longer thought of as depending on changing the existing social relations of production and ending class. Production itself is seen as a totalizing concept (productivism) and put under suspicion not only by conservatives but also by such marxists (small "m") as Fredric Jameson (*Postmodernism or, the Cultural Logic of Late Capitalism* 406). Freedom is thus said to be obtained by working within the current system of wage-labor, along with some reforms, which are often represented as "difference." "Our political and theoretical interest," J. K. Gibson-Graham write, "is in creating alternative (and potentially emancipatory) economic futures in which *class diversity* can flourish" [*The End of Capitalism (as we knew it)* 52, emphasis added, xi]. The goal, in other words, is no longer classlessness but class difference and heterogeneity ("class diversity"), which is seen as a resistance to capitalism's "class homogeneity," especially since "the revolutionary task of replacing capitalism now seems outmoded and unrealistic" (263). In the *a-revolutionary* world, discursive difference suspends the "economic essence" of the social and rewrites class not in relation to production but in terms of a post-class belonging, what Derrida calls "a link of affinity"—a link of affects "suffering, and hope" but without "belonging to a class" (*Specters of Marx* 85). Class, as the social structure of the divisions of labor and their contradictions, is dispersed by being rewritten as the flows of affect.

Spiritualizing the social and turning class into an affect has become an epistemological epidemic in the Left North, which now speaks in quasi-religious idioms of "forgiveness," "democracy-to-come," and "hospitality" (Derrida, *Of Hospitality*). The guide to understanding the social, for example, for Gibson-Graham—whose *A Postcapitalist Politics* has become a manual for the generic Left in the U.S.—is "Zen master Shunryu Suzuki" who teaches that "in the beginner's mind there are many possibilities, in the expert's mind there are few" (8). They advocate a new elementalism of seduction and pleasure to overcome the legacies of the Enlightenment, which is seen to be the real pathology of modernity. This new, Left spiritual-fundamentalism is a mixture of a very old "New Age" sentimentality, quasi-religious banalities, and ecstasies over the ineffable, as well as an equally dated Lacanian psychoanalysis of desire and/as lack. This is a rather strange mix because the discursive Left in the North represents itself as cutting edge and markets the purported "newness" of its post-class views as the sign of their Truth (at the same time that it announces Truth as an obsession of the dead past). Gibson-Graham, for instance, write that "the crisis of modernist class politics is a crisis of desire" (13) and then suggest that class resistance is shaped either by desire getting stuck or being liberated (13).

Affects are seen as shaping class and its material relations, but class is not recognized as conditioning affects. Consequently, affects are considered autonomous and elemental, having no history. Quoting Hannah Arendt, whose conservative views along with the reactionary thoughts of Carl Schmitt have become new sources of ideas for the U.S. Left, Gibson-Graham write, "We need to foster a 'love of the world'" (6). Instead of being outraged at class exploitation, they propose we abandon militancy, which they seem to think of as negative energy. In its place, they call for "seducing, cajoling, enrolling, enticing, inviting," as well as adopting "playfulness, enchantment and exuberance" in order to develop an interest in "unpredictability, contingency, experimentation…and the possibilities of escape" (7). "Escape" is an integral part of Left pleasure-activism in the North; because the Left gets easily bored with the task at hand—like the class whose interests it normalizes. Much like the entrepreneur—who is worried about his commodities going out of style and his profits falling, and is therefore always on the look out for new commodities to market—the Left North constantly seeks newer and newer objects of desire and joy

Gibson-Graham, Resnick, and Wolff, therefore, find Fredric Jameson's notion of "ressentiment"—his idealist, Nietzschean term for what he calls a "primal class passion" ("Marx's Purloined Letter" 86)—to be too unjoyful. They argue that it limits a whole range of affective and bodily intensities and also marks the worker as a victim. Instead, they offer a portrait of the worker as a hopeful laborer and, in a desiring interpretation, describe exploitation as the "affective intensity" linked to "bodily intensity" in "performing surplus labor" (*Class and Its Others* 14-15). Their translations of class from an objective fact of history (structure) into the subjective, temporal pains and joys of the worker (sensations) entail their tying bodily intensities to affects that differ from those "familiar emotions" attributed to the proletariat—namely anger and outrage (which actually have always energized workers in their radical actions). Instead they associate workers with new feelings of "creative excitement, pleasure, hope, surprise, pride and satisfaction, daily enjoyment" (15). Under the alibi of a joyous participation, "envisioning and acting," which, they argue, should replace "blaming and moralizing" (15), they deploy "hope" and "daily enjoyment" to reconcile workers with their existing conditions of exploitation and teach them another lesson in joyful fatalism: immersion in the *jouissance* of class reconciliation. Hope is the opium of the revisionists.

Replacing class with affect has become a routine interpretive transference (Probyn, *Blush: Faces of Shame*) by which the "corporeal" is naturalized as a site of agency and resistance against the "conceptual" and thus as the locus of energy for liberating the subject into what Lauren Berlant calls "formlessness" and "unpredictability." She treats them as signs of the autonomy and freedom of the post-class subject who transgresses rationality and its ordering norms ("Critical Inquiry, Affirmative Culture" 447). The visceral, along with the corporeality of affective singularity, take the place of the abstractions of collectivity and class, which are assumed to be sites for controlling and oppressing desire. The cure for abstractions is the turn to the senses and the ecstatic, spontaneous contingencies of affects—which are not recognized as the historical outcome of class relations but are seen as marks of the sovereignty of intensities (Massumi, "The Autonomy of Affect"). The social is no longer seen as shaping affects, instead it is now thought that the social is actually made by the affective, by intimacy. The intimate every day (Berlant, ed., *Intimacy*) is a resistance to the homogeneities of abstract reason and also a celebration of the heterogeneous concrete. The social as the realm of the senses and affects, according to Berlant, is to be approached not by the rationality of the "think tank," but through what she calls the "feel-tank"—where feelings, empathy, aura, and sentiments are attended to ("Critical Inquiry, Affirmative Culture" 450).

With a cynical wit, that is a feature of class reconciliation, Berlant sensualizes the economics of the alienation of labor and, "only partly as a joke," translates it into the affects of depression, apathy, hopelessness, and exhaustion (451). Alienation of labor is converted from being the material outcome of wage labor and exploitation into an unrepresentable affect that borders on depression and can be cured only by participating in the therapeutic ironies of such gatherings as "The International Day of the Politically Depressed" (451) and wrapping oneself in T-shirts that heal alienation by irony: "Depressed?... It might be Political" (451). Berlant's "depression" and Gibson-Graham's ecstasies of "seducing" and "cajoling" (*A Postcapitalist Politics* 6) are all elements of a poetics of "affects and emotions" (1-21) that has displaced class struggle in the prosperous global North where social change is no longer perceived to be an effect of changing social structures through revolution but by a change of heart, change one's affects and desires (Nelson, *Manifesto of a Tenured Radical* 133). Social change, as bell hooks puts it, is "a vision of participatory economics within capitalism that aims to challenge and change class hierarchy" (*Where We Stand: Class Matters* 156). It is not class but class elitism that she opposes. So in place of class struggle, she believes changing the world means one has "To love the poor among us, to acknowledge their essential goodness and humanity" because this is "a mighty challenge to class hierarchy" (164). The affective in Left economics, as we will discuss later, is turned into the logic of "immaterial labor" and is said to displace material labor in the new capitalism (Hardt and Negri, *Multitude* 108-115).

The implications of the post-class-Left's desires for spiritualism and its ethical self-transformations are nowhere more clear than in Cornell West's theory of racism. He also seeks a solution to class injustice in love and does not see capitalism as responsible for racism. His objections are, therefore, directed at "profit-hungry corporations." For West, the problem is not capitalism and its structural class contradictions but rather the soul-less corporations that distort capitalism with their greed (lovelessness). The issue, he writes, is not "relative economic deprivation" but the "existential and psychological realities of black people" (*Race Matters* 19-20). The real problem is not that capitalism exploits people but that the culture of the market weakens "caring and sharing, nurturing and connecting" (*Democracy Matters: Winning the Fight Against Imperialism* xvi).

Class in these discourses of the Left is the unrepresentable desire and difference (Butler, "Merely Cultural"), and class struggle, as the dynamics of social change, is supplanted by "ethical self-transformation" (Gibson-Graham, *A Postcapitalist Politics* xxv). Ethics is one of what Trotsky calls the "philosophic gendarmes of the ruling class" (*Their Morals and Ours* 48), whose function is to deduce the laws of the social life from private desires and substitute the singular for the collective.

Capitalism Is Not What You Think

Dominant theories of class are theories of the death and waning of class (Pakulski and Waters, *The Death of Class*). These interpretations assume that capitalism has so completely changed from its early industrial phase and its production practices have been so radically transformed—especially after the collapse of Fordism in the 1950s—that class is no longer relevant to the understanding of "new" social relations. These relations are said to have been fashioned either outside production relations (Laclau, "Structure, History and the Political 202) or by new forms of labor and the centrality of consumption (along with the meanings and identities it creates), as well as by new (information) technologies (Hall, "The Meaning of New Times"). Contemporary capitalism, in yet another version of this metastory, is said to be the effect of a "mobile, flexible, computerized, immaterialized and spectral labor," whose referent is no longer use-value (Negri, "The Specter's Smile" 8), which Jean Baudrillard claims is a relic of the metaphysics of utility (*For a Critique of the Political Economy of the Sign* 133). Negri further argues that post-industrial capitalism has moved beyond the "law of value," which was formative in an earlier phase, and "time" is no longer a measure of value in post-industrial capitalism ("The Specter's Smile" 8, 10; "Twenty Theses on Marx" 157; *Marx Beyond Marx: Lessons on the* Grundrisse 171-190).

Negri argues that the new capitalism has rendered Marxist ontology obsolete ("The Specter's Smile" 13) and contends that Marx's class analytics—"his ontological description of exploitation" (10)—has become extraneous to new capitalism. The transformation of capitalism is so deep in his view that even the most sophisticated contemporary theories, such as deconstruction, have become outdated in their critique of capitalism because they are situated in the same old ontology (13) and are thus "exhausted" (10). What is needed, according to Negri, is a "post-deconstructive" ontology (12) because "we are at the beginning of a new epoch" ("Twenty Theses on Marx" 154). Deconstruction and the theories based on it may have activated the singular and waged a war against totality as a resistance against capitalism, but today's capitalism has itself become the home of heterogeneity, singularity, and difference following the "mutation of labor" (8) and the emergence of a changed "labor paradigm" (8). Capital actually needs difference because it increases its rate of profit by appealing to the unique preferences of individuals in the market. Capitalism has gone beyond itself and deconstructed deconstruction. New capitalism, and not deconstruction, is, for Negri, the promoter of difference and defender of heterogeneity against the old industrial capitalist order of mass production and homogeneous identities. Derrida, in Negri's words, is "a prisoner of the ontology he critiques" (13).

Negri's theory of "new" capitalism, like his theory of "empire," is a tissue of clichés; it is based on ideas developed in capitalist think-tanks, sponsored speculations, and a deep-rooted idealism that borders on mysticism. For instance, he regards capitalism to be "a radical 'Unheimlich'" (9)—an unrepresentable whose laws of motion are aleatory because they are grounded in immaterial labor, which defies the "law of value," and thus are beyond the understanding of reason and also beyond the reach of deconstruction's linguistic demystifications. His claim that capitalism has outdone deconstruction is an extension of this crypto-romantic epistemology, which regards philosophy to be autonomous from the social relations of production and thus thinks of deconstruction as an independent theory of culture and language that is now outdone by another autonomous force, namely capitalism. Capitalism and deconstruction, in other words, are represented in Negri's theology of culture as two different autonomous developments—one economic, the other cultural. However, deconstruction is not separate from capitalism but is its cultural extension. Like all philosophies and theories, deconstruction is the cultural articulation of the material base of the society in which it is produced. Deconstruction is the cultural arm of capitalism.

By advancing singularity, heterogeneity, anti-totality, and supplementarity, for instance, deconstruction has, among other things, demolished "history" itself as an articulation of class relations. In doing so, it has constructed a cognitive environment in which the economic interests of capital are seen as natural and not the effect of a particular historical situation. Deconstruction continues to produce some of the most effective discourses to normalize capitalism and contribute to the construction of a capitalist-friendly cultural common sense in which capitalism's economics and economic practices (layoffs, reduction of pay

Getting Class Out of Culture

and benefits, abolishing of pensions) are all received as matters of complexity, unpredictability, uncertainty, and the inability of reason to explain the uncanny workings of the social. Consequently, it places the subject of labor in a position where instead of becoming a militant against capital, he becomes a contemplative ethical subject grappling with the undecidable and meditating on his own responsibilities.

If deconstruction seems "exhausted" and not as powerful in its naturalization of capital today as it was at the beginning of Neoliberal economics, this is not because capitalism has gone beyond itself and outdone deconstruction. It is because capitalism has become more itself in recent years: its class contradictions have increased. Negri's views on the changing relations of labor in capitalism are an extension of his theories on imperialism. In *Empire* (co-written with Michael Hardt), Negri argues that imperialism (like industrial capitalism) is a thing of the past. What was imperialism is now empire, which is "a decentered and deterritorialized apparatus of rule" where "hybrid identities, flexible hierarchies, and plural exchanges through modulating networks of communication" are managed (*Empire* xii). The wars in Iraq and Afghanistan—not to mention the proxy wars in Somalia and the war-to-come in Iran—all prove that capitalism has not moved from imperialism to empire; rather it has become more imperialist. Capitalism is now, more than ever before, more deeply and extremely itself. This may be why Derrida regards Negri's insistence on the need for a new ontology, commensurate with a new capitalism, to be a sign not of progress but of regress—a new desire for old metaphysics ("Marx & Sons" 257-62). Like all superstructural practices, deconstruction is adjusting to the class situation in capitalism, and the publication of such texts as Derrida's *Politics of Friendship*, in which the idea of democracy-to-come is further developed, is part of this cultural adaptation to the economic base. Derrida's recent writings, in other words, are responses to the "new" capitalism, in which class contradictions can no longer be explained away by theory. This is one reason why in recent years the end of theory has been announced as yet another cutting edge event both by conservative journals, such as *Critical Inquiry* in its special issue on the "Future of Criticism" (Winter 2004), and by left writers like Terry Eagleton in *After Theory*. Even using anti-reason arguments (e.g., Derrida, "*Différance*"), theory can no longer provide epistemological cover for the growing global class antagonism, for the new imperialism, or for the collapse of "human rights." "New" capitalism now needs a more effective discursive shield—a new cultural poetics instead of theory. Derrida's *A Taste for the Secret* and *Of Hospitality* are among his contributions to this new poetics. *Of Hospitality* is a narrative poem on capital as "law without law" (83) and a lyrical dispersing of class contradictions into "forgiveness," "friendship," and "hospitality."

Panculturalism is one of the consequences of the "death of class" arguments which maintain the centrality of culture in new capitalism as a result of the events cataloged by Negri, Stuart Hall, and others, such as the emergence of labor that travels the Internet, the development of information technologies, and the growth of consumption—especially as a production of cultural meanings and identities (e.g., Hall, "The Centrality of Culture: Notes on the Cultural Revolutions of Our Time"). As Jameson writes, "everything in our social life—from economic value and state power to practices and to the very structure of psyche itself—can be said to have become 'cultural'" (*Postmodernism, or, the Cultural Logic of Late Capitalism* 48). Thus, there is no place within culture from which one can critique class and its exploitative relations; culture exceeds its critique and absorbs the economic (class) in the proliferation of its meanings.

Negri's panculturalism is his device for the inversion of materialism into a new subjectivism ("Twenty Theses on Marx" 159-160, 172-173). It has the aura of spirituality and the aroma of mysticism. Like his theory of labor and the law of value, it is grounded in "a radical 'Unheimlich.'" Playing with Derrida's trope of spectrality, he equates the spectral with the every day and declares that "there is no longer any outside" and that we are all immersed in a radical uncanny (9). Therefore, even though he recognizes that "we're entirely within this real illusion," and that we need to get back to the "question of life, spirit, or the spectral," he finds the task to be unfeasible: "But how will it be possible to follow this task through, immersed as we are in the world of specters?" (9). In other words, one is immersed in "a radical 'Unheimlich'" (which is really an allegory of Negri's notion of a capitalism beyond capitalism). All one can do is to play cultural resistance inside the system—a goal that sounds like an insurgency against capital (Antonio Negri, *Insurgencies*) but is actually a confirmation of capital, part of the global North's system maintanence strategies. As long as the inside is the home of the anti-capitalist activist—"*without an outside any longer possible*" (13), capital has nothing to worry about. Derrida goes much further and remakes the inside into an imperial inside (as we discuss more fully below).

Panculturalism in all its versions is ultimately based on post-Fordist theories (Aglietta, *A Theory of Capitalist Regulation: The U.S. Experience*), which are essentially culturalizations of the social in which consumption is seen as displacing production. The "mode of regulation," around which all panculturalist theories evolve, is the desire, expectations, and culturally contradictory behavior of individuals in their relation to the regime of accumulation. In pancultural theories, economy is not perceived as an objective, impersonal force but as always dependent on culture. "If post-Fordism exists," Stuart Hall writes, sharing the skepticism and beliefs of the poststructuralist cultural turn, "then it is as much a description of culture as of economic change. Indeed, that distinction is now useless" ("The Meaning of New Times" 128). Theorists of the "regulation school"—the ground of panculturalism—are, in the words of Alan Lipietz, the "'rebel sons' of Althusser" in revolt against what they see to be Marxist class determinism ("From Althusserianism to 'Regulation Theory'" 99). One of the consequences of "regulation theory" for class is that the contradictions of capital are no longer seen as "structures" but as "unstable tensions" (100), which is a not very subtle way of rewriting class from a structure of conflicts into an open-ended process without antagonism.

Contrary to widespread assumptions that culture is now material and independent from the relations of production, culture, we argue, continues to be the superstructural articulation of labor relations. It has not and does not shape the economy. The suggestion that "through design, technology and styling, 'aesthetics' has already penetrated the world of modern production" (Hall, "The Meaning of New Times" 128) confuses cultural adjustments in the regimes of commodification with changing the logic of capitalist production, which is always the logic of profit and never of aesthetics and meanings. Capital itself produces the aesthetics required to represent the profitable as desirable: under capitalism "needs are produced just as are products" (Marx, *Grundrisse* 527).

Culture is always an effect of production, but it is also true that once cultural practices emerge from the material base of the social, they "also exercise their influence upon the course of the historical struggles" (Engels, "Letter to Joseph Bloch" in Marx and Engels, *Selected Correspondence* 395). As the history of aesthetics shows, the idea of aesthetics as errant tropes resisting market norms is itself a by-product of production as it adjusts cultural desires to the shifting ratios of profitability.

Worried More About Essentialism Than Capitalism

"For us," J. K. Gibson-Graham write, "creating a knowledge of class implies not only a concern about exploitation and economic difference, but a commitment to an anti-essentialist theoretical position" (*The End of Capitalism* 54-55; on anti-essentialist "reframing" also see pp. 24-45 and *A Postcapitalist Politics* xxx, 105-106). Philosophically, this commitment is a reaffirmation of the familiar Nietzschean critique of metaphysics ("…categories that refer to a purely fictitious world," *The Will to Power* 13). It argues that to give primacy to class in social analysis is a symptom of a will to power concealed as a desire for truth. To put it differently, it is a logocentrism that seeks presence and certitude by transferring the difference within class to an outside (e.g., capitalism) in order to construct labor as the plenitude of an objective society that cannot exist because of the constitutive role of what Ernesto Laclau and Chantal Mouffe call "antagonism." "Antagonism" is "the presence of the 'Other'" which "prevents me from being totally myself" (*Hegemony and Socialist Strategy* 125). The "other" is "the Real," which is the fundamental "lack" of "me." In other words, in "antagonism... the relation arises not from full totalities [e.g., "classes"], but from the impossibility of their constitution" (125). This, among other things means that

> the social only exists as a partial effort for constructing society—that is, an objective and closed system of differences—antagonism, as a witness of the impossibility of a final suture, is the "experience" of the limit of the social…. Society never manages fully to be society, because everything in it is penetrated by its limits, which prevent it from constituting itself as an objective reality. (125, 127)

To be clear, according to Laclau, "society does not 'exist'" as an objective system of differences such as classes (*New Reflections on the Revolution of Our Time* 183).

The post-class social theory of the Left converges with such conservative theories as those articulated, for example, by Margaret Thatcher, who also argues that "there is no such thing as society" rather "there are individual men and women" ("Interview"). She is, in short, putting forth another claim for the singularity (contingency) of what makes society. Thatcher implies that only in capitalism is the full difference of the individual materialized, and therefore, as she puts it, "There Is No Alternative" (TINA) to capitalism and its political cover (democracy).

The impossibility of an alternative (an "outside") to the existing class relations is perhaps nowhere more subtly implied than in the writings of Jacques Derrida who has deeply influenced the way class is understood and written about in contemporary cultural critique. Derrida rejects all radical transformations that seek to go beyond what exists because, he argues, the "beyond" is an illusion of presence that assumes it brings one closer to Truth. What is needed is not a "beyond" but a rewriting of what *is* in terms of internal differences. Derrida advocates a gradual rewriting ("little by little," *Positions* 24) and not a radical move because any radical move to construct an alternative to what exists will, he contends, subject one to the dangers of proceeding "too quickly...immediately jumping beyond oppositions" (*Positions* 41) such as class. Derrida believes that gradual change should always take place within the current system and by making relationships different within that system since there is no outside to the system, or to put it more precisely, "the outside is the inside" (*Of Grammatology* 44). To change relations within a system, he deploys what he calls a "double science" (*Positions* 41; *Dissemination* 4)—a double move by which the terms of the system are overturned and then re-written back into the system with a difference (*Positions* 41-42). Classes, accordingly, are never abolished but become different from themselves. They thus lose their purported foundationalist authority and fade into "another dimension of analysis and political commitment, one that cuts across social differences and oppositions of social forces (what one used to call, simplifying, 'classes'" ("Marx & Sons" 239).

He claims the binary theory of class is in disorder because fundamental shifts in capitalist modernity have "ruined" not only "the concept of class struggle" but also "the identification of a social class" ("Politics and Friendship" 204), so much so, that "any determining reference to social class, to class struggle" now seems to "belong to another time" (204). He goes on to argue that "the idea of social class," even in its "refined" form of (Althusserian) "overdetermined groups of classes" is quite "inappropriate for understanding" the contemporary situation whose analysis requires "much more subtle instruments" (203). Consequently, "any sentence in which 'social class' appear[s]" is "a problematic sentence" for Derrida (204). "Class" is a leftover, he says, "if not from the nineteenth, at least from the first half of the twentieth century" (204). To become suitable for the contemporary, class has to be "considerably differentiated" (204) and complicated. The "differentiation" he demands in order to make class more complex actually turns class from an economic element of social life into a cultural poetics of heterogeneity. So, while Derrida, like many other critics, uses "class," he so thoroughly empties it of its economic content that it becomes a cultural meaning and, like all cultural meanings, according to Derrida, remains indeterminate and uncertain.

He does this by rewriting "economics" as "aneconomics" and thus undercutting the material base of class. In its classical sense, "economy" constitutes "the material basis of [the] world" (Marx, *Capital* I, 175); it is the real relations of production and exchange of the material means of life. Derrida regards this to be "the economist dogma of Marxism" ("Politics and Friendship" 205), and rewrites it "by bringing in all sorts of elements that were not simply forces of production or effects of ownership or appropriation" and included "non-productivity, non-appropriation" (205). Economy, in other words, is resignified as a cultural poetics, namely "something heterogeneous both to productivity and unproductiveness" (205), which overturns Marx's concepts of "productive" and "unproductive labor" (*Theories of Surplus-Value*). Consequently, the economy is no longer an inquiry into the material basis of life and the "relations between classes" (Engels, "Review of Karl Marx" 472), but "différance (with an 'a') is in an economy that counts with the aneconomics" (Derrida, "Politics and Friendship" 206), and produces class as a sign—the site of the overflow of meanings, which exceed any explanations such as "class analysis."

It is important, however, to point out that in keeping class (as "indispensable" 204) but turning it into a scene for the play of traces, Derrida is exemplary of a larger tendency of the Left in the global North where it has become customary—as proof of its resistance to capitalism—to maintain class but to treat it as a cultural sign without decidable meanings. At the same time, the Left deplores and rejects the use of class as a materialist concept that explains the extraction of surplus labor at the point of production and how this brings about the conditions that determine life under capitalism. The rejection of class as a materialist analytics usually takes the form of an argument that concludes such a materialist view of class is "ossified and simple," if not simplistic (Hutnyk, *Bad Marxism* 190). Class, therefore, only becomes "useful if thought about in the double sense of both markers of status-based resource privilege and as a system marking differential usage, distribution and expropriation of resources" (190). Production—the main materialist determinate of class relations—is completely erased from such a neo-Weberian view, which claims class "does not make as much sense if rigidly restricted to a bipolar opposition," as Marx and Engels argued in the *Manifesto of the Communist Party* (Hutnyk, *Bad Marxism* 190). Materialist theory, however, maintains that class is the effect of relations of property and not an unanchored sign crisscrossed by difference. This is seen as reductive but is also thought to be deployed only by the naïve, the dogmatic, and Stalinists. (By the way, the cure for Stalinism, according to Derrida, is to read more Heidegger, "Politics and Friendship" 208.) To prove that it is neither dogmatic nor Stalinist, the Left in the North has turned economics into an applied Heideggerian metaphysics of being-in-between (Cullenberg, et al., eds., *Postmodernism, Economics and Knowledge*) and has also invented a spiritualistic Marxism in which class, as a marker of labor relations and thus a source of economic value, is considered to be "trafficking in ineluctable essences." This post-material Marxism seems to suggest that "catachresis" and not class struggle is the dynamics of sociocultural emancipation (Spivak, *Outside in the Teaching Machine* 12, 127).

Hutnyk's notion that class "does not make much sense" is based on the popular claim in the mass media and by think-tanks of the North that, as we have already mentioned, capitalism has changed, and in the "new" cybereconomy of a globalized culture, class has become a "class-process" (Gibson-Graham, Resnick, and Wolff, "Toward a Poststructruralist Political Economy" 6-10), which means it is not a structure of social antagonism and therefore not determined by "property ownership" (Gibson-Graham, *The End of Capitalism* 179). These views of class are, in the last analysis, an extension of the capitalist theory that social conflicts are not caused by labor relations or, as Ernesto Laclau puts it, "class antagonism is not inherent to capitalist relations of production" ("Structure, History and the Political" 202). The culturalist theories of class are ultimately all grounded in the myth that labor has become "immaterial" (Hardt and Negri, *Multitude*)—a fantasy that is ontologized by Giorgio Agamben, who regards labor as a "solidarity that in no way contains an essence" (*The Coming Community* 19). The Left in the prosperous North is clearly more worried about essentialism than capitalism. Its vision of the future is, therefore, "a vision of economic heterogeneity rather than of an alternative (noncapitalist) homogeneity" (Gibson-Graham, *The End of Capitalism* 179).

The anti-metaphysics of difference, which underlies the philosophical argument about the end of class and which critiques class as a fiction of presence and a will to truth, is itself a version of the metaphysics of presence which we call the metaphysics of the negative: it is an argument against "presence" that relies itself on the presence of an absence, namely the inaudible ("a") in "différance" in Derrida's *Margins of Philosophy* (5). As we discuss in our critique of metaphysics, this anti-esentialism, in other words, is itself an essentialism of the negative.

Displacing Class with Inequality

The North-centric Left (the metaphysics of capitalism) has avoided class by focusing on inequality, which emphasizes individual differences and obscures the structures of conflicts that form collective labor relations. In his *A Short History of Neoliberalism*, David Harvey writes that class is "always a somewhat shadowy (and some would even say dubious) concept" (31). Class is a "shadowy" concept for Harvey because the owners of the means of production are now so diverse. For example, in England the old aristocracy is displaced by brash "entrepreneurs"; in Indonesia, Malaysia, and the Philippines, "economic power became strongly concentrated among a few ethnic Chinese"; and in Russia, "seven oligarchs" rose in the aftermath of the counter-revolution in the Soviet Union (32). For Harvey class is irrelevant because, he implies, how could such diversity—lifestyle in England, ethnicity in Indonesia, power in Russia—be explained by "class"? The change in class morphology—the fact that new subjects occupy the structural position of ownership—is hard evidence for him that class has lost its explanatory power and should therefore be abandoned as the marker of social structure. Class is consequently replaced by inequality, a move that has gained great popularity with the Left in the North (e.g., Michaels, *The Trouble with Diversity: How We Learned to Love Identity and Ignore Inequality*). Thus, the problem of capitalism for Harvey is that "the net worth of the 358 richest people in 1996 was equal to the combined income of the poorest 45 per cent of world's population—213 billion people" (34-35) and not that it is a system of wage-labor, which is the cause of inequality.

Class, of course, is not simply inequality that can be overcome by providing further opportunities for all within the existing social system because the system itself produces inequality. Inequality is the statistical index of social differences without conflicts. Class is the structural relations of labor grounded in antagonism over the appropriation of surplus labor—exploitation. To make everyone equal under capitalism simply means to exploit everyone equally. It does not put an end to the exploitation of humans by humans because capitalism is structured around private ownership of the means of production of social surplus. When one talks about the equality of "all" (which is actually the exploitation of all), all does not mean all; it means all who have to sell their labor to subsist. All is everyone except the owners of the means of production who exploit the labor of others. Equality within capitalism does not end exploitation and free people from necessity—fulfilling the needs of all (Marx, *Critique of the Gotha Programme*). By obscuring class in inequality and representing society as differences without antagonism ("meanings," "values," "desires"), the Left claims there is no need for revolution because, under capitalism, reform can make the unequal equal through opportunities.

Beyond Class Binaries

In materialist theory, class is constructed at the point of production which, among other things, means it is based on labor relations in history. With the rise of private property, ownership of the means of producing commodities—which embody surplus labor—enables some to exploit the labor of others. The materialist theory of class is, therefore, a binary theory: it argues that people in class societies are divided between those who sell (or are forced to give free) their labor power to live, and those who purchase (or appropriate by force) the labor power of others and profit from it.

In their *Multitude*, Michael Hardt and Antonio Negri call the classical materialist theory a "unity" theory and place it in opposition to "plurality" theories of class that "insist on the ineluctable multiplicity of social classes" (103). In their usual manner, they take an eclectic path out of the binary and write "that both of these seemingly contradictory positions are true should indicate that the alternative itself may be false" (104). In the end they, like Derrida, formally concede that class is indispensable for understanding the social (Derrida, "Marx &

Sons"), but at the same time they undermine its very materialist possibility, which is the only possibility that actually matters. Hardt and Negri demolish class, in other words, not by giving up class—in fact they say that the "multitude" is a class concept (103)—but by the inversion of class from an economic category to a political concept: "Class is determined by class struggle"(104). It is not the materialism of the relations of property that produce classes, which in turn start class struggle; instead the subjectivity of people lead them to struggle and through that struggle form classes (103-104). Hardt and Negri actually find that "the old distinction between economic and political" is an obstacle to understanding class relations (105). Their dismissal of the binary, here and in their class theory, is in part based on Negri's call for a "post-deconstructive" ontology ("The Specter's Smile" 12), which implies that the binaries are undone by a capitalism that travels on the Internet. Thus, they can no longer account for its singularities which constitute not only its cultural practices but also its class formations. There are as many singular classes as there are class struggles, and there are as many class struggles as there are subjectivities. Class, for Hardt and Negri, is an effect of the multitude which is "an irreducible multiplicity; the singular social differences that constitute the multitude must always be expressed and can never be flattened into sameness, unity, identity, or indifference" (105). Class in the new capitalism is another name for singularity which is the undoing of the collective.

Using different languages, the contemporary discourses on class repeat this narrative in which the classical materialist binary theory of class is represented as essentialist and in need of deconstruction. One of the most influential critiques of binary class theory, as we have already indicated, is by Jacques Derrida, whose general theory of class and specifically his deconstruction of binary class theory we will discuss and critique at several points in this book. Here, however, we would like to outline what is often called the "class-as-process" theory and point to its underlying logic and class politics.

The class-as-process theory is the work of Stephen A. Resnick and Richard D. Wolff who, in their groundbreaking book *Knowledge and Class*, critique the "dichotomous theory of class" (112) for its determinism and foundationalism (109-163) and propose an anti-essentialist and "overdeterminate" (114, 116) class theory situated in the multiple processes involved in the extraction and distribution of surplus labor. Their views are reinterpreted under the strong influence of poststructuralist social theory by J. K. Gibson-Graham in *The End of Capitalism (as we knew it)* (49-56), who repeat their argument for a theory of class "without an essence" (55). We leave aside here how their version of anti-essentialism, like all other versions, collapses and becomes a new essentialism in which a trans-historical notion of surplus labor becomes the foundation of a new pro-capital social theory.

Since class-as-process theory views class as an effect of "producing and appropriating surplus labor" (52), and because in all societies surplus labor is produced and appropriated, class-as-process theory makes class the immanent feature of all societies throughout history (58). Even in such societies as early communism and post-capitalist socialism, in which the social surplus labor produced is appropriated not by private owners but by society as a collective, there is class according to this view. There is no outside to class—ever, anywhere.

Class-as-process is a rather crude translation of Althusser's post-class theory of ideology into class theory. For Althusser ideology is not a "false consciousness" by which the exchange of labor power for wages is seen as being a fair exchange. Instead, he writes that ideology is "the imaginary relationship of individuals to their real conditions of existence" (*Lenin and Philosophy* 162). Ideology for Althusser, who draws on Lacan and Freud for his main concepts, is basically a theory of subjectivity (170-177). This is another way of saying that, for Althusser, "ideology has no history" (159) because "human societies secrete ideology as the very element and atmosphere indispensable to their historical respiration and life" (*For Marx* 232). Similarly, for Gibson-Graham, class is an organic part of all societies and not a specific historical stage in them (*The End of Capitalism* 58-59). All societies, they contend, secrete class.

Given their affirmation that capitalism is here to stay (263), it would be "unrealistic," to use Gibson-Graham's word, to struggle to end class rule. The practical thing to do is to learn to live with it. Consequently, the mark of an activist agency in the class-as-process theory is not a militancy to overthrow class because that requires a revolutionary act, which they claim is "outmoded" (*The End of Capitalism* 263). Instead, they call for an intervention in the homogeneity of class to make it heterogeneous and plural (52, 58). Class stays; its modalities and forms multiply (52, 58). This view of class, which is represented as cutting edge (Gibson-Graham, *A Postcapitalist Politics* 1-21, 66-68, 90-92), is interesting not because of its arguments but mostly for what it says about the way the Left in the global North has accommodated and normalized the class interests of capital. The goal of class-as-process, for example, as Gibson-Graham state, is not to "eradicate all or even specifically capitalist forms of exploitation" but to contribute to "self-transformative class subjectivity"—and change the emotional components of exploitation (53).

As always, there is more. Class-as-process is a discursive device for dissolving what Marx calls "the antithesis between lack of property and property." He argues that this antithesis "so long as it is not comprehended as the antithesis of labour and capital, still remains an indifferent antithesis, not grasped in its *active connection*, in its *internal relation*, not yet grasped as a *contradiction*" (*Economic and Philosophic Manuscripts of 1844*, 293-94).

Grasping this contradiction is grasping the binary theory of class and realizing that class is a relation of owning: the owning of labor by capital. As such, it is the other of human freedom because it is grounded in the exploitation of humans by humans—private property is the congealed alienated labor of the other. Using the epistemological alibi of anti-essentialism, class-as-process obscures the constitutive role of private property (ownership of the means of production) in the construction of class divisions. Thus, in the name of opposing economism, it actually protects the economic interests of capital: "class in our conception is overdetermined, rather than defined by property ownership and other sorts of social relations" (Gibson-Graham, *The End of Capitalism* 179). Private property, they contend, is only one of many factors that make class (55, 179), and it is no more significant in this construction than, for example, "affects and emotions" (*A Postcapitalist Politics* 1-21).

But private property is the sensuous "expression of estranged human life," and class is its concrete effect in the every day. "The positive transcendence of *private property* as the appropriation of *human life* is therefore the positive transcendence of all estrangement—that is to say the return of man from religion, family, state, etc. to his *human*, i.e. *social*, existence" (Marx, *Economic and Philosophic Manuscripts of 1844*, 297). Ending the contradiction of the binary of property and propertyless is the end of class and the end of alienation: it is the beginning of human freedom from necessity.

Class-as-process naturalizes private property and the estrangement of humans—from their work, from others and from themselves—by making class the plural effect of "the intersection of all social dimensions or processes—economic, political cultural, natural" (Gibson-Graham, *The End of Capitalism* 55). By pluralizing class, the class-as-process theorists undermine the importance of private property in constructing class relations and thus absolve capital—whose history is a history of accumulation of private property and is "dripping from head to toe, from every pore, with blood and dirt" (Marx, *Capital* I, 926).

Other critics, who argue class has become irrelevant to contemporary society, claim that, owing to changes in technology and structural transformations in capitalism, the differences within classes have so proliferated they have exceeded the differences between classes, thereby making the binary labor theory of class obsolete. These views go even further and state that the very premise of binary theories of class—namely, private ownership as determining class relations—has lost its significance in shaping class relations. We live, they argue, in post-property times in which property has been displaced by access (Rifkin, *The Age of Access*).

The increasing differences within classes, however, do not demolish the binary class structures under capital. The "differences that flourish within classes," as John O'Neill argues, "do not challenge but even confirm the differences between classes. Poverty is colorless and genderless however much it marks women and racial minorities" ("Oh, My Others, There Is No Other!" 81).

Destruction of Collectivity

The North Left is somehow under the illusion that contemporary capitalism is opposed to difference, heterogeneity, and singularity. Therefore, it has persuaded itself that if it supports these values, it has opposed capitalism. But these are the very virtues that capitalism now promotes because, among other things, they propel consumption and bring up capital's rates of profit. They also break up collectivity and thus any sustained, thought-through struggles against capital.

Negri in fact uses these new cultural strategies of capitalism to obscure the continuity of capital's exploitation of labor. The myth of capital as a homogenizing force has provided a center for Left identity and allowed it to achieve its own coherent identity while advocating differential identity for others. J. K. Gibson-Graham, for instance, rely on this very outdated view of capitalism to fight what they imagine to be a very updated war against class collectivity and put in its place a notion of "community" as a cultural space for cultivating conforming subjectivity rather than transforming social relations (127-163). Their community is actually quite representative of capitalism's poetics of difference.

Grounding itself in difference, singularity, and its moral imperative—"ethical self-transformation" and "(re)subjectivation" (*A Postcapitalist Politics* xxv)—the Left in the global North has legitimated de-regulation (of the market) and valorized contingency and anti-binarism, all in the name of resistance to normative (homogenizing) practices. Derrida's notion of "equality" demonstrates with unusual clarity the way in which the Left's ostensible opposition to capital is essentially an affirmation of capital's values. Derrida, like all persons of the Left, is for equality, but he adds "I am trying…to think out an equality that would not be homogeneous, that would take heterogeneity, infinite singularity, infinite alterity into account…equality calls for a consideration of a certain infinite heterogeneity, an infinite distance" (Derrida, "Politics and Friendship" 213). Equality—collectivity—in other words, is the negation of individuality. This is what capitalism is not only arguing for in its theoretical writings (e.g., Hayek, *The Road to Serfdom*), but also in its daily advertising for its commodities.

Recall Margaret Thatcher's statement: "There is no such thing as society, there are individual men and women," which sums up these tendencies. They are, what Pierre Bourdieu calls, "a programme of methodical destruction of collectivities" ("The Essence of Neoliberalism").

In his "late writings," Derrida radicalizes Thatcher's purging of social life from collectivity by, for example, telling one of his interlocutors: "do not consider me 'one of you,' 'don't count me in,' I want to keep my freedom, always: this, for me, is the condition not only for being singular and other, but also for entering into relation with the singularity and alterity of others" (Derrida and Ferraris, *A Taste for the Secret* 27). He goes far beyond Thatcher and, to use Bourdieu's words, calls "into question any and all collective structures." Thatcher at least adds "families" to "individual men and women," but Derrida is adamant that even "family" is an obstacle to singularity: "When someone is one of the family" he loses "himself in the herd" (27). For Derrida, not only is one singular but so is everyone else, and all relations are relations of singularities. Since the social is seen as an assemblage of singularities, human freedom is not obtained through collective class struggles but by waging "a war on totality" and activating "difference" (Lyotard, *The Postmodern Condition* 82). This allows one to protect one's individual freedom, which is "the right to remain silent, to refuse to answer" to others (Derrida and Ferraris, *A Taste for the Secret* 26). Under the heading, "Deconstructing Classes," Ernesto Laclau takes this cult of the individual a step further and argues that capitalist social relations of property do not produce class antagonism in workers, and therefore any class awareness is formed in the consciousness of the individual worker outside these relations through private experiences (Butler, Laclau, and Zizek, *Contingency, Hegemony, Universality* 201-204, 296-301). Culture—not economic exploitation—is seen as shaping the relation of the individual to capitalism, and culture is assumed to be self-producing.

The fact, however, is that culture and politics are always effects of social relations of production:

> In acquiring new productive forces men change their mode of production; and in changing their mode of production, in changing the way of earning their living, they change all their social relations. The hand-mill gives you society with the feudal lord; the stream-mill society with the industrial capitalist.
>
> The same men who establish their social relations in conformity with their material productivity, produce also principles, ideas, and categories, in conformity with their social relations. (Marx, *The Poverty of Philosophy* 166)

Derrida and Thatcher seemingly belong to two radically different if not opposite sides of culture and politics. Their different local idioms, however, have obscured the fact that the ideological effects of their writings and practices are identical. "Lyotard, Roland Barthes, Michel Foucault and Jacques Derrida" according to a special report in the conservative magazine, *The Economist* (December 19, 2006), "were all from far left" yet they "gave modern retailers, advertisers and businessmen" the tools to reinvent capitalism in the 1980s and 1990s ("Post-Modernism Is the New Black"). In other words, the "post" (as in poststructuralism, postmarxism, postcolonialism…) and

> 'neo-liberal' free market economics which had developed entirely independently of each other…pointed to the same direction…. Both sought to 'emancipate' the individual from the control of state power or other authorities…. Both put restoring individual choice and power at the heart of their 'projects.' ("Post-Modernism Is the New Black")

There is, as John O'Neill puts it, a "convergence of a postmodern leftism with neoliberal defenses of the market" ("Economy, Equality and Recognition" 85). They are different cultural manifestations of the same material logic—uncovering these connections is the task of ideology critique.

Dominant cultural theory has displaced the critique of ideology with a poetics of representation (Giorgio Agamben, *Means without End*; Foucault, "Truth and Power" 118-120, 132-133; Jameson, *Postmodernism* 46, 201, 261, 399) and has represented the task of writing class back into culture as a will to metaphysics by treating transformative politics that aims at anything more than modifying cultural representations as an "old" metaphysics (Derrida, *Politics of Friendship*). Politics, to be more precise, has become a quasi-religious and faith-based apologetics for capitalism. Its lexicon no longer evolves around material life and how it is conditioned by human labor, but instead meditates on "forgiveness," "hospitality," "friendship," etc., which inevitably lead to converting questions of "justice" into an ineffable beyond all representations (Derrida, "Force of Law: The 'Mystical Foundation of Authority'" 25). A homily on "law without law" is a code for a spiritualism that obscures "debt and economy" (Derrida, *Of Hospitality* 83) and takes the place of a polemic for freedom from necessity (Marx, *Critique of the Gotha Programme*).

Derrida's political theory recasts the notion of politics in cultural critique: it textualizes what is regarded to be an essentialist politics and rewrites it as a sign without any specific referent. Anti-essentialist politics is, in Derrida's words, without "a programme, an agenda, or even the name of a regime" ("Politics and Friendship: A Discussion"). In other words, it is a way of talking about politics that is not political—a politics without end whose only "ends" are preventing the formation of any content through endless talking to avert such closure by any referent (class, labor, capital,...). To act politically is to encounter the undecidable where a decision has to be taken without pre-knowledge, without a political "program" (e.g., "socialism"). A politics that does not know itself beforehand is an event that "does not await the deliberation, consciousness, or organization of the subject" ("Letter to a Japanese Friend" 274). On other hand, a politics that knows ahead of time that it is, for example, for freedom from necessity is not seen as politics but as simply carrying out a program. To have a thought-out goal (to transform the world) is to forfeit politics.

But Derrida's notion of politics as a discourse of non-closure is itself a class closure. By keeping politics open to endless difference, it closes it to what actually shapes difference. It is a closure to the determining, and by refusing to recognize determination itself as a difference—a difference of the non-determining play from itself—it excludes it from the open space of politics. What is advertised as "open" is open only to that which is not opposed to openness as a strategy of delay and stalemate—a way of keeping things the way they are in the name of plurality and non-closure. This is a plurality that is not open to the plural. Its non-closure is grounded in a closure to the determining; thus the play of *différance* itself is placed beyond difference and essentialized. This, of course, is not simply a logical contradiction but an effect of the class contradictions that a non-closural politics attempts to close out.

The absence of class in recent social critique is not simply a discursive matter caused by the influence of "theory." Or to put it more clearly, like all discursive matters it has material causes. It is the outcome of the material defeat of labor by capital after World War II (Dumenil and Levy, *Capital Resurgent: Roots of the Neoliberal Revolution*). Bringing class back into the understanding of social and cultural relations and their practices is the first step in constructing the critical knowledges that contribute to social change and to building different social relations: "without revolutionary theory there can be no revolutionary movement" (Lenin, *What Is to Be Done?* 369). Class analysis is fundamental to producing such a theory because all social practices are class practices.

TAFT-HARTLEY ACT AND THE "DEATH OF CLASS"

The contemporary cultural catchphrase, the "death of class," has its material roots in capital's battles after World War II aimed at crushing the labor movement, which was resisting capital's practices to increase the productivity (i.e., exploitation) of workers in order to bring up the rate of its profits. Walter Reuther clearly articulated the goal of the postwar labor movement:

> The kind of labor movement we want is not committed to the nickel-in-the-pay-envelope philosophy. We are building a labor movement, not to patch up the world so men can starve less often and less frequently, but a labor movement that will remake the world so that working people will get the benefit of their labor. (Dubofsky and Dulles, *Labor in America* 349)

World War II provided capitalism with massive profits and enabled it to re-acquire some of the social influence, political power, and cultural hegemony it had lost during the Depression. Wars are intra-class conflicts among the international bourgeoisie over cheap labor, material resources, and markets. However, they are carried out by the workers who are recruited through the narratives of "nation"—which have the ideological role of uniting everyone culturally so that the material interests of different classes vanish and all suddenly have the same cultural interests regardless of their class, namely, to defend the country and its freedom. Mythologies of patriotism and freedom spiritualize the class interests of the owners and produce a "false consciousness" that persuades workers to fight to protect the class interests of their own exploiters.

The war "yielded spectacular profits for big business corporations (as well as smaller profiteers)" (Le Blanc, *A Short History of the U.S. Working Class* 93). At the same time the growing class antagonism, which was caused, for the most part, by the high exploitation of the workers, was heavily repressed during the war by various labor laws and no-strike clauses in the name of defending freedom. Toward the end of the war and especially in the years immediately after, class antagonism emerged into the open, and labor and capital became involved in one of the most sustained and hostile class struggles in the history of capitalism. In her brilliant *Selling Free Enterprise,* Elizabeth A. Fones-Wolf meticulously analyzes the postwar class struggles between labor and capital in the U.S. with considerable intellectual rigor and scholarly thoroughness. She writes that although the high exploitation of workers was described as necessary war-time "productivity" and was tied to individualism, freedom, and the "American way of Life," it was clear to workers that it was "SPEED-UP" and that capital wanted "more work for the same pay" (5, 8, 71). Workers were prepared to fight capital because the labor shortage, among other historical factors, had given them new power to stand up against capital.

The class solidarity of workers against their exploitation by capital surfaced through an unprecedented series of massive strikes in the 1940s and 1950s. In the strike wave of 1945-46, for example, over 4.5 million workers participated in protesting capitalist practices against labor (Le Blanc 93-97). In their strength and popularity, these strikes were unequaled in U.S. labor history. One critic described them as "so threatening as to look like nothing less than catastrophic civil war" (Whiting Williams, "The Public Is Fed Up with the Union Mess" 97). Perhaps the most consequential of them was a 116-day strike in 1946 against GM which was led by, among others, Walter Reuther. Reuther, who had served as director of the UAW's General Motors department, called for economic justice and demanded that the workers' wages and prices be linked to profits. He connected the wage of workers to the compensation of CEOs and argued that wages could be raised without raising prices for the public and putting pressure on people, which was, as usual, management's excuse for keeping wages low to remain competitive. He called on GM to "open the books" and make decisions in an open manner within a democratic workplace in which all could participate in discussions and decision making. Reuther's call was a historical argument for alternative labor relations in which workers were not subjugated by capital.

Capital was determined to crush any movement that gave such power to the workers. However, the colossal labor resources necessary for World War II created a shortage of labor that limited capital's options to do so. Therefore, by appealing to patriotism and using the National War Labor Board (NWLB), capital forced labor to surrender its right to strike (Rayback, *A History of American Labor* 378), and through its allies in government it manipulated the new laws governing the fair treatment of workers in order to contain labor. When, for example, in July 1942, the workers of "Little Steel" companies demanded a $1.00-a-day increase in their wages, the NWLB concocted a formula by which it restricted all wage increases—regardless of the cost of living—to no more than 15 percent. The result was that "the rise in living costs continued to exceed the allowable increase in wages under the Little Steel formula" (Dubofsky and Dulles 318). Having already had the right to strike taken away, the majority of workers in the AFL and CIO were left without any defense, and their status as wage-slaves of capital was once again masked behind all the patriotic and moral rhetoric of capitalist cultural politics.

However, mine workers whose injuries and fatalities had dramatically increased because of the long hours of work necessary for the high production level became very "angry over war profiteering at the expense of worker's needs" (Le Blanc 94) and challenged the "Little Steel" formula and the no-strike pledge. Under the leadership of John L. Lewis, they went on strike in 1943 and asked for a $2.00-a-day increase and pay for travel-time underground. To break the strike Roosevelt deployed the patriotic formula: "Tomorrow the Stars and Stripes will fly over the coal mines. I hope every miner will be at work under the flag." He used the same rhetoric in dealing with railway workers preparing to strike: "American lives and victory are at stake" (quoted in Dubofsky and Dulles 319, 322). Lewis, who had actually ordered workers back to work, was accused of lack of patriotism, and his argument that war and even national emergency cannot be used as an excuse to exploit workers was condemned by many including other union leaders as pure arrogance.

The coal miners' collectivity became such a powerful symbol of labor's threat that it quickly grew to be the focus of a new anti-labor move by capital. Owners sought to contain labor which, because of labor shortages, had found new strength in capital's deepening dependence on labor. Capital, however, managed to represent its class interests as the interests of the nation and get the Smith-Connally Act of 1943 through Congress. The act was described by CIO president Philip Murphy as "the most vicious and continuous attack on labor's right in the history of the nation" (Dubofsky and Dulles 321). It constrained work stoppages and prohibited union contributions to political campaign funds; this effectively reduced labor's political influence but left business contributions unlimited and unconstrained. The Smith-Connally Act was the first clear class legislative-manifesto of capital against labor.

The end of the war brought huge layoffs of workers, and those who kept their jobs found their paychecks reduced (because of the return to regular work schedules under "reconversion" programs) at the very time that the cost of living was going up and the profits of capital were soaring. Government's reports stated that "corporation profits during the war period had been two and a half times the prewar average and were heading toward the highest levels in history" (328). Consequently, the class antagonisms of labor and capital grew to the point that their contestations over wages, prices, and profit could not be settled within the existing legal structures. The clashes between labor and capital became so intense that, as we have said, they were described as "so threatening as to look like nothing less than catastrophic civil war" (Whiting Williams 97).

Through its allies in Congress, capital sought to invent new legal structures to protect its interests and contain labor. Lacking the lobbying power of capital, labor thus resorted to strikes. To defeat labor, capital depicted its own class interests as values that were universal and direct expressions of human nature and portrayed labor as totalitarian anti-capitalists who were against the "American way of life," which was interpreted in terms of free enterprise, individualism, anti-collectivity, and competition, all of which were condensed into the code of "patriotism."

The war of capital against labor, therefore, was fought on two fronts: legalizing the class interests of the owners as national interests, and spiritualizing them as the "higher realities" of a culture which was exceptional, and above all others, in its pursuit of freedom and individual liberty through free competition in a deregulated market.

Through a series of bills and legislation in Congress (e.g., the Case bill of 1946 and the Hobbs Act which followed after it was vetoed by Truman), capital tried to legalize its class interests as national interests but was not fully successful until after the Republican Party's victory in the 1946 midterm election, which gave capital decisive control of Congress. The outcome of this electoral victory was the Taft-Hartley Act of 1947—perhaps the most anti-labor law in modern democracies. The National Maritime Union of America in a pamphlet published in December 1947 called it "The Taft-Hartley Slave Law."

The Taft-Hartley Act (The Labor Management Relations Act of 1947, United States Code, Title 29, Chapter 7) limited strike practices (e.g., mass picketing); denied foremen the protection of federal law; prohibited unions from contributing to political campaigns; gave states [Section 14 (b)] the right to pass laws against union shops ("right-to-work" laws); authorized the president to impose a "cooling-off" period with court approval, and required that votes on the last offer by a company before a walk-out could become legal. It also demanded that union officials should have no affiliation with the Communist Party nor be a sympathizer of Communist causes.

Each of these provisions had great economic and political impact on labor, civil liberties, and equal democratic citizenship. Giving the right to states to outlaw unions, for example, was nothing less than legalizing union busting. Taft-Hartley left working people without any defense of their rights while it made protecting the class interests of the owning class part of the laws of the land. The "cooling-off" period, to point to yet another issue, was aimed at eliminating the "often important element of surprise from strike 'strategy,' a 'status quo condition is established for the union while the employers gather every conceivable weapon for use against the proposed strike'" (Le Blanc 98). The clause against any Communist affiliation for labor was not only a violation of free speech but an assertion of capital's hegemony over labor. The capitalist sympathizers of Fascism and Nazism, such as Henry Ford, had never been asked to denounce or even to explain their politics (Wallace, *The American Axis: Henry Ford, Charles Lindbergh, and the Rise of the Third Reich*).

The Taft-Hartley Act aggressively articulated the agenda of (post-) modern capitalism in the U.S. and the North, in general. It legalized the violent crushing of labor in all social arenas—from factories to schools. The underlying ideology of the act was that labor and unions were activists of a totalitarian collectivism that, in the words of H. W. Prentis, the president of the National Association of Manufacturers (NAM), had produced "an ominous rise in class consciousness" which directly threatened the social order because, as Earl Bunting, NAM's managing director put it, to deal with social and labor issues "on the basis of…class is repugnant to our ideals" (Fones-Wolf 43, 71). Labor, in the cultural and legal discourses of postwar capitalism, was represented as the enemy of individualism, difference, democracy, and, above all, "freedom." The Taft-Hartley Act was aimed at containing labor's agenda which was based on economic equality, human rights, full employment, industrial democracy, expansion of social security, a national health program, unemployment insurance, and a higher minimum wage. In Van A. Bittner's words, labor's goal was "the achievement of the brotherhood of man through the limitation of the competitive and the development of the cooperative" (*CIO News*). Big business regarded these goals as signs of an invading socialism in which "man's dignity and independence is lost to him, and he becomes a slave to the state" (Fones-Wolf 220).

However, the Taft-Hartley Act proved to be much less effective in the actual everyday containment of class tensions and conflicts in the workplace and in establishing the management power for which big business had fought. Major strikes, such as those by mine workers (1950), the steel industry (1952), longshoremen in New York (1953), and others by smaller unions, demonstrated that legislation alone was not able to carry out capital's agenda. A more comprehensive strategy with universal scope and effectivity was needed. To crush labor, capital turned to culture.

THE TURN TO CULTURE

The impact of the strikes against GM and Reuther's call for economic equality were so terrifying to capital and so profound in their social and political implications that, in commenting on the 1946 strikes, Sumner H. Slichter wrote that the U.S. was "shifting from a capitalistic community to a laboristic one—that is to a community in which employees rather than businessmen are the strongest single influence" (quoted in Brody, *Workers in Industrial America* 174). To prevent this potentially different economic model and its social relations from ever becoming a reality in the U.S., capital launched a multi-front cultural campaign against labor. In its fight against labor, capital depicted its own class interests as natural and not the product of a particular stage in history and represented "free enterprise" as emanating from human nature and its desire for freedom. Around this theme, it organized a massive and sophisticated cultural campaign for "reshaping the ideas, images, and attitudes through which Americans understood their world" (Fones-Wolf, *Selling Free Enterprise* 285). The cultural campaign took two related but different forms: the populist and the theoretical.

On the populist level, it was a cynical manipulation by capital of the feelings and sentiments of people in order to turn them into enemies of labor (their own families and neighbors) by focusing on deeply personal issues—from faith to going out on strike; from bringing up children and their schooling to even discussing family matters as intimate as the relations of husbands and wives, by which wives were in fact encouraged to influence their husbands on wages and factory matters. This level of the campaign was conducted in an everyday language with an intensely sensuous imagery through cartoons, films, newspaper articles and editorials in local papers, and company magazines and newsletters, as well as company organized family picnics and birthday celebrations for workers and their families. In her *Selling Free Enterprise*, Elizabeth Fones-Wolf gives a full account of these activities.

On matters of faith, for example, a mode of social activism known as the "Social Gospel" had emerged in the church since the turn of the century. Committed to economic fairness, the Social Gospel gained strength and popularity especially during the Depression and the war. So much so, that in 1942, a conference of the Federal Council of Churches' Commission on the Bases of a Just and Durable Peace advocated "experimentation with various forms of ownership and control, private, cooperative and public" (King, "The Reform Establishment and the Ambiguities of Influence" 126). The sympathies of the activist church for the poor and the weak alarmed capital, which thought such sympathies would strengthen labor's cause. It therefore attacked social activism by the church as a form of ignorance and tried to discredit its very logic. *Fortune* magazine, for instance, asked, "how much do churchmen really know about economics?" (Fones-Wolf 229). At the same time, in community after community, through pro-business media, capital attacked the activist church's cultural values by labeling them "socialist tendencies" and argued that they were "doctrines inimical to the American system of freedom" (220). The role of the church, accordingly, was said to be teaching personal salvation, individual morality, and religious individualism in a market-oriented society and to oppose "the rising tide of collectivism" and a system "in which man's dignity and independence is lost to him and he becomes a slave to the state" (220). The question of economic fairness was thus translated by the cultural arm of capital into the idea of totalitarian priests determined to deprive people of personal salvation and prevent their pursuit of individual choice through the free market.

On the theoretical level, the attacks on labor focused on the material logic: the question that Sumner H. Slichter had raised, namely that the U.S. was "shifting from a capitalistic community to a laboristic one—that is to a community in which employees rather than businessmen are the strongest single influence." This second cultural front developed new arguments for the legitimacy, permanence, and transhistorical moral and social authority of capitalism as an economic regime that was seen as the condition of possibility for human freedom. This is what, for example, F. A. Hayek's writings did. Not only did they provide the grounds for a Neoliberal economics that marginalized Keynesianism, but they also offered an ethics and a philosophy for capitalism (*The Fatal Conceit: The Errors of Socialism*). In a subsequent move, post-theory ("post" as in postcolonialism, postmarxism, poststructuralism, etc.) translated Neoliberal economics into a new philosophy of representation that made discourse the primary ground of social reality. Discourse was not simply a "text" in its narrow sense but

> the ensemble of the phenomena in and through which social production of meaning takes place, an ensemble that constitutes a society as such. The discursive is not, therefore, being conceived as a level nor even as a dimension of the social, but rather as being co-extensive with the social.... There is nothing specifically social which is constituted outside the discursive, it is clear that the non-discursive is not opposed to the discursive as if it were a matter of two separate levels. History and society are an infinite text. (Laclau, "Populist Rupture and Discourse" 87)

Class in post-theory was turned into a trope whose meanings are wayward and indeterminate—a metaphor for a particular language game (Jenks, *Culture* 74). This move has de-materialized class by hollowing out its economic content and turning its materialism into "a materiality without materialism and even perhaps without matter" (Derrida, "Typewriter Ribbon" 281). This de-materializing has taken place through a network of "post" interpretive strategies: such as "destruction" (Heidegger, *The Basic Problems of Phenomenology* 22-

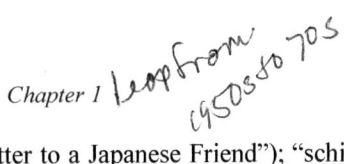

23); "deconstruction" (Derrida, "Letter to a Japanese Friend"); "schizoanalysis" (Deleuze and Guattari, *Anti-Oedipus: Capitalism and Schizophrenia* 273-382); "reparative reading" (Sedgwick, *Touching Feeling* 123-151), "cultural logic" (Jameson, *Postmodernism or, the Cultural Logic of Late Capitalism*); "performativity" (Butler, *Gender Trouble*); "immaterial labor" (Hardt and Negri, *Multitude*), and "whatever (qualunque)" (Agamben, *The Coming Community*).

The goal of both the populist and the theoretical campaigns against the labor movement—which capital often referred to as "socialistic schemes" (Fones-Wolf 52)—has been the blurring of class lines by depicting class antagonisms as cultural differences, and to persuade people that, as Wallace F. Bennett, chairman of the National Association of Manufacturers put it, "We are all capitalists" (quoted in Fones-Wolf 70-73). In other words, as far as capitalism is concerned, there are no class differences in the U.S. and what makes people different are their values, lifestyles, and preferences.

We call this obscuring of class relations by cultural values and the play of language the "cultural turn." The term "cultural turn" is often used to designate a particular movement in social and cultural inquiries that acquires analytical authority in the 1970s and is exemplified by such books as Hayden White's *Metahistory* and Clifford Geertz's *The Interpretation of Cultures*, both of which were published in 1973. White describes history writing as a poetic act and approaches it as essentially a linguistic (tropological) practice (*Metahistory* ix). The view of history and social practices as *poiesis*—which is most powerfully articulated in Heidegger's writings and is re-written in various idioms by diverse authors from Cleanth Brooks through Jacques Derrida to Giorgio Agamben—constitutes the interpretive logic of the cultural turn. Geertz's argument that culture is a semiotic practice, an ensemble of texts (*Interpretation of Cultures* 3-30), canonizes the idea of culture as writing in the analytical imaginary.

The cultural turn is associated by some critics with the social movements of the 1960s and 1970s, whose cultural activism they assume energized rebellion against "scientific" social and cultural inquiries and ushered in the cultural turn with its linguistic reading of culture and emphasis on the subjective (Bonnell and Hunt, ed., *Beyond the Cultural Turn* 1-32). Other critics have also related the cultural turn to the radical activism of the post-1968 era and to postmodernism as well as to a tendency among radical intellectuals, as Larry Ray and Andrew Sayer put it, to approach language no longer as reflecting "material being" but to read it (in Heidegger's words) as the "house of being" (*Culture and Economy after the Cultural Turn* 1).

These and similar explanations of the cultural turn are insightful in their own terms. However, "their own terms" are not only historically narrow but are conceived within the very terms that they seem to critique: they are, in other words, accounts of the cultural turn from within the cultural turn. As a result, in spite of their professed interest in material analysis, their interpretations, like the writings of the cultural turn, remain culturalist. They too analyze culture in cultural terms—that is, immanently. Culture cannot be grasped in its own terms because its own terms are always the terms of ideology. Therefore to understand culture, one needs to look "outside."

The cultural turn, we argue, is not a specific recent event brought about by what is often believed to be a radical (postmodern) break with the modernist metaphysics of "science" and a mistrust of foundationalism, in general, that has led to a new understanding of language as difference. Nor is it the effect of what Stuart Hall calls "cultural revolutions of our time," whereby "culture" has freed itself from material relations outside itself and acquired a materiality of its own, making it "primary and constitutive" ("The Centrality of Culture" 215). Rather, it is the most recent articulation of a structural feature of all class societies.

In the history of all class societies, whenever social contradictions and class antagonism reach a crisis level, a cultural turn emerges that obscures class relations and thus eases social tensions in order to protect the economic interests of the class in dominance. It does so by constructing an autonomous world apart from the material every day through language, which it depicts as being independent from the constraining referents in the outside world. This world, which exists almost exclusively in language, is said to be a sphere of "higher values"—freedom, individuality, choice, forgiveness—and is represented as the site of the real meaning of life: a meaning that is superior to daily concerns about material interests and is thus transcendent to the worldly in general. The world manufactured by the cultural turn is a world charged with spirituality (aesthetic, ethical, religious) and assumed to be a world whose values are beyond change. Change itself is thought to be a re-writing of what already is, a re-figuration of the inside (Derrida, *Positions*; Lyotard, "Rewriting Modernity").

The cultural turn is a necessary feature of all class societies because it discursively "solves" the social contradictions that these societies cannot solve in their material practices and still remain a class society of privilege for some. In capitalism, it generates an imaginary re-patterning of the social by displacing class with "difference," "performativity," and "desire," thereby remaking the social: erasing it as an effect of labor and rewriting it as an effect of meanings, affects, hospitality, and the unrepresentable.

When the social contradictions in the early phases of capitalism affected almost all aspects of social life in Britain, a cultural turn emerged that withdrew from the city and its class conflicts by emphasizing nature as the site where authentic spiritual values and "the essential passions of the heart find better soil in which they can attain their maturity" (William Wordsworth and Samuel Coleridge, "Preface" to *Lyrical Ballads* 9). As in all cultural turns, it focused on language in order to "throw over" the "incidents and situations from common life" (the actual class conditions)

> a certain colouring of imagination, whereby ordinary things should be presented to the mind in an unusual way; and, further, and above all, to make these incidents and situations interesting by tracing in them, truly though not ostentatiously, the primary laws of our nature: chiefly, as far as regards the manner in which we associate ideas in a state of excitement. (8-9)

In the name of a return to "real" reality and honoring the language "really used by men" (8), the cultural turn that emerged in the late 18th century and is often labeled Romanticism, manufactured a reality that is cleaned of the city's class struggles. It obscures the historical real—the urban and its shifting class conflicts—by the imaginary of the rustic where "the passions of men are incorporated with the beautiful and permanent forms of nature" (9).

Another cultural turn emerged almost a century later when the "barbarous indifference" of the "powerful few" had turned the major European cities, such as Manchester, into scenes of "starvation" and the "long continued want of proper nutrition" of those who lived in the "filth, ruin, and inhabitableness" of the slums, on the one side, and, on the other side, those who lived lavish lives in "villas with gardens" on "the breezy heights" (Engels, *The Condition of the Working-Class in England* 59-102). This cultural turn also buried the plight of the every day under aesthetic fantasies (John Ruskin, *Modern Painters*, 1843; *The Stones of Venice*, 1851-53; and Walter Pater, *Studies in the History of the Renaissance*, 1873; *The Renaissance: Studies in Art and Poetry*, 1877). Pater's expression, "the love of art for its own sake," appeared in the "Conclusion" of the first and third editions of *The Renaissance*, but the absence of the "Conclusion" from the second edition is itself a symptom of the class conflicts that surrounded its interpretation. The aesthetic slogan points to the logic of the cultural turn and the manner in which the social fissures and class antagonisms of the late 19th century were hidden under aesthetic values by such writers as Theophile Gautier, Baudelaire, Mallarme, Wilde, and Poe. This cultural turn reached its most effective moment in the inversion and mystification of capitalist labor practices in the early part of the 20th century, particularly around the Great Depression, in the anti-mimetic writings of such High Modernists as T. S. Eliot, *The Waste Land*; James Joyce, *Ulysses, Finnegans Wake*; Virginia Woolf, *To the Lighthouse, The Waves*; Faulkner, *The Sound and the Fury*; Samuel Beckett, *Murphy*; Gertrude Stein, *The Autobiography of Alice B. Toklas*. After being critiqued and purged of its more organicist aspects (de Man, *The Resistance to Theory, Aesthetic Ideology*), which have proven to be useless for postwar capitalism, aesthetics is again the underlying logic of the cultural turn today (Joughin, ed., *The New Aestheticism*.

The post-war cultural turn is not a new, unique phenomena but a reoccurring of a familiar feature of capitalism. It is neither the result of disciplinary conflicts (scientific/interpretive) nor the outcome of radical activism (civil rights, women's movements, queer protests, etc.). Knowledge conflicts and social activism are themselves aspects of the cultural turn, which is, like previous cultural turns, the effect of the material conflicts over appropriations of social surplus labor by private owners. The post-war cultural turn, with which we are concerned in this book, has its origins not in culture (language, theory, epistemology) but in the Taft-Hartley Labor Relations Act of 1947, which is a class act.

As we suggested before, the cultural turn to demolish the labor movement and represent capitalism as the embodiment of human freedom took two different forms: the populist and the theoretical. We have already outlined the contours of the populist campaign, but before moving to an analysis of the theoretical level of this campaign, which is our main focus, we would like to expand on that outline. A key source for much of our own discussion, as we have already indicated, is Elizabeth Fones-Wolf's *Selling Free Enterprise* since her extensive archival research provides an authoritative and detailed account of the strategies and machinery of capital's war against the labor movement.

On the populist level, capital used such cultural devices as pamphlets, cartoons, speeches, radio, and television to translate "freedom" into community concerns and quietly convert "class consciousness" into "company consciousness," which it has equated with the "American Way of Life." GM in its employee magazine, for example, used an "'old codger,' who 'looks like every one's grandfather' to mouth glittering generalities about free enterprise. According to the UAW, the idea was 'to get the corporation curse off what the company is telling you, and to make it look as if it were just your old man giving you the benefit of his years of experience'" (Fones-Wolf, *Selling Free Enterprise* 111). The purpose of this "homey, intimate appeal" was to persuade workers to identify their social, economic, and political well-being with a specific company (Ford, GM, DuPont), and by extension with capitalism. The goal was to forge a post-class unity of workers with capital, or, as Wallace F. Bennett, chairman of the National Association of Manufacturers put it, "we" should not allow "classes" to compartmentalize "us" (Fones-Wolf 70-73). Ideological fights were necessary, according to J. Warren Kinsman, chairman of the National Association of Manufacturers' Public Relations Advisory Committee and vice-president of DuPont, because "in the everlasting battle for the minds of men," they were the only ones "powerful enough to arouse public opinion sufficiently to check the steady, insidious and current drift toward Socialism" (Fones-Wolf 52).

The principal site of cultural work against labor and the selling of free enterprise was the factory. The immediate issues were such fundamental workplace questions as the right to manage wages, benefits, and their relation to profit. Labor had challenged management's total control, and Walter Reuther had proposed that labor-capital co-manage the workplace (Lichtenstein, *The Most Dangerous Man in Detroit: Walter Reuther and the Fate of American Labor*), but capital insisted on total managerial control.

At the core of the campaign to persuade people that "We are All Capitalists," and therefore have the same class interests, was capital's representation that success in one's career was the result of individual effort and not the outcome of collective work as maintained by the labor union philosophy. It equated labor with collectivism and collectivism with totalitarianism, which was against the "American way of life." In economic education classes, the "American way of life" was, itself, interpreted and associated with such business values as profit and the free market. Attendance in these classes was mandatory in some companies:

> During December 1951, half of the adult population of the industrial town of Latrobe, Pennsylvania, took regular breaks from work to study economics on company time. Employees from nineteen firms gathered in small groups to

watch a series of films and to participate in discussions that focused on the values and symbols associated with the American way of life, including patriotism, freedom, individualism, competition, and abundance through increasing productivity. (Fones-Wolf 1)

These and similar economic education programs, such as "How Our Business System Operates," were developed by IBM, Johnson & Johnson, and DuPont as part of a massive re-education of workers, their families, and the general public to accept capitalism as an integral part of the "American way of life." The economic education of workers had some impact on them. After attending "How Our Business System Operates" sessions, a worker said: "I realize what could happen under socialist government, and now I am going to do all I can to prevent government from going socialistic" (85, 84). The purpose of the cultural turn here was to use these classes to help construct an economic common sense that workers would automatically fall back on to explain their "working day" (Marx, *Capital*, I, 340-416) without any further thinking. After having gone through an "economic education" class in his company (the Toyad Company), another worker, Paul Palmer, concluded: "People benefit when the tools of production are in the hands of private individuals rather than under the control and supervision of government" (Fones-Wolf, 85).

These classes taught the necessity of profit and argued that it had "the same purpose as wages a husband brings home" (Sutton et al., 74-89). Teaching "economics" to workers was an attempt to cover up the radical differences in class interests between capital and labor. However, in spite of some success, the awareness of a gap remained and intensified for the most part, and workers were quite skeptical about the lessons they were taught. The UAW made it clear such programs were aimed at "selling corporation's ideas more than its product" (Fones-Wolf 179). The claim, for example, that profit was the same as wages and, therefore, increasing productivity would be beneficial to all, as well as part of American values, was not accepted, as we have said, by those workers who regarded these attempts by management's as "speed-up": getting more work out of workers but paying them the same wages (71).

To overcome such objective class awareness of the difference between "wages" and "profit," the cultural turn articulated a grand epistemological project to discredit the objective itself by representing it as an illusion. The material every day was turned into a zone of piety, feelings and sentimentality by such corporate-sponsored movements as "Spiritual Mobilization," and by what one management manual called strong "appeals to the heart" (Fones-Wolf 163). The idea of objective reality (e.g., low wages and high profit), it was implied, was based on a false philosophy. Instead, an authentic and pious life was lived above material concerns according to personal values and a subjective relation to God, country, and company.

One of the main discursive means by which the cultural turn spiritualized class relations was the "human relations" management theories of Elton Mayo and Abraham Maslow, who argued that (class) conflicts were not objective or natural acts but were the effects of the mind—subjective misunderstanding and miscommunications (Mayo, *Social Problems of an Industrial Civilization*; Maslow, *Eupsychian Management*; *Maslow on Management*). The ideological goal of "human relations" management was to transcode economics into the non-economic and teach workers that the real meaning of life was in the satisfaction of non-material "higher needs" not in receiving higher wages (Jacoby, *Modern Manors: Welfare Capitalism since the New Deal*). By emphasizing the affective, management attempted to produce a friction-free workplace in which class antagonism was replaced by cultural differences so that "Happy relationships shall prevail between the Corporation and its employees" as one corporate head declared (Fones-Wolf 75).

The class contradictions that human relations management theories attempted to solve through affective care were, of course, not solvable by such discursive ploys as giving workers "personal recognition," or manufacturing "community" feeling by organizing picnics or a "Fishing Derby," as Boeing did. The contradictions were reproduced in their solution. At the same time as capital tried to teach that the real purpose of life was in spiritual values, it tried to seduce workers away from trade unions by actually providing what is basically a private welfare program in which workers were not only given higher wages but also such benefits as pensions, healthcare, vacations, and similar material incentives. These contradictions—selling spirituality through material rewards—are repeated in the theoretical discourses of the cultural turn.

Worker participation in decision making was another part of human relations management which ostensibly addressed workers' "higher needs" to be respected and included in important consultations. Consequently, they felt good about themselves and the company, and productivity was increased "without restructuring work or the line of authority within the shop." Management, as many have observed, wanted the "workers to accept what management wants them to accept but to make them feel they made or helped to make the decision" (Fones-Wolf 76). The same was true about profit sharing: it made workers feel they had a share in the company, but the main goal was to strengthen the "spirit of capitalism" and make them an ideological ally of capital. Strange J. Porter, personnel director of a Syracuse machine company, argued that profit sharing combined with other affective attention to the worker will do more to establish the worker's "inherent identity with free enterprise...than anything we merely preach about" (quoted in Fones-Wolf 89). To substitute "company consciousness" for "class consciousness," capital included workers' families in factory events and organized family days. The ostensible purpose was to overcome workers' alienation by forging a new group identity for them. In actuality it was aimed at recruiting wives to the cause of capital. Timken Roller Bearing executive R. L. Frederick wrote: "You would be surprised at the pressure that a woman can place upon her husband if he is considering going out on strike for half a cent an hour, or vested right...Mrs. Employee will often made it clear that she doesn't care for that" (quoted in Fones-Wolf 95).

Manufacturing a common sense that embodied "company consciousness" based on individualism, freedom from government regulations, the importance of profit, competition, and private enterprise while opposed to "statist collectivism," however, was a global and not local goal of capital. The cultural turn thus targeted the community, schools, churches, and other social sites.

In the community, business mangers tried to "create an impression of neighborliness" and erase the image of business that they thought labor had put in people's mind, namely, that capital was "'out to skin the shirt off workingmen' and that business was 'as cold blooded as a fish in a cake of ice'" (Fones-Wolf 160). To do this, businesses worked to mobilize communities in defense of Americanism by forming alliances with The American Legion and other patriotic groups to attack communism through community activities as well as by publishing in 1948 *A Program for Community Anti-Communism Action*, and distributing "The Red Package," a folder that explained the evils of Communism. "Protecting American freedom became intertwined with protecting American business" and many members of communities were recruited as "missionaries of the free enterprise" (Fones-Wolf 161-62).

Education for capital is a process of training children in the skills needed by business. Control of the school curriculum, therefore, has been one of the main goals of capital. When capital and its education theorists talk about "academics," they mean, for the most part, the "fundamentals" of literacy that enable people to join the workforce as efficient workers. But teaching skills without inculcating values was not enough: children also had to be taught to support the system of free enterprise through lessons in individualism, individual liberty, free choice, and patriotism—"the American way of life." This curriculum of skills and values was opposed by critical pedagogues who not only considered it to be a program for producing a docile labor force but also questioned the free enterprise system itself.

In order to make capitalist values integral to education, postwar business did several things. It supported private education because it argued that academic independence was the "counterpart of economic freedom" and in supporting private education it was supporting individual freedom (195). Along the model it had used in factories, it organized economic education programs for schools through formal lessons as well as by distributing such comic books as "Watch Out for the Big Talk" to students. This comic book taught students not to trust "Big Plan" malarkey about "cradle to grave" security and remember that American heroes such as Benjamin Franklin achieved success through individual initiatives (208). Students, therefore, should insist: "None of those 'planned economy' pipe-dreams for us" (208).

In addition capital set up educational conferences, seminars, and exchange programs for faculty and students. In the exchange programs, for example, selected faculty would spend several weeks at a corporation, participating in discussions and seminars on the "philosophical basis of free enterprise" (196). The goal was to convince teachers that education was a means for increasing productivity (197, 202). To put it another way, the exchange programs were designed to teach teachers how to teach students that higher productivity (i.e., a higher ratio of surplus labor) should be a goal of every student (future worker)—which is another way of teaching that the exploitation of labor by capital is for the common good.

Like its approach to education, capital's support for religion has always been instrumental and cynical: God is "a good partner to have in the firm" (Fones-Wolf 224). The partnership seems almost natural given that religion's traditional focus on the individual and individual salvation is essentially a theological justification for the class interests of owners. The minority of clergy who opposed business's brutal competitiveness and its disregard for social solidarity and collectivity, such as those who formed the "Social Gospel" movement in the early part of the twentieth century and their successors after the war were savagely attacked and discredited by capital. The "Social Gospel" and the postwar Federal Council of Churches, as we briefly discussed, were actively involved in economic and political struggles in contrast with church tendencies that emphasized "piety, personal salvation, and individual morality" (219). The Federal Council of Churches, it is worth emphasizing, argued for "experimentation with various forms of ownership and control private, cooperative and public" (King 126).

In order to discredit such social activism, capital duplicated the programs it had used in the factories and especially in the schools. For example, it organized seminars, conferences, and exchange programs aimed at halting the "subversive force that would destroy (our) way of life and at the same time blow out Christianity and American business" (Fones-Wolf 221). Capital's ideological war was aimed at making the clergy teach that the only way to improve life for the poor was to increase productivity, which is a code word for more work without a pay increase. The goal of business was to argue for individual freedom and, in doing so, acquire moral and ethical authority for its exploitation of "free" people (workers) who "freely" enter into a wage contact with capital (Marx, *Capital* I, 280). To give its anti-labor position a philosophical ground and scientific legitimacy, capital published *Christian Economics* which called for "the church to speak up for capitalism and kept up a steady drumbeat of warnings that the survival of religion depended upon the survival of capitalism" (Fones-Wolf 223). As a result of such efforts supported by donations to the church, capital was able to promote a new surge of piety (the phrase "Under God" was added to the pledge of Allegiance at this time) and revive the church's suspicion of labor as agents of Bolshevism. Capital's war against the collectivity of workers was so effective that many ministers came to view labor as un-American and un-Christian and to see the "CIO as the 'mark of the beast' and the 'work of the devil,' and that the CIO stood for 'Christ Is Out'" (228). In the new anti-labor climate, the Federal Council of Churches, itself, accommodated capital and issued a statement making it "perfectly clear the irreconcilable conflict between Christianity and the Communist philosophy as set forth by the Russian state" (231) and its new lay president, Charles Taft—brother of Republican Senator Taft—was urged to drive out "the socialists, pinks and reds" from the organization. The most aggressive anti-labor work of the church, however, was done by the new National Council of Churches, which had displaced the Federal Council of Churches, and was effectively run by J. Howard Pew, the former chairman of Sun Oil Corporation, who asserted: "We never can hope to stop this country's plunge toward totalitarianism until we have gotten the ministers 'thinking straight'" (Fones-Wolf 237). This meant marginalizing labor and erasing class from the scene of social debates.

Perhaps the most famous instance of capital's populist cultural propaganda against labor was the *General Electric Theater* hosted by Ronald Reagan:

> Beginning in 1954, the future president of the United States spent eight years in the employment of General Electric, hosting a television program and speaking to employee and local civic group audiences as part of the company's public relations and economic education program. During that time, Reagan fine-tuned a message that he would repeat in the late seventies, warning of the threat that labor and the state posed to our 'free economy.' (Fones-Wolf 289)

Capital not only organized populist rallies such as the "soldiers of production" and sponsored shows like the *Ford Sunday Evening Hour*, it also invested huge funds setting up "research" fellowships; supporting such conservative think-tanks as the "Hoover Institute," the "American Heritage Foundation" and the "American Enterprise Institute"; and sponsoring arts exhibitions, classical music concerts, and intellectual publications.

The cultural activism of capital against labor, however, was not limited to conservative thinkers. It also energetically recruited Left intellectuals and "socialists of the heart." The defense of free enterprise from the Left has always been of great cultural value to capitalism. When Left intellectuals defend the market directly—in the guise, for example, of "market socialism" (*Market Socialism: The Debate among Socialists*, ed. Ollman; *Why Market Socialism? Voices from Dissent*, ed. Roosevelt and Belkin)—or denounce the enemies of capital as totalitarian, as violators of human rights, and for repressing the play of cultural meanings and thus singularity and heterogeneity (e.g., Sidney Hook, Ernesto Laclau, Jean-François Lyotard, Jacques Derrida), their discourses seem more authoritative and sound more credible coming from the supposed critics of capital than do the discourses of conservative authors.

To put it precisely: the Left has been valuable to capitalism because it has played a double role in legitimating capitalism. It has criticized capitalism as a culture, but has normalized it as an economic system (e.g., Deleuze and Guattari, *Anti-Oedipus: Capitalism and Schizophrenia*; Duncombe, ed., *Cultural Resistance Reader*; Kraus and Lotringer, eds., *Hatred of Capitalism*). It has complained about capitalism's so-called corporate culture, but has normalized it as a system of wage-labor that is grounded on exchange-relations and produces the corporate culture. The normalization of capitalism by the Left takes many forms, but all involve the justification of exploitation, which the Left represents as redemptive. They are all versions—with various degrees of conceptual complexity—of Nicholas D. Kristof's argument in his "In Praise of the Maligned Sweatshop." He writes that the sweatshops in Africa set up by capitalists of the North are in fact "opportunities" and advises that "anyone who cares about fighting poverty should campaign in favor of sweatshops." His argument is summed up by two sentences printed in boldface and foregrounded in his essay: **"What's worse than being exploited? Not being exploited"** (*The New York Times*, 6 June 2006, A-21).

What has made this double role of postwar Left writers so effective for capitalism is the way their innovative writing, unorthodox uses of language, and captivating arguments have generated intellectual excitement. Jean-Paul Sartre, Theodor Adorno, Jean-François Lyotard, Jacques Derrida, Judith Butler, Jean Baudrillard, Jacques Lacan, Michel Foucault, Gilles Deleuze, Giorgio Agamben, Slavoj Zizek, and Stuart Hall, to name the most familiar authors, have each used quite different, but still intellectually intriguing idioms, to de-historicize capitalism. In highly subtle and nuanced arguments, they have translated capitalism's authoritarian economic practices—which quietly force workers to concede to the exploitation of their labor—into cultural values of free choice and self-sovereignty (at the same time that they question traditional subjectivity). Their most effective contributions to capitalism and its economic institutions have been to represent capitalism as a discursive system of meanings and thus divert attention away from its economic violence to its semantic transgressions—its homogenizing of meanings in, for example, popular culture or its erasure of difference in cultural lifestyles. They have criticized capitalism, in other words, for its cultural destruction of human imagination, but at the same time, they have condoned its logic of exploitation by dismantling almost all the conceptual apparatuses and analytics that offer a materialist understanding of capitalism as an economic system. More specifically, they have discredited any efforts to place class at the center of understanding and to grasp the extent and violence of labor practices. They have done so, in the name of the "new" and with an ecstatic joy bordering on religious zeal (Ronell, *The Telephone Book*; Strangelove, *The Empire of Mind: Digital Piracy and the Anti-Capitalist Movement*; Gibson-Graham, *A Postcapitalist Politics*).

Left thinkers, for example, have argued that "new" changes in capitalism—the shift, they claim, from production to consumption—have triggered "a revolution in human thought around the idea of 'culture'" which, under new conditions, has itself become material, "primary and constitutive" (Hall, "The Centrality of Culture" 220, 215), and is no longer secondary and dependent on such outside matters as relations of production. Consequently, Hall and others have argued that the analytics of base/superstructure has become irrelevant to sociocultural interpretations because the "new" conditions have rendered such concepts as objectivity, cause and effect, and materialism questionable. "The old distinction" between "economic 'base' and the ideological 'superstructure'" therefore can no longer be sustained because the new culture is what Fredric Jameson calls "mediatic" (*Postmodernism* 68). According to Hall, "media both form a critical part of the material infrastructure...and are the principal means by which ideas and images are circulated" (Hall 209).

The logic of Hall's argument is obtained by treating the "material" as materialist. Media, however, are "material" only in a very trivial sense, they have a body of matter, and are a material vehicle (as a "medium"), but media are not "materialist" because, as we argue in our theory of materialism below, they do not produce "value" and are not "productive." They distribute values produced at the point of production. The un-said of Hall's claim is that production and consumption/distribution are no longer distinguishable and more significantly, labor has itself become immaterial—which is now a popular tenet in the cultural turn (Hardt and Negri, *Multitude*). But, even Paul Thompson, who is not without sympathy for the turn to culture, argues that "labour is never immaterial. It is not the content of labour but its commodity form that gives 'weight' to an object or idea in a market economy," and, he adds,

> While it is true that production has been deterritorialised to an extent, network firms are not a replacement for the assembly line and do not substitute horizontal for vertical forms of coordination. Network firms are a type of extended hierarchy, based, as Harrison observes, on concentration without centralisation: 'production may be decentralised, while power finance, distribution, and control remain concentrated among the big firms' (*Lean and Mean: The Changing Landscape of Corporate Power in the Age of Flexibility*, 1994: 20). Internal networks do not exist independently of these relations of production, and forms of cooperation, such as teams, are set in motion and monitored by management rather than spontaneously formed. ("Foundation and Empire: A Critique of Hardt and Negri" 84)

Relations of production have shaped and will continue to shape the cultural superstructure. Changes in its phenomenology—the textures of everyday lifestyles, whether one listens to music in a concert hall, on the radio, or through an iPod—should not lead to postmodern Quixotic fantasies about the autonomy of culture from its material base [Ebert, *Cultural Critique (with an attitude)*]. As Marx writes,

> the Middle Ages could not live on Catholicism, nor could the ancient world on politics. On the contrary, it is the manner in which they gained their livelihood which explains why in one case politics, in the other case Catholicism, played the chief part.... And then there is Don Quixote who long ago paid the penalty for wrongly imagining that knight errantry was compatible with all economic forms of society. (Marx, *Capital* I, 176).

In order to represent media as material, that is, as economic, Hall reduces the economic to finance and banking. His interpretation of the economic (and therefore of the base) is exemplary of the way the cultural turn has converted the material/economic into the cultural and placed (mostly aesthetic) values in place of labor. In Hall's scheme, media are economic because they "sustain the global circuits of economic exchange on which the worldwide movement of information, knowledge, capital, investment, the production of commodities, the trade in raw material and the marketing of goods and ideas depend" (209). The economic in his narrative is exchange (of what is obviously produced somewhere else). It is, in short, "trade," which in Neoliberal economic theories is the source of wealth (Hayek, *The Fatal Conceit*; Milton Friedman, *Capitalism and Freedom*). The dynamic of Hall's economics is the movement of capital across borders through banking systems, stock markets, and other financial activities. The media

> truncate the...distances across which commodities can be assembled, the rate at which profits can be realized (reducing the so-called 'turn-over time of capital'), even the intervals between the opening time of different stock markets around the world—the minute time-gaps in which millions of dollars can be made or lost. (210)

The fact that the media make money does not turn them into material/economic agents. Money, itself, is not a material object (as positivists maintain), nor is it the materiality of a "sign" or the sign of materiality, as such Left writers as Gayatri C. Spivak have argued and who, after some relays, represent economics/economy as a structure of writing—textuality in play ("Speculation on Reading Marx: After Reading Derrida" 41). Economy is "the material basis of the world" (Marx, *Capital* I, 175), and its structure is not one of representation but of objective class interests, or as Engels puts it, "economics deals not with things but with relations between persons, and in the last resort, between classes, these relations are, however attached to things and appear as things" (Engels, "Review of Karl Marx, *A Contribution to the Critique of Political Economy*" 514). Media speed up the process of realizing "profit" made at the point of production. Thus, they remain secondary and dependent on the materialism of the relations of production. The quiet, mediated redefinition of the material and economic and the consequent substitution of banking for production put money in place of surplus labor, trade in place of exploitation, and investment in place of class relations. Hall is, of course, repeating a cultural notion of the economic, wealth and work popularized by bourgeois economics in which "supply and demand" constitute the fundamental law and "trade" is the driving force in creating value (Adam Smith, *The Wealth of Nations*).

In the analytics of "base and superstructure," however, the base is not finance capital. It is the totality of the relations of production that are formed in connection with a particular level of productive forces. It is not about the "turnover time" of capital; it is about "production" of capital. The source of wealth is not "interest"—a representation legitimated by Jacques Derrida (*Specters of Marx*) and canonized in cultural theory (Jameson's "Culture and Finance Capital"; Kumar, ed., *World Bank Literature*). Money does not produce (more) money. Profit is the effect of the particular social relations of capital and labor that produce surplus value and not from trade or investment.

Hall's erasure of base/superstructure—as well as most of the other Left theory discourses aimed at demolishing the materialist analysis of culture—depends on a theory of materialism that equates materialism with materiality. But materiality in these Left narratives is actually a mode of matterism: the medium of cultural practices. Since all cultural acts take place within a medium (eating, filming, writing, religion, etc.), they are assumed to be material, and in most Left theory, this becomes the same as materialism. Equating the "material" (materiality) with "materialism" is one of the major contributions of Left writers to the legitimation of capitalism. The issue here is not simply such innocuous subjects as the status of filmic apparatus or the tropes of a text or its affects. What is at stake here are the conditions of historical possibility for all of these factors and their connections to the social relations of production within which they become what they are. In other words, the question of materiality and materialism is, in the end, a *class question*. By equating materiality and materialism, the Left obliterates the class lines dividing consumption from production, wages from profit, and capital from labor. In doing so, it normalizes the capitalist ideology that "We are all capitalists" and, therefore, concedes that there is not outside to the existing social relations.

The analytics of base/superstructure explains *why*—why the way people think is conditioned by the way they live and how this is determined by their place in the social division of labor.

Left theory has normalized the market's inversion of this relation, and in subtle ways and through interminable relays, it has implied that in the "new" times, the way people live is the effect of the way they think. Thought is given an independent existence that, furthermore, is endowed with the agency to produce the social world. Here the ideas of the Left converge with those of the Right (Gilder, "Triumph Over Materialism") because both are products of the same class interests. The Left in the global North has become the advance guard for the market's inversion of materialism into objective idealism (materiality): it has accepted as given that if something exists in the mind it is real, and what is real is material and what is material is real. But, "it is not the consciousness of men that determines their existence, but their social existence that determines their consciousness" (Marx, *A Contribution to the Critique of Political Economy* 21).

To marginalize materialism, the cultural turn represents it as an object-ism, namely, an attempt to build a pre-figural origin for an ontology. Subsequently, by following its familiar formula, it "deconstructs" what it has constructed as an ontology ("materialism") into the rhetorical effects of tropes and concludes that materialism is spectral representation, inscription, and memory.

But where speculation ends, materialism begins.

Materialism is the worldliness of human practices—practices that constantly revolutionize (the relations of) production and make human history, namely, the progress of humans toward freedom from necessity. Materialism is the objective, productive activities of humans involving them in social relations under definite historical conditions that are independent of their will and are shaped by struggles between contesting classes over the surplus produced by social labor. A materialism that excludes historical processes is a theology of the corporeal.

Materiality, on the other hand, is the objective idealism of the cultural turn which, in the speculative tradition of Feuerbach, produces a spiritualized "materiality without materialism and even perhaps without matter" (Derrida, "Typewriter Ribbon" 281). It is the contemplative corporeality of difference, which is

Getting Class Out of Culture 41

the effect of the textual sensuality of language—the medium of representation, the body and its affective resistance to conceptuality and determinate meanings. In the turn to culture, materiality becomes a performativity, a species of meaning, an effect of archives, of memories, which is another way of saying: it is the effect of "matter as a sign" (Butler, *Bodies That Matter* 49).

Matter, however, is not a sign or any other physical body, nor is it the self-alienated spirit or an invention to support atheism (George Berkeley). To identify matter with an object, an indivisible atom or any immutable substance/motion, or to equate it with a quanta of light, zero-dimensional point particles, or one-dimensional "strings" ("superstring theory"), is to make the local modalities of matter absolute and to yield to the urge for physicalism and its metaphysical twin, (unchanging) substance, in bourgeois philosophy and its ontology and epistemology. Matter is objective reality in history—materialism; it is not corporeality—matterism. Owning a house and not owning a house are both social relations and both are materialist—articulations of labor relations in history. Matter is the shared property of the totality of different and transforming elements, historical processes, and social practices; these are independent from the will of the individual and exist in conflicts (motion) objectively outside the consciousness of the agent. The cultural turn disperses matter into substance (body, language, sign…) and thus dehistoricizes it—separates matter from production and its contradictions—and consequently "substantiates" the class interests of the owners.

Matter is history not corporeality: it is the dialectics of the objective. "There are no ghosts." The ghosts have, however, been let loose on the contemporary in the writings of such Left thinkers as Jacques Derrida, who claims, "I vote Socialist in France" ("Politics and Friendship" 212). Derrida's writings—which have a conceptual boldness, intellectual liveliness, and writerly eagerness that, at times, borders on ecstasy—have strengthened the underlying logic of capitalism directly (e.g., using the allegory of "singularity" to bolster capitalism's entrepreneurial individualism) and indirectly (e.g., dismantling the oppositional logic of binaries that marks the owners from workers and the powerful from powerless). They have been master-lessons in class collaboration for the global North since the 1960s. These lessons have had a profound impact on almost all forms of social and cultural writings (as we will thus discuss both here and throughout this book).

Derrida's notion of the specter and spectrality shades the lines separating the "real" and the "imaginary" (*Specters of Marx* 10) and more radically undercuts any claim for the objectivity of class interests: the real is always haunted by its spectral other which puts its self-sameness in question and implies class is never free from its own self-difference; thus its claim for coherence and objectivity is doubtful. "The specter was there (but what is the *being-there* of specter? What is the mode of presence of a specter…?)" (38). Derrida reads class spectrally (55, 85-87, 90) and subtly and obliquely opens up what he regards to be the self-difference (within) class through the relays of such spectral intermediaries as "gift," "hospitality," "democracy-to-come," "supplementarity," and the

"New International." His ghosting of class is an integral part of his philosophical efforts to keep capitalism as a functioning and expanding system hospitable to "democracy-to-come." Like Milton Friedman (*Capitalism and Freedom*), he seems to believe that global capitalism brings, what is regarded by the owning class to be, economic freedom and is said to be the condition of political freedom (Derrida, *Philosophy in a Time of Terror* 123). However, unlike Friedman, Hayek and other traditional proponents of capitalism, the task of system maintenance is performed by Derrida in a fresh and unorthodox manner and in intellectually exciting vocabularies of nuance and fine distinctions. Derrida deploys the rapturous terms of "dangerous" supplementarity, spectrality, undecidability, traces, and *différance* that have become part of a performativity of destabilizing, anarcho-readings of the social. The brilliance of his pro-capital interpretations of the social is that he has stabilized the system of wage-labor by de-stabilizing some of its cultural signs and thus creating the image of radical transformation. The semiotic rebellion of his anarcho-readings becomes a screen that covers over the second layer of his interpretations which secure capitalism as an economic system. For instance, he puts in question capital's culturally violent treatment of the "immigrant" (which he often rewrites as the more innocuous "foreigner") but not the global economic regime that produces immigrants—mostly people looking for jobs—the system that puts no restrictions on the free movements of capital across borders but severely limits the movements of workers. The immigrant thus becomes a purely affective entity (the "singularity of the new arrival, of the unexpected visitor") in his readings which, in effect, clear capital by sentimentalizing the "foreigner" and erasing historicity (*Of Hospitality* 83). His readings unsettle the cultural by putting its signs in play but keep classes in their place, preserved as they are (with, as we will see, a "difference" that makes no difference at all).

His arche-strategy proves quite useful in maintaining the system; it defuses oppositions within the system (thus establishing steadiness and stability) by what he calls "double-science" (*Positions* 41) or "double session" (*Dissemination* 4), which writes "difference" into the system and in doing so it claims to have balanced the relations of power in the system. After deactivating the binaries, he expands the system by erasing its boundaries of inside/outside (*The Truth in Painting*). Derrida's insistence that "the outside is the inside" (*Of Grammatology* 44) is a philosophical alibi by which he re-makes the inside as an imperial inside. Although he puts the "is" under erasure in order to inscribe "difference" into the system to equalize the relations between binaries, his "double-science" actually annexes the outside to the inside, and the resulting imperial inside sets the laws of the social according to its own immanent needs and requirements. His inside/outside argument provides the cognitive context for reading global capitalism in its own terms—an imperial inside without regulations (from outside). The self-sovereignty of the inside is further emphasized in Derrida's deconstructive readings in which the text is said to provide its own theory of reading and deconstruct itself ("Letter to a Japanese Friend") without any intervention from an outside. The logic of "self-deconstruction" is, of course, the logic of the voluntary: leave capital alone, it will voluntarily re-form itself.

Derrida suspends the oppositions within the system by converting its class antagonisms into discursive differences and through such conversions stabilizes the system. The conversions are completed through elaborately detailed and often highly entertaining readings, in which he renovates "old" concepts, ideas, and interpretive modes that have lost their historical usefulness for capitalism, translating them into more useful ones. For instance, the notion of a coherent identity is no longer a primary subjectivity in new capitalism because it is incompatible with the emerging needs of consumer capitalism, which requires a discontinuous identity that moves from one fractured identity to another. Each fragment of identity has different desires and appetites, which add to consumption and the rate of profit for capital. While capitalism may no longer need coherent identities when it comes to interpellating subjects as consumers, it certainly needs them when it calls the subject to fight its wars as a soldier—fighting in the name of freedom (of trade), democracy (de-regulation of the market), and human rights (the right to obtain and maintain private property)—so that capital can have unfettered access to cheap labor and resources. Coherent identity is required for the ideological indoctrination of "soldiers of production." Derrida's "double-science" therefore never discards the old but maintains it (with a difference) and brings the old and new together (for capitalism) in a fluctuating cohabitation that cannot be read in terms of either "new" or "old" but is always in an uncertain in-between-ness of the old-as-new and the new-as-old. Derrida's deconstruction is a discursive machine for renovating capital's old concepts, translating them into "difference" and thus "new" terms. It keeps the old and the new together so that they can be used situationally.

Through "double-science," identity, for example, is situationally treated as coherent or fractured according to the pragmatics that maintain the system. In his defense of Paul de Man's Nazi writings, for instance, Derrida deploys "Paul de Man" both as a stable identity (otherwise no defense of the "later" Paul de Man would be necessary) and also as a fractured identity whose parts are autonomous, and thus the later Paul de Man cannot be said to be a continuation of the former Nazi sympathizer (*Memoires: For Paul de Man*). Paul de Man is a coherent identity that is also fractured, and what seems a rather absurd patching is described as self-difference, which is a capacious concept accounting for almost all fissures in Derrida's own fissural writing.

Referential language—to take another contribution Derrida has made to capital's self-balancing—implies the existence of an objective reality, such as class, that is independent of language and, therefore, not a capital-friendly apparatus of knowledge. Capital discards referential language when its referent is class and the social antagonisms formed by objective production practices. Yet it needs this very referentiality in language when its managers issue orders to its workers because it is only through clear reference that capital makes sure the orders are clearly understood and carried out. Derrida's double-science revives the referential by using the differential and keeps both in a relation of uncertainty available to capital. Language is neither referential nor differential—it is always in the shift and oscillations between the two because nothing is either literal or metaphorical; everything is a hybrid, which is another way of saying that deconstruction is an engine producing hybrids to renovate the conceptual apparatuses of capital.

The shifts, hesitations, and oscillations of meanings and values in the hybrids are made part of the system and declared marks of the profound and unexplainable "undecidablity" of the real (*Limited Inc* 116, 148). The undecidable is a space that accommodates—in the form of an ethics of responsibility—the unpredictability of the market, in the face of which capital must make decisions about the most effective routes to profitability. Through undecidability, Derrida turns these decisions into a high (melo)drama of responsibility (*The Gift of Death; Politics of Friendship*), which endows capital with a moral consciousness, whose agonies never cease.

Derrida's contributions to capital's social logic are exemplary of the writings of the Left in the global north (socialists of the heart). They revamp capital's dated concepts in daring new languages and through boundary-breaking readings within the system's own conventions, codes, and habits of knowing. They always keep the system intact while re-arranging its details inside.

The effort to enlist Left intellectuals to join the cause of capital has been widespread and global. At times, these highly sophisticated strategies have even involved such state agencies as the CIA.

In *The Cultural Cold War: The CIA and the World of Arts and Letters*, for example, Frances Stonor Saunders describes how the CIA in the postwar years—through such programs as "The Congress for Cultural Freedom" and in the name of intellectual freedom—used Left intellectuals to fight socialism and planned economies by directly or indirectly funding such journals as *Partisan Review, Kenyon Review, New Leader*, and *Encounter*, which were edited by and/or published the writings of Stephen Spender, Irving Kristol, Frank Kermode, Philip Rahv, Sidney Hook, Daniel Bell, Isaiah Berlin, Hannah Arendt, Dwight Macdonald, Mary McCarthy, Arthur Koestler, and Raymond Aron. The CIA's efforts were not limited to the support of these intellectuals, who represented themselves as being above party politics and free iconoclastic thinkers, or to the print media. The CIA also supported "art for art's sake" and sponsored numerous exhibitions of abstract art to combat "realism" and art with a social content, as we discuss in the next chapter. The CIA translated and distributed the works of writers, including classic American authors such as Melville, Emerson, Franklin, and Thoreau, whose writings legitimated the free market through celebrations of spiritual freedom and unfettered individualism. It routinely sponsored concerts, supported symphonies and ballets, and sent African American singers and jazz musicians, such as Marian Anderson and Louis Armstrong, to Europe. Saunders argues that the support for African-American artists was motivated by the need to represent American capitalism as free from racism.

As James Petras makes clear in his own discussion of these issues, the deployment of culture and its valorization were part of a world-historical "class warfare" ("The CIA and the Cultural Cold War Revisited"). Petras writes that "some of the biggest names in philosophy, political ethics, sociology, and the arts, who gained visibility from CIA-funded conferences and journals, went on to establish the norms and standards for promotion of the new generation, based on the political parameters established by the CIA. Not merit nor skill, but politics—the Washington line—defined 'truth.'" The cultural common sense of the Left today is constructed in these postwar cultural wars conducted by the CIA and corporations in defense of American capitalism. These Left intellectuals now act, as Petras puts it, as "ideological gatekeepers," excluding from cultural contestations the critical intellectuals who "write about class struggle, class exploitation, and U.S. imperialism." Critical intellectuals are considered to be involved in ideological work and polemical writing, not objective inquiries and scholarship. Capitalism, through its institutions, has convinced intellectuals that "sustained political engagement...is incompatible with serious art and scholarship."

Left intellectuals in the North, in the name of freeing repressed meanings and identities from the metaphysics of presence and power, have dismantled all critique-al understanding of capitalism. The Left is so useful in capital's attack on labor because it represents capitalism not as an economic regime based on wage labor, but as a set of cultural practices that even out "differences" by homogenizing meanings. Capitalism is assumed to be culturally repressive because it homogenizes cultural meanings and not for exploiting the labor of others. Of course, this is not the case: capitalism is at the forefront of advancing singularity and difference in order to secure its exploitation of labor. What is needed is not more singularity but collectivity.

In the mythologies of the Left that depict capitalism as a regime of homogenization, the cure for capitalism's assumed in-difference is more activism for difference by activating heterogeneity through, for example, consumption and other lifestyle strategies—which is, of course, exactly what capitalism needs for the increased accumulation of capital. With great "subtlety," Left writers in the "cultural turn" portray consumption as a creative, "producerly" act of meaning-making (Fiske, *Reading the Popular* 95-113) and resistance against capitalism (de Certeau, *The Practice of Everyday Life*). In the narratives of the "cultural turn," consumption is a transformative practice that, from within culture itself, changes economic and political processes (Canclini, *Consumers and Citizens*). By proposing the cultural and political outcomes of capitalism as causes of in-difference, the cultural turn occludes them as effects of economics, enabling it to substitute cultural "inequality" for "class." Thus, while it puts in question matters of race and other cultural identities, it erases the economics of class. In other words, it obscures the exploitative structural relations of production while unveiling repressed cultural meanings and identities.

The ideas expressed in Reagan's shows, speeches, and writings on the defense of "free" enterprise, freedom of choice, individualism, and anti-communism (Skinner et al., eds. *Reagan, In His Own Hand*) are rearticulated in the postwar years in the sophisticated theoretical and cultural writings of the

"New Critics" (T. S. Eliot, Ezra Pound, R. P. Blackmur, Cleanth Brooks, Yvor Winters, John Crowe Ransom, and Allen Tate), the anti-communist texts of New York intellectuals (Lionel Trilling, Sidney Hook, Dwight Macdonald, Philip Rahv, Norman Podhoretz), the anti-historical writings of the "Myth Critics," such as Northrop Frye, and the formalist texts of such structuralists as Levi-Strauss.

As the postwar Keynesianism was displaced by monetarism and Neoliberalism, anti-socialism once again become the ideology of the Left in the global North. Anti-labor ideologies were recast in the quasi-anarchist radical Left idioms of hospitality "to-come" (as in "democracy-to-come"), anti-totalization, desire, lack, and logocentrism in the writings of such authors as Jacques Derrida, Jean-François Lyotard, Jacques Lacan, Michel Foucault, Gilles Deleuze and Felix Guattari, Paul de Man, Richard Rorty, Stanley Fish, Judith Butler, Ernesto Laclau, Philippe Lacoue-Labarthe, Stuart Hall, Slavoj Zizek, Giorgio Agamben, and Alain Badiou. Their writings have contributed to the construction of a Left pro-market ideology that now also shapes the curricula of knowledge as well as the management of the university—a space that before the hegemony of the Left was largely outside commodification.

In spite of the local differences in topic, idiom, and the specifics of the arguments, the writings of the cultural turn are essentially a rewriting of an old Hegelian metaphysics ("All that is rational is real, all that is real is rational," *Philosophy of Right*) as a new ideological consensus: all that is cultural is real; all that is real is cultural. The cultural turn is the representational apparatus of postwar capitalism; it provides the concepts and interpretive devices for what Bret Cochran calls, "the businessman's intellectual reconquest of America" (*American Labor in Midpassage* 2). The cultural turn deploys culture as a trope to interpret almost all aspects of social life from work and elections to foreign policy, healthcare, economics, family, environment, and architecture. The postwar primacy of culture, which emerges in the mid 1940s and reaches its height of theoretical influence from the early 1970s to the mid-2000s, has now become the canonic interpretive code—often with a linguistic twist—in social and cultural analysis (e.g., Elspeth Probyn, *Blush: Faces of Shame*; Lee Edelman, *No Future: Queer Theory and the Drive*; Ella Shoat, *Taboo Memories, Diasporic Voices*; N. Katherine Hayles, *My Mother Was a Computer*).

2

Class Binaries and the Rise of Private Property

Binaries—indeed, all oppositions—reproduce material class divisions on various levels of social life. Since structures of owning are fundamental to the accumulation of capital, binaries cannot be eliminated in actual contemporary social relations without transforming the relations of capital and labor. Consequently cultural discourses deploy a range of interpretive strategies articulating the quasi-concept *différance* and its network of tropes, such as hybridity, heterogeneity, singularity, in-between-ness, etc. (Derrida, *Margins of Philosophy*), in order to represent binaries as effects of a metaphysics of Truth, which is assumed to be the working of a will to power (Nietzsche, *The Will to Power*). The class origins of binaries are thus obscured through either discourses of power relations (Foucault, *History of Sexuality* I, 90-102) or a textual displacement, such as "deconstruction," by which the material is converted into the cultural and the cultural itself is written as a knot of nomadic signs whose meanings are always in play. Binaries, we argue, are the outcome of the rise of private property, and the discourses of metaphysics are only one of many cultural vocabularies that have been used in class societies to either naturalize binaries (as in Descartes's *Meditations*—especially the "sixth meditation") or to make them culturally suspect (as in Derrida's *Of Grammatology* and his *Of Hospitality*). In order to understand the interpretive logic by which binaries are translated from a material structure into a writing effect through the machinery of *différance*, we need to examine the working of this machinery.

THE SPECTER OF METAPHYSICS AND BINARY PANIC

As postwar capitalism becomes more complex in its global production relations, its class contradictions increase. It thus requires newer forms of cultural representations that can articulate a believable rhetoric to justify its progressively more exploitative labor practices and, at the same time, imbue it with social legitimacy and ethical authority (as a champion of liberty). The current cultural turn is a radical response to this radical demand. It is entirely different from traditional cultural analysis in which culture was only one of the factors taken into account. It reverses the relationship between the vocabularies we use to describe things and the things themselves.... This is not the same thing as saying that...[practices] are 'embedded' in a particular socio-cultural context, or that they are 'socially constructed.' (du Gay and Pryke, ed., *Cultural Economy*, 2)

To put it differently, the newest phase of the cultural turn represents class upside down by claiming that meaning arises not from material practices but from the sign itself, from language: "The names of things are also sobriquets. Not from the thing to the word, but from the word to the thing; the word gives birth to the thing" (Bakhtin, *Essays and Dialogues on His Work* 182). In the cultural turn, classes become "metaphors for particular language games" (Jenks, *Culture* 74). As a result of the "cultural revolutions of our time" (Stuart Hall, "The Centrality of Culture" 220-225), culture is now understood to be an assemblage of differential, contingent, and autonomous events that are not controlled "by destiny or a regulative mechanism" (Foucault, "Nietzsche, Genealogy, History" 154) other than their own immanent and aleatory working.

The radicality of the cultural turn, however, is not simply in "reversing" the relation of the material and cultural or language and reality, because such a reversal still leaves the governing structure intact. Rather, it puts in question the structure of the relationship and casts doubt on any reliable relation between the two, namely the possibility of any decidable representation. The cultural turn textualizes the two and resituates them in a new relationship through *différance*.

In his *The Other Heading: Reflections on Today's Europe*, Jacques Derrida writes:

what is proper to a culture is not to be identical to itself. Not to not have an identity, but not to be able to identify itself, to be able to say, 'me' or 'we'; to be able to take the form of a subject only in the non-identity to itself or,...only in the difference *with itself [avec soi]*. There is no culture or cultural identity without this difference *with itself*. (9-10)

The "difference" (*différance*), in question here, it should be clear from our discussions so far, is not the traditional difference or dissimilarity between two settled identities but a radical difference that activates difference within an identity and, by turning it into an instance of instability, makes it difficult for difference to serve with any certainty as a secure term in any relation of opposition between two steady identities (Derrida, *Margins of Philosophy* 1-27). The cultural turn has more and more vigorously taken "culture in difference *with itself*" as its interpretive norm and since the early 1970s, has forcefully represented itself as a critique of the metaphysics of culture—cultural essentialism (S. Hall, "The Problem of Ideology: Marxism without Guarantees" ; Fish, *The Trouble with Principle*; G. Hall and Clare Birchall, ed., *New Cultural Studies*).

The "problem" with metaphysics, from the perspective of the contemporary cultural turn, is that metaphysics considers Truth, which it obtains through a binary logic, to be a coherent totality in plentitude, outside representation and unaffected by such accidents as language, difference, affects, and thinking.

Class Binaries and the Rise of Private Property 49

Truth, in metaphysics, is the ground of thinking, not its subject. Although Truth, as first principle, is different in each version of metaphysics ("Form," in Plato; "Spirit" in Hegel; "Art" in Nietzsche; "Being" in Heidegger; "Affect" in Freud, or "Existence" in Sartre), each one is considered to be self-evident. If, however, the cultural turn's critique of metaphysics is read reflexively—that is, if its own practices are included in its own critique—it will be clear that the anti-metaphysics of the cultural turn is itself a version of metaphysics, what we call the metaphysics of the *negative*. Like all metaphysics it interprets the world through a first principle—representation, i.e., the difference of language—by which it establishes the Truth of other cultural practices.

The cultural turn critiques class as a concept because it regards its "truth" to be a "problematic" matter (Derrida, "Politics and Friendship" 204) mostly because "a social class" is said to be an objective totality outside the difference of language and therefore "homogenous, present and identical to itself" (Derrida, "Marx & Sons" 237). Its objectivity, in Derrida's narrative, is established by grounding it in the lucidity of an "economy" founded on "production" and "appropriation" without difference (Derrida, "Politics and Friendship" 205). For the cultural turn, such a view of class is an inherited metaphysics. In order for class to become viable for the "realities of techno-scientific capitalist modernity," it needs to be "considerably differentiated" by a "*différance*" that produces "an economy that counts with the uneconomic" and displays class's immanent heterogeneity ("Marx & Sons" 239, 204, 206). The cure for metaphysics (of class) is *différance*—the opacity that language displays in the proclaimed lucidity of Truth.

The same self-evident first principle is also at work in Derrida's reading of Rousseau:

> what one calls the real life of these existences 'of flesh and bone,' beyond and behind what one believes can be circumscribed as Rousseau's text, there has never been anything but writing, there has never been anything but supplements, substitutive significations which could only come forth in a chain of differential references, the 'real' supervening and being added only while taking on meaning from a trace and from an invocation of the supplement, etc. And thus to infinity… (*Of Grammatology* 159)

In his theory of ideology, Paul de Man is even more insistent on the self-evident priority of the difference of language:

> What we call ideology is precisely the confusion of linguistic with natural reality, of reference with phenomenalism. It follows that, more than any mode of inquiry, including economics, the linguistics of literariness is a powerful and indispensable tool in the unmasking of ideological aberrations, as well as a determining factor in accounting for their occurrence. (*Resistance to Theory* 11)

With the priority of language as its first principle, the (anti-)metaphysics of the cultural turn regards "presence"—the grounding property of metaphysics which is placed outside the text—to be itself a textual construct marked by difference. The "I," to take what is perhaps the most familiar instance of presence in established metaphysics, is textualized in the anti-metaphysics of difference as an absent presence constructed by signs:

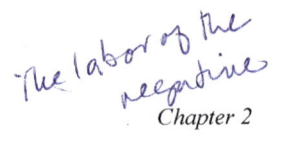

> Where there is an 'I' who utters or speaks and thereby produces an effect in discourse, there is first a discourse which precedes and enables that 'I' and forms in language the constraining trajectory of its will. (Butler, *Bodies That Matter* 225)

To be quite explicit: the primary reality that shapes all other realities in the metaphysics of the negative is not the categories of traditional ontology—such as "soul," "substance," "causality," "form," "experience" or "existence"—but the anti-ontology of language. As we see in Butler's text, language undoes the coherence of "first principles" (such as the "I") in traditional metaphysics, showing how they are fissured by their differences within. Butler assigns to language the Truth of a "first principle" that, in her words, "precedes" and "constrains" (i.e., determines) other realities such as "I."

The cultural turn's claim to be an anti-metaphysics of culture is based, for the most part, on its deconstruction of culture-as-totality (culture-as-presence) and demonstrating that culture is itself a tissue of language differences that cannot act as the origin or site of Truth. This is the core of its argument against classical cultural studies—which it claims treats language as if it were a transparent reflection of an objective culture outside and not an autonomous play of signs that construct what is seen as objective culture. In the cultural turn, the difference of culture from itself loosens culture's claim to Truth. In other words, the singular (the trope) unknots the general (the topic), and the fraction undoes the whole. This privileging of difference as a self–evident principle that "instigates the subversion of every kingdom" (Derrida, *Margins of Philosophy* 22) is itself a claim to Truth—the Truth of the negative—which "belongs neither to the voice nor to writing" (5) and is therefore an anti-essentialist essentializing of the "neither-nor," a foundationalism of in-between-ness.

The contemporary anti-metaphysics of culture critiques traditional metaphysics for attempting to retrieve presence (Truth) from the void of absence. However, its own arguments are also grounded in obtaining presence from an absence, namely the inaudible /a/ in "*différance*" (Derrida, *Margins of Philosophy* 3-27). From the missing /a/, the plenitude of [a] is recovered in the oscillations "between two differences" (*Margins of Philosophy* 5). This space of non-belonging gives rise to all meanings ("culture"); it puts in ruins the familiar first principles of Truth, Objectivity, History, Reference, and Consciousness. But in their ruins, it constructs a new metaphysics of *différance* (with an "a") which, although absent from speech, is the presence on which culture as "writing" ("culture in difference from itself") is based. *Différance* is the certainty of the uncertain, the decidability of the undecidable, the law of "a law without law" (*Of Hospitality* 83).

Not only is *différance* not outside difference, but it is constructed through the very binary logic that it critiques: the identity of *différance* (difference in flux within) depends on the binary that opposes it to difference (difference in stability between). Without the binary opposition between "a" (movement) and "e" (static), there will be no "a." *Différance* which

> cannot be 'relieved' [*relevé*], resolved, or appeased by any philosophical dialectic; and which disorganizes 'historically,' 'practically,' textually, the opposition or the difference (the static distinction) between opposing terms. (Derrida, *Dissemination* 6-7)

is itself grounded in an opposition. This anti-metaphysics is the metaphysics of the negative. It is an essentialism that always "disorganizes" and whose instability is stabilized always and beforehand. As always stable yet always destabilizing, it is an unchanging essence outside history, textuality and what it calls *différance*, which it deploys to rewrite the other. It is writing in the absent presence of negative spacing.

The critique of metaphysics (of class) in the cultural turn is based on the primacy of representation and is as much a metaphysics as the metaphysics it critiques. Like all metaphysics it is the discursive apparatus of the class interests of owners. The critique of metaphysics in the cultural turn suspends the explanatory concepts of a materialist understanding of culture and rewrites them as indeterminate meanings. It is an epistemological alibi through which the materialist content is hollowed out of class, and class is rewritten as undecidable within an equally aporetic and self-undermining economic that is seen as "something heterogeneous both to productivity and unproductivity" ("Politics and Friendship" 205). The cultural turn puts classes—as objective materialist relations of property that mark the binary divisions of the contemporary social—in ruins by reading them as effects of a productivist metaphysics grounded in what Derrida, in a related context, calls the "economic dogma of Marxism" ("Politics and Friendship" 205). Classes are put in ruins not by showing they are empirically unverifiable or theoretically unavailable but through an interpretive violence that privileges representation (*différance*) and holds that "*there is nothing outside of the text*" (Derrida, *Of Grammatology* 158).

Différance puts in question the concepts and categories whose Truth is said to be produced by a closure of metaphysics. It does so not to demolish them but to "deconstruct" them, to change them through a recognition of their difference from themselves which undoes their hold on their putative Truth. The "de" in "deconstruction" is not "the demolition of what is constructing itself, but rather what remains to be thought beyond the constructivist or destructionist scheme" (Derrida, *Limited Inc.* 147). More explicitly, Derrida argues that "deconstruction" is a "rethinking" with a "difference": "to deconstruct the metaphysical and rhetorical" is not "to reject and discard them" but "to reinscribe them otherwise" (*Margins of Philosophy* 215).

What is "otherwise"? Derrida writes that the "otherwise" is a "deconstructing, dislocating, displacing, disarticulating, disjoining, putting 'out of joint' the authority of the 'is'" ("The Time Is Out of Joint" 25). In other words, he maintains that deconstruction is a rethinking of (the ethics of) power relations that organize the way things "are"—the "authority of the 'is.'" But it turns out that "otherwise" obscures property under the sign of power. The deconstruction of "is" seduces the understanding of "is" away from what makes authority authoritative—gives "is" its power of being. Power ("authority of") is not obtained, abandoned, or lost by cultural discourses, as in the "two beloved sentences" Derrida reads in "The Time Is Out of Joint" (25). The material ground of power (the authority of "is") is private property, which structures power relations not only in the feudal monarchy in which Hamlet's struggle for power and legitimacy is situated but also in the specter of America that hovers over Derrida's text: "what Hamlet says to me today in America" (25). In reading the power relations in *Hamlet*, Derrida disperses property—which he has already made problematic by the play of the "proper" and its indeterminate meanings (*Margins of Philosophy* 207-271)—in a discourse (of interpretive) power that reads *Hamlet* through the fiction of "America is/in deconstruction" (25, 26, 37). After deconstructing power as an "is," the task of politics becomes the poetics of change: "change the world without taking power" (Holloway, *Change the World without Taking Power*).

Derrida's "otherwise" rewrites the old order of "having" solid objects (feudalism and the America of industrial capitalism) as new flows of meaning of the is-ness ("just what is America...?") in cybercapitalism—which is at the cutting edge of "the new realities of techno-scientific capitalist 'modernity' of world society." "Class" in these new realities has become a totality without difference ("Marx & Sons" 239) and therefore "more and more inappropriate" ("Politics and Friendship" 203). Derrida's writing contributes to the construction of an interpretive situation in which techno-scientific capitalism is read as "post-property," as a place in which "having" is displaced by "access" and "the material gives way to the immaterial" (Rifkin, *The Age of Access* 14-15).

Derrida's writings are master lessons in erasing class from contemporary cultural critique—in replacing private property with power, and then exchanging power for affective relationships, what he calls "friendship," "forgiveness," and "hospitality." J. K. Gibson-Graham, for example, annotate these lessons through Hannah Arendt's spiritualism of "love of the world" as the "pleasures of friendliness" (*A Postcapitalist Politics* 6). Affective activism becomes a powerful contribution of the cultural turn to marginalizing class. It is the un-said, for instance, of the new progressive business management theories. These theories ostensibly attempt to increase the freedom of workers in the workplace, but they actually erase militancy in the workplace and advocate such "tactics" as, in Gibson-Graham's words, "seducing, cajoling,...enticing, inviting" (6) workers to give up class struggle and instead cultivate "trust, conviviality, and companionable connection" (6) with management—the agents of capital.

The cultural turn updates old concepts by re-writing the oppositional binary relations in culture (e.g., class oppositions) as effects of *différance*. This discursively undoes the structure of material antagonisms constitutive of capitalism and floats the class contradictions of capital as an excess of meanings fissuring the binary class structure. The opposition of binaries are represented not as differences from each other but as the "difference" within each one. This move defuses the antagonism between owners and workers into a plurality of differences in which the structural class opposition loses its own difference, becoming *différance*—as difference within, a metaphysics that puts its own Truth outside its own critique.

As we have seen, displacing the opposition (between classes) by difference (within classes) is carried out through what Derrida calls "a double science," which overturns the hierarchy between the two terms and shows, for example, that speech acquires its seeming stable identity—through which it opposes itself to writing—from writing itself. Writing, in other words, is not "outside" speech but is the difference within speech, which now becomes a generalized writing (as *différance*). The new concept of writing (as a generalized *différance*) "simultaneously provokes the overturning of the hierarchy speech/writing, and the entire system attached to it, and releases the dissonance of writing within speech, thereby disorganizing the entire inherited order" (*Positions* 42). This renovation never questions the system from its outside—in the political economy of labor— but from inside, in the economies of signification: "The movements of deconstruction do not destroy structures from the outside. They are not possible and effective, nor can they take accurate aim, except by inhabiting those structures...operating necessarily from the inside" (Derrida, *Of Grammatology* 24). This is one of deconstruction's great contributions to system maintenance in capitalism which is all the more effective now because—as we suggested in our discussion of the Left and capitalism—it claims that the "double science" is an applied science of emancipation, a science that is said to be much more radical than ("say") socialism (Bennington, *Legislations: The Politics of Deconstruction* 50).

The cultural turn deploys the analytics of difference to deconstruct class. In the production system, it sees the worker not as a stable "inside" but as a contingent effect of what is, in the metaphysics of labor, considered "outside"—the owner. The owner, in other words, is the difference within—the difference of the worker from himself (which has been projected onto an "outside" so as to acquire a pure identity for the worker). The worker is considered a generalized owner (as *différance*), and the two are not in a relation of opposition but are forms of difference. *Différance* makes both possible and, as such, it relates them to each other (*Positions* 27). In the system of production, consequently, the worker is no longer considered prior to the owner, which is another way of saying labor is not the sole source of value.

Différance updates the worker—displacing him from an "outdated" economic category and as a militant for freedom from necessity: "the [bearer] of a particular class-relations and interests" (Marx, "Preface to the First Edition of *Capital*" 92) into a "new" cultural category, a spectral identity. Such an identity is acquired out of flows of cultural meanings produced through consumption, and from immaterial labor, which produces linguistic expressions (meanings) as well as affects (Hardt and Negri, *Multitude* 108). The worker, in other words, is updated as a bearer of *différance* in the new immaterial labor (Hardt and Negri,

Empire 280-303), which is the practice of an "aneconomic," namely "something heterogeneous both to productivity and unproductivity" (Derrida, "Politics and Friendship" 206, 205).

Theories of immaterial labor, from Daniel Bell (*The Coming of Post-Industrial Society* 165-265) to Michel Hardt and Antonio Negri (*Empire* 280-303), do not deny materiality, at least in its objective idealist sense of "matter"—the "matter" of the body and mind involved in producing. However, they rewrite the history of labor, and this is their ideological work: immaterial labor (i.e., knowledge, information, affect) is represented as a new form of labor superseding material labor. But immaterial labor is an outgrowth of the surplus of material labor, which provides capitalism with the time and means by which the immaterial is produced. Immaterial labor, in short, is a product of material labor. The products of immaterial labor (information, affects...) are second-order products: products of a product. They are effects of the class relations by which humans are exploited by humans. The dominant views of immaterial labor, such as those put forth by Bell as well as Hardt and Negri—to take two politically opposed but economically allied labor theories—are not genealogies of labor, contrary to what they claim (Bell, *The Coming of Post-Industrial Society* 47-123, 162-64; Hardt and Negri, *Multitude* 103-115). They are class theories. They do not analyze the emergence of a new form of labor in the history of capitalism but instead obscure the source of value and the structures of exploitation in capitalism (Hardt and Negri, *Multitude* 113, 150). Immaterial labor is the outcome of over-productivity (exploitation) of material labor and not an autonomous source of value. In rewriting the history of labor under capitalism, theories of immaterial labor are inventions of spectral histories that obscure the continuity of capitalism's present with its past which is "dripping from head to toe, from every pore, with blood and dirt" (Marx, *Capital* I, 926).

The "double science" rewrites the worker as a difference without opposition and without any mooring in labor. It absorbs exploitation in the traces of signs—the "a" of *différance*—and demolishes the ground of militancy, reducing class struggles to negotiations. The machinery of "double writing" is an updated theory of representation (language) that puts in question the availability of any objective reality (such as class) outside representation. It contends that knowing the outside requires going through the relay of language, which is caught in its own loops of self-reference. Therefore, any knowledge it provides is primarily a knowledge of its own workings and not of the objective world outside it. "The outside is the inside" (Derrida, *Of Grammatology* 44); we have called this the *imperial inside*.

In updating language as a self-referential structure of signs in play, the cultural turn makes representation and its various apparatuses (language, film, sound in music, color in painting, laboratory procedures in science, etc.) the issue and shifts the focus of analysis away from what is represented. Class critique, in the discourses of the cultural turn, is no longer a subject of inquiry in terms of analysis of the relation of labor and capital, but is now seen as a tissue of tropes—a mode of writing that should be analyzed not for *why* it does what it does but according to *how* it does it. Consequently, class analysis becomes an epistemological issue that is then turned into a question of rhetoric. In the end, class critique becomes a piece of writing, which, like all writings, is a play of tropes and deconstructs itself (de Man, *The Resistance to Theory* 115-121), and class itself becomes a metaphor in a language game.

Language in the "double science" is a language of difference at odds with the referential language of mainstream culture under earlier stages of capitalism. Referential language is essentially a "realist" language whose "reference" to its outside is layered and ambiguous. However, with sophisticated interpretive strategies, the referent could still be read through the ambiguity (e.g., Wordsworth and Coleridge, *Lyrical Ballads*; George Eliot, *Middlemarch*; Charles Dickens, *Bleak House*). One can, of course, read the ambiguous differently, as for example, Paul de Man does (*The Rhetoric of Romanticism*), and argue that ambiguity is not an accident of clarity but is essential to the workings of language, whose meanings are marked by their undecidability which cannot be resolved by any norm outside language. This is what the cultural turn does. For the cultural turn, there is no such thing as "realistic" language because "mimesis" is "one trope among others" (de Man, *The Resistance to Theory* 10). All texts are non-realistic—they do not refer to their "outside" but are allegories of their own self-referentiality or, to be more precise, of their own "unreadability" (non-reference). They both assert and deny their own authority, thus destroying the foundations of any choice for reading them realistically/referentially, as de Man demonstrates through the undecidability of the "genitive in the title of Keats's unfinished epic *The Fall of Hyperion*" (*The Resistance to Theory* 16).

Texts do not have merely ambiguous referents (concealed realism) but are undecidable narratives of their own textuality—they are constitutively non-realistic. De Man's reading is a variation on the metaphysics of difference. He essentializes "the literary" as by nature the site of the freedom of language from referential constraints and for "the autonomous potential of language" (10). The literary is where the "negative knowledge about the reliability of linguistic utterance is made available"(10). The text is updated as an allegorizing of reference to be of use in the culture of contemporary capitalism which is beset by growing class antagonism. The updated (deconstructed) idea of text obscures reference to the "outside" of language, which is the arena of class struggle. Instead the text turns back on itself and self-reflexively reads itself as an instance of self-difference which, it implies, is the fate of all social categories (such as class) because they are all language constructs. The analytical focus of culture critique is thus diverted away from critical understanding of social relations and toward the formal relations of language itself.

The history of modern linguistic realism (referentiality) is the history of class relations in capitalism. It is significant, of course, that influential theories of anti-realism in language are conceptually grounded in a theory that was developed in the late 19th century at the height of capitalism's colonial violence and was made public in the form of lectures to a new generation of European cultural elite just before the outbreak of the intra-class wars of imperialist conflicts in World War I. (The lectures were put in print in 1916 as Ferdinand de Saussure's *Course in General Linguistics*.)

"Realism" in language becomes more and more perturbing to capitalism as it develops into a more complex system of labor relations and commodity exchanges and becomes a more aggressive imperialist power. Its material relations consequently produce a cultural superstructure in which language is constructed as a medium whose message is its own materiality—one with a low referentiality that approaches zero degree. As we have already suggested, one of the effects of the class contradictions of capital is that it needs both a language with a high degree of reference (to reduce misunderstanding and increase efficiency of workers) and one with zero degree of reference (to occlude the realities of the "working day"—Marx, *Capital* I, 340-416). This is one reason, for example, de Man emphasizes that the "referential function of language is not being denied" but simply suspended, because "it is not a priori certain that language functions according to principles which are those, or which are like those, of the phenomenal world" (*The Resistance to Theory* 11). Language, in other words, is not denied referentiality; rather its reference is made contingent. This is the theory of reference that the contradictory social relations of capitalism require. Language's contingent reference blurs the line of "naïve opposition between fiction and reality" (11) and thus removes the historically determinate relation between language and its outside. Reference, contrary to contemporary theories, is not a matter of a "natural" or "formal" relation between signs and the world but is a historical and materialist relation (Rossi-Landi, *Language as Work and Trade*, and *Linguistics and Economics*). Clearly, it is not language as such that is the issue for the cultural turn but its uses in shading the lines between the real and the fictive—to put in play what it dismisses as "mimesis," the determined relation of language to reality.

Putting forward a playfulness of the sign, as the anti-logic of reference, is a historical necessity for the culture of capital because it provides a space in language (through self-reflexivity, the slippage of tropes, and spectrality of the trace) in which intense social contradictions are folded in irony, elusiveness, and uncertainty. The resulting semantic dimness, gray interpretations, and undecidable readings render class antagonisms as instances of linguistic indeterminacy and uncanniness of meaning. Through such cultural apparatuses, capitalism-as-imperialism makes unclear its very clear exploitation and, in a protective move, dismisses the very idea of clarity (mimesis) as a remnant of a simple industrial and linear past.

The black-and-white rhetoric of moral clarity of state propaganda ("You are with us or against us") is commonly used by the Left to justify its linguistic complicity with capital's demand for uncertainty (Laclau, "The Politics of Rhetoric"; Butler, "On Linguistic Vulnerability"), but this does not contradict what we have just said. The unyielding clarity of state language is a mask camouflaged as transparency. It covers up the clarity of capitalist violence with the excessive explicitness of its own language, thereby making people suspicious of clarity itself. Clarity thus becomes ironic, and the common sense becomes the shelter for indirection: "nothing in real life is so black-and-white." The clarity of the state, in other words, is a strategy for discrediting clarity altogether, making a wordplay (just as the Left does) out of the clarity with which the practices of capitalism are put on display. Both the state and the Left end up in the same place—nothing can be so crude as to fall into the binary of 'one' or the 'other'— what matters is the in-between. George Bush's clarity ("axes of evil"), for example, makes clarity so suspicious that when the violence of capital in the West Virginia coal mines is clearly exposed, it is rendered unbelievable. In the unclarity composed by Right and Left, capital finds a linguistic safe haven.

To put it more "clearly," linguistic and referential elusiveness—in public debates over the class practices of capitalism—is produced by hiding the obviousness of capital's violence under cover of the extreme clarity of state propaganda, much the same way that the letter in Poe's "The Purloined Letter" is hidden in clear view.

The Minister (the state) in Poe's narrative deposits "the letter immediately beneath the nose of the whole world, by way of best preventing any portion of that world from perceiving it." Lacan's and Derrida's readings of the story are exemplary updatings of the theory of reference for imperial capitalism by obscuring reference in desire and/as lack and thus essentializing the signifier in a chain of absences. Lacan's and Derrida's privileging of the undecidable (unclarity) is actually a much more straightforward (clear) masking of clarity than the state's double masking—a layered masking under the unmasked. The state, it turns out, is a much more sophisticated connoisseur of the irony of undecidability than the Left (of the global North). The theorist and the state both disperse the rigid clarity of class antagonism in the manufactured unclarity of language and translate the decided exploitation of labor by capital into an undecidability. Theorists of the Left represent the undecidable with surprising linguistic naiveté as constitutive of language itself. The state, however, knows that it is always cunningly constructed: language is always an extension. No matter where one stands in relation to reference, the debates over language have already achieved their goal: to shift the focus from the content of representation to its medium, from the represented to representation (techne of writing) itself. The change of focus, from the represented (content) to the medium of representation, effectively turns analytical attention away from class to language.

Anti-realist writings, such as Laurence Sterne's *The Life and Opinions of Tristram Shandy*, had already started earlier on the margins of the culture of capital because in each mode of production there are residues of the past as well as emergent elements of the future. Both the residue and the emergent, however, are articulations of class interests and not free-floating cultural meanings. This means the diversities in a mode of production will eventually be subordinated to the interests of the class in dominance by "exploding them little by little everywhere" (Marx, *Grundrisse* 510).

The marginal, anti-realist tendencies in language and the arts became more and more central as monopoly capital became more powerful and the growing class conflicts in imperialist capitalism led to the emergence of modernism and its valorizing of complexity and anti-realism. In high modernism not only did anti-representational writings become more central in the cultural productions of capital (Charles Baudelaire, *Les Fleurs du mal*), but at the height of modernism and the expansion of European imperialism and colonialism, Saussure's theory of language was developed, which canonized the anti-realist view of representation by displacing reference with difference:

> in language there are only differences. Even more important: a difference generally implies positive terms between which the difference is set up, but in language there are only differences without positive terms. (de Saussure, *Course in General Linguistics* 120)

As we have suggested, around the time of the Great Depression—the first major crisis of capitalism after the first world-wide imperialist wars—anti-referential writing became the norm for the advanced cultural guard of capitalism (T. S. Eliot, *The Waste Land*; James Joyce, *Ulysses*, 1922, and *Finnegans Wake*, 1939; Virginia Woolf, *To the Lighthouse*, 1927, and *The Waves*, 1931; Faulkner, *The Sound and the Fury*, 1929; Samuel Beckett, *More Pricks Than Kicks*, 1934, and *Murphy*, 1938; Gertrude Stein, *The Autobiography of Alice B. Toklas*, 1933). As capitalism's system of exchange becomes more opaque, anti-representational language "represents" its opacity as the natural circumstances of living and the normal conditions and modes of knowing. Language, as we have said, is the extension of social relations. In a market society (where the logic of production is inverted), language inverts the material logic of the social, representing it as the anti-logic of desire which is lack, a missing presence.

The idea of language as anti-referential difference became popular in the 1960s. Derrida's first influential lecture in the U.S., "Structure, Sign, and Play in the Discourse of the Human Sciences," for example, was delivered at the Johns Hopkins University conference on "The Language of Criticism and the Sciences of Man" in 1966 and became available in humanities classrooms through a popular paperback edition of the conference lectures in 1970 as *The Structural Controversy* (ed. Macksey and Donato). It continues to be the hegemonic theory of representation in the global North (e.g., Gibson-Graham, *A Postcapitalist Politics* 53-78).

Anti-referential language provides the cultural climate in which representation is no longer considered to be related to the world "out there" but is seen as a construction of that world "in here"—inside language. In short, language and its meanings are treated as autonomous from the material base of culture, and therefore, "What is important is learning to live in the speaking of language" (Heidegger, *Poetry, Language, Thought* 210), because "The speech of mortals rests in its relation to the speaking of language" (208), and "*Language speaks as the peal of stillness*. Stillness stills by the carrying out, the bearing and enduring, of the world and things in their presence...language goes on as the taking place or occurring of the dif-ference for world and things" (207). The autonomy of language and the freedom of its meanings set the subject of language free:

Man speaks only as he responds to language.
Language speaks.
Its speaking speaks for us in what has been spoken. (210)

Representing language as the "house of being" (Heidegger, "Letter on Humanism" 193) ontologically clouds historical materiality, for the social is the house of being. Language does not speak; it is spoken by subjects of class—class speaks (through language).

The role of anti-referential language and art in advancing the cause of capital is, perhaps, nowhere as clear as in the treatment of abstract expressionism in the postwar years. Abstract expressionism is often regarded to be an absolute text, a self-referring textuality with zero outside. It is considered a text that self-reflexively deploys its own metaphysics of textuality, putting it into play so that it transforms metaphysics into an open trope, and instead of being centered by it, decenters it. However, what is depicted as an ecstasy of sheer color is like the joy of the absolute signifier in writing, an articulation of the interests of the class in supremacy, although the class affiliations are difficult to see in the sensuous rapture of the aesthetic.

Nelson Rockefeller points to the class relations in abstract expressionism by describing it as "free enterprise painting" (Saunders, *The Cultural Cold War: The CIA and the World of Arts and Letters* 258). Painting that has zero outside—that is anti-mimetic—is indeed an enunciation of capitalist values, of "anti-Communist ideology, the ideology of freedom, of free enterprise. Nonfigurative and politically silent, it was the very antithesis to socialist realism" (254). In its emptiness, the blankness of abstract expressionism represents the historical content of social relations as spectral meanings, as versions of a metaphysics. Such blankness aggressively suspends the social in the tropics of the cultural: "society does not 'exist'" (Laclau, *New Reflections on the Revolutions of Our Time* 183).

The ideological implications of the blankness of abstract expressionism are so strongly pro-capital that, as Saunders argues, the CIA used it as part of its cultural arsenal to fight socialism and all forms of socialist arts and writings. MoMA (the Museum of Modern Art)—the main site for the popular dissemination of postwar abstract expressionism—was a close collaborator with the CIA in advancing the cause of the indeterminacy of the sign (signifier, color, musical note) on behalf of capitalism and in fighting against socialism. In her 1974 article in *Artforum* on "Abstract Expressionism: Weapon of the Cold War," Eva Cocroft discusses the ideology of blankness and writes that

> links between cultural cold war politics and the success of Abstract Expressionism are by no means coincidental.... They were consciously forged at the time by some of the most influential figures controlling museum policies and advocating enlightened cold war tactics designed to woo European intellectuals.... In terms of cultural propaganda, the functions of both the CIA's cultural apparatus and MoMA's international programs were similar and, in fact, mutually supportive. (Quoted in Saunders 263)

Abstract expressionism is exemplary of art-without-referents. It is held up, like anti-referential writing, as an instance of free art and, by extension, of human freedom from all that may constrain it by tying it down to an idea, a direction, or a "cause" (which is represented as the embodiment of metaphysics). Its only commitment—as Bill Readings puts it in the quasi-religious idioms he uses to describe the "new" university—is to the "empty name of Thought" (*University in Ruins* 160). Like abstract expressionism and the textuality of the negative in Derrida, Readings's university of Thought (which supplants the university of ideas and the university of culture) is a space of activity without referent: in which "Thought...does not masquerade as an idea" (160) and whose aim is to keep Thought as an open space for thinking about Thought. This notion of pedagogy, as we have discussed at length in *Hypohumanities*, produces a workforce for capital that is "Thoughtfully thoughtless"—it thinks but has no ideas, thinks about thinking about Thought. Self-reflexivity is the last space left under capitalism for the subject of estranged labor.

The anti-mimesis of abstract expression is itself a reproduction of the industrial capitalist cultural ideal of *l'art pour l'art,* which is itself a reconstruction of the Kantian idealist notion of "purposiveness without purpose" at a higher level of class antagonism. It is perhaps the most popular example in the postwar years of euphoric emptiness, which is reproduced, as we have shown, across numerous cultural forms of quasi-transcendental blanknesses: from textuality without an outside and the university of Thought to community without community; from materiality without matter to empire without imperialism. State support of self-mimesis, art about its own nomadic signs—through the CIA and its various cultural institutions on behalf of capitalism—goes beyond support for a particular school or textuality or art. It is support for apolitical theories of art and apolitical intellectuals who disseminate them. The cultural turn is, above all, about an interpretive strategy that represents the world as a textuality without text—activities without referents (meanings)—and objects without objectivity.

The anti-mimetic text is a response to a need: capital after the Bretton Woods agreement, which founded the financial ground for globalization, needed more agile, effective, and aggressive discursive practices to normalize its social contradictions on a global level. Anti-mimetic art "blanks" out these contradictions in an orgy of the singularity of signs, whose abundance of color/meanings exceeds all representations and becomes a performativity of the "impossible," which reflexively becomes the only possible subject of discourse. It dismantles the "old" reference theories by marking them as residues of a metaphysics of presence. It does not abolish reference—no human practice can—it simply updates it by redirecting it to refer to its own processes of reference. In other words, it displaces the mimesis of the outside by the mimesis of the inside: "The outside is the inside" (Derrida, *Of Grammatology* 44). It becomes a faith-based textuality whose being is being itself. The anti-mimetic is the representational technology of a capitalism that considers itself to have gone beyond capitalism, becoming a knowledge capitalism without labor (capitalism without content). To be even more blunt: anti-mimesis is not simply a theory of writing; it is the discursive device for nulling labor in class societies.

In the postwar years, as culture moves from the mid-1940s—the time of the Bretton Woods agreements—to the time of NAFTA, WTO, and beyond, it faces deeper and deeper class contradictions and is emptied out of all its social contents. It becomes a textured sensuality, which is treated as its materiality. This is the time of the rise of so-called "cultural materialism," "cultural economy," and "political economy of the sign." Consequently, culture as the superstructural articulation of the social relations of production—as the arena where class conflicts are articulated and fought out—is now thought to be "instrumentalist" (Sterne, "The Burden of Culture" 80-84) and is displaced by a notion of culture as discursive strolling: a "meaningless, nondirected activity" (99). Post-instrumental culture is a digressive digression, a way of talking free from the burden of saying anything, a non-mimetic, "loiterly" act—a lusting, desiring "moving without going anywhere," a delightful "dilatory" and "digressive" activity, a writerly ecstasy or "loiterature," which is another name for culture as "peripatetic desire" (Chambers, *Loiterature* 3-25). Culture is no longer an explanatory concept but a figure that intervenes in itself and rids itself of commitment—of cultural politics. Its politics becomes politics in "the last instance" which, like Althusser's moment of economic determination, will never arrive (Sterne 82). The unburdening of culture from culture is intensified in the linguistic turn within the cultural turn by theorizing culture as a form of "writing"—culture as spacing, difference, and singularity. In the cultural turn, culture, as we have shown, is a textuality of the negative, a site of meaningfulness without meaning and thoughtful unthoughtfulness.

"Meaningless, nondirected activity," however, far from being anti-instrumental, or even meaningless, is the instrumentality of a "new" capitalism in which non-employment and imposed leisure, for instance, play an important economic role. "Meaningless, non-directed activity" is the only meaningful and directed activity in the wasteland of time produced by layoffs, on one side, and high consumption, on the other, where the two are connected by a popular culture that teaches people that their "meaningless and nondirected" activities are signs of their freedom and their arrival at "higher" realities beyond the normative rules of culture. Under capitalism, however, there is no outside to instrumentalism, and all "rebellions" against instrumentalism—from Horkheimer and Adorno's Left anti-instrumentalism to contemporary late aesthetic non-instrumentalism—are strategies for inventing more effective forms of instrumentalism to naturalize the alienation of labor under capitalism as meaningful activities without meaning, activities without destination, nomadic sensualities.

These sensualties are the aesthetic instrumentalities of consumption, which is an absolute necessity for capital and is thus represented in the cultural turn not as passive consumption but as active production. Through consumption, the consumer is seen as inventing herself as an active cultural agent in the process of consumption by producing new "meanings" from commodities. By disfiguring jeans ("tie-dyed, irregularly bleached, or particularly 'torn'"), for example, the wearer of jeans becomes active because the disfiguring turns her into a resistance consumer who re-makes commodities by changing their meanings (Fiske, *Understanding Popular Culture* 1-21). The contradictions in such practices—resisting capitalism yet perpetuating it by purchasing its products—are themselves justified by critics like John Fiske, who calls such contradictions "semiotic richness" (5). Social contradictions, in other words, are dissolved in the polysemy of commodities because class, for Fiske, is in the last instance a knot of cultural meanings and not a social category (1). Fiske further exalts consumption by calling the consumer who produces different meanings from common commodities "producerly" (*Reading the Popular* 115-117). What Fiske and other critics in the cultural turn have done is a translation of the capitalist economic theory that holds "how much one buys—rather than how much one makes—is a better measure of economic well-being" and that by such a measure, working people are "even doing better than the upper crust" (*The New York Times*, December 12, 2006).

Consumption is valorized in the cultural turn as an act of resistance and is thus used to give a new identity to the consumer who can then support capitalism by his "resistance" to it. What Fiske and his mentor, de Certeau, and many others have done is to translate consumption from a passive activity into an active passivity. In doing so, they forge a new subject position for the shopper—a "producerly" passivity. This subject position, however, is historically determined by labor relations and has its origin in the transformation and commodification of labor with the rise of capitalism. Structurally, capitalism needs a space of self-reflexivity within which the subject obtains by contemplation what is denied him in existing social relations. The archetype of this subject position is Kant's maxim of a "purposiveness without purpose" (*Critique of Judgment* 17-31, 68-73), which is periodically reproduced in the North, depending on the level of class tensions. Walter Benjamin's late-modernist revision of Baudelaire's modern *flâneur* (*The Arcades Project*) is perhaps the best-known instance of the reproduction of the Kantian slogan. Anti-instrumental culture is a perpetual discursive machine for producing a subject of caprice and quirky consumption for capitalism—"a botanist of the sidewalk" in Baudelaire's words. The cultural turn is the poetics of "a botanist of the sidewalk."

CLASS AND THE CALL OF BEING

The cultural turn naturalizes the anti-labor views of the Taft-Hartley Act through a wide range of discourses from popular culture to philosophy. Heidegger, whose writings bring considerable authority to the interpretive logic of the cultural turn, provides a master lesson in anti-labor cultural critique in his analytics of *dwelling/building* (*Poetry, Language, Thought* 145-161). He depicts the plight of workers ("truck driver" and "working woman," 145) not as a result of the absence of freedom from necessity but, in effect, as lack of spirituality. As in all ideologies, he explains the material by the ineffable, the worldly by the ghostly, through rewriting "building" (the material house) as "dwelling" (the holy singularity). His interpretation thins and dissipates the material objective ("building") in the religious, the spiritual, and the subjective ("dwelling") by means of "thought." As he writes in "Letter on Humanism," "Thinking" overcomes the objective by engaging Being for Being: "l'engagement par l'Être pour l'Être" (194). The material relations of production involved in "building" are transformed into the immateriality of "dwelling"—the primal call of Being (*Poetry, Language, Thought* 148).

As Heidegger attenuates the objectivity of "housing" by converting it into the spirituality of "dwelling," the historical alienation of "the truck driver" and "the working woman" produced by wage labor (the relations of the "owner" and the "workers" in "building") is re-Thought as an inability to listen to the silences of language (148). The relation to language, according to Heidegger, and not the social division of labor is what brings about the estrangement of the subject. Heidegger writes that

> Man acts as though *he* were the shaper and master of language, while in fact *language* remains the master of man. Perhaps it is before all else man's subversion of *this* relation of dominance that drives his nature into alienation." (146)

Spiritualizing the social by transcoding "housing" into "dwelling" enables Heidegger to rewrite the "housing shortage" (161), which is an effect of property relations, as the existential absence of the holy—forgetting the being-in-the-world. He mystifies the wretchedness of not having any actual shelter ("house") by evoking the "*real plight of dwelling*" which "does not lie merely in lack of houses" (161) but lies in the fact "that mortals ever search anew for the essence of dwelling, that they *must ever learn to dwell*" (161). Housing (the material) itself is represented by Heidegger as a building alienated from Being, while "dwelling...is *the basic character* of Being" (160). Significantly, it is in "dwelling" (the spiritual), for Heidegger, that the homeless overcomes the "hard and bitter...hampering and threatening" lack of "housing" (the material) and is disalienated into Being (161).

After having been subjected to a "concernful deliberation" (*Being and Time* 412) by which he divides Being into "*present-at-hand*" (67) and "*readiness-to-hand*" (98), the objective emerges in his writings as numinous and transcendental with a halo of otherworldliness. An objective "hammer," for instance, which "circumspectively" is "too heavy or too light," loses these qualities after his caring reading, because

> we have now sighted something that is suitable for the hammer, not as a tool, but as a corporeal Thing subject to the law of gravity. To talk circumspectively of 'too heavy' or 'too light' no longer has any 'meaning'; that is to say, the entity in itself, as we now encounter it, gives us nothing with relation to which it could be 'found' too heavy or too light. (*Being and Time* 412)

Underneath the object ("hammer") there is always a deeper objectivity (the "corporeal Thing") which is transobjective "Being-in-itself" (98), and unlike the being that is present-at-hand, it is appropriate to Dasein's character (67).

Transforming the objective into the otherworldly and reversing the relation of the material to the cultural takes place through "thinking." Social goals, such as objective access and equality (housing), are rendered trivial compared to the spiritual raptures and affective ecstasy of the dweller in Being.

For Heidegger, thinking is always "thinking of Being" ("Letter on Humanism" 196), and it is the cure for material dispossession: "as soon as man *gives thought* to his homelessness, it is a misery no longer" (161). To cease to think of Being as an issue is, accordingly, to cease to be human, for whom being ("dwelling") is a question, and to become a thing ("housing") whose being is already decided ("Letter on Humanism" 213-214). By existentializing "thingness" (house), Heidegger dematerializes the social relations of property—what turns humans into things. He, therefore, clouds the fact that the contemporary every day (the "there" and "here" of Being-in-the-world where there is a "housing shortage") is a reified every day in which the producers ("subject") and the products ("object") are at odds with each other not because producers cease to think of Being as an issue but because of the "conversion of things into persons and the conversion of persons into things" under wage labor in the "working day" (Marx, *Capital* I, 209, 340-416). "Thing-ness," which according to Heidegger is the mark of the transmogrification of human (for whom being is an issue) into non-human (whose being is already determined), is not the effect of a lack of engagement with Being but the outcome of what Marx calls the "personification of things and the reification (*Versachlichung*) of persons" (1054). It takes place because the compulsion of capital for surplus labor makes the former "homed" and the latter "homeless." Heidegger's reading is not a subtle interpretation of "dwelling"/"housing" and displacing of the absolute which excludes the difference of Being-in-the-world. Rather, it is a crude masking of class binaries which depersonify humans and personify objects by denying the objectivity of material labor.

THE "LONG BOOM" AND CLASS: FROM BRETTON WOODS TO THE RISK SOCIETY

The "Long Boom" in the postwar years is often depicted as a break in class struggles—the end of class militancy and class antagonism as well as a time of social harmony and the exhaustion of ideology (Bell, *The End of Ideology*)—not only in official and mainstream analyses but also in Left-liberal narratives such as Eric Hobsbawm's *Age of Extremes*, and perhaps most significantly in "socialist" accounts. In his *The Future of Socialism*, for example, Antony Crosland argues that the Long Boom is proof that "Capitalism has been reformed almost out of all recognition" (517). In other words, capitalism is a series of breaks, discontinuities, and fissures. This is, of course, a recurring narrative in the history of capitalism as we have seen in Negri's writings.

Discontinuity is valorized in the cultural turn (e.g., Foucault, *History of Sexuality*; Castells, *The Rise of the Network Society*) because it maps the social as an assemblage of fragmentary and unconnected events and, among other things, represents capitalism as continuously starting a "new" phase that enables it to disconnect itself from its exploitations in the past and always remain a "new" capitalism. Theories of discontinuity, in other words, are spaces in which capital cleanses itself from its history, which is "dripping from head to toe, from every pore, with blood and dirt" (Marx, *Capital* I, 926). Narratives of a break conceal the continuity of capitalist structures of exploitation and obscure the "uninterrupted" class struggles of the "oppressor and the oppressed" whose "constant opposition" to each other produces the transformative motions of society (Marx and Engels, *Manifesto of the Communist Party* 41).

In the "new" capitalism associated with the break of the Long Boom, the relation of capital and labor is assumed to have changed from militancy and conflict to what Derrida calls "friendship" *(Politics of Friendship)*. Structural crises, such as the Depression of the 1930s, are believed to have vanished for good, and the working class itself is said to have rapidly undergone a process of "embourgeoisement" that has transformed it into a new middle class (Drucker, *Post-Capitalist Society)*. The "most striking feature" of the Long Boom is "a quite breath-taking growth in production" (Armstrong, Glyn, and Harrison, *Capitalism since 1945,* 117). In short, the Long Boom is seen as "capitalism's great leap forward" (Beaud, *A History of Capitalism 1500-2000,* 213-261).

The Long Boom is also represented as the embodiment of industrial capitalism (Fordism) whose collapse produces a new fissure in the history of capital and gives rise to another new economic order that is variously called by such names as "postindustrial" (Bell, *The Coming of Post-Industrial Society)* or "postFordist" (Aglietta, *A Theory of Capitalist Regulations: The U.S. Experience)* and whose "cultural logic" is named "postmodernism" (Jameson, *Postmodernism or, the Cultural Logic of Late Capitalism*). In the fissures of the Long Boom, industrial capitalism is "newed" as postindustrial; the digital emerges, and in the ruins of nation, the new transnational world order takes shape—a "new" world order in which the nature of labor itself is supposed to have changed, and the material itself has become cultural (Jameson, *Postmodernism*).

"Old" (manual) labor capitalism is believed to have been displaced by a new "knowledge capitalism" that reshapes all variants of capitalism—from paramilitary Anglo-American capitalism to Swedish social capitalism; from French state capitalism to Japanese national capitalism—into a "global knowledge-based economy" (Burton-Jones, *Knowledge Capitalism* 20-22). One feature of knowledge capitalism, according to these theories, is that for workers not only have they become well-off, but also their very mode of work has changed. The "old" style "proletariat" is being replaced with a "new" style "cybertariat" (Huws, *The Making of a Cybertariat*).

66   Chapter 2

Capitalism, of course, advances by increasing production (surplus labor) through "constantly revolutionizing the instruments of production and thereby the relations of production, and with them the whole relations of society" (Marx and Engels, *Manifesto of the Communist Party* 45). These changes, however, also increase the class gaps and thus intensify the class antagonisms that threaten the very existence of capitalism. Although the wages of workers—which are taken as objective proof of changes in postwar capitalism—have increased in absolute terms during the Long Boom, the gap between workers' wages and executive pay and profits has dramatically increased (Perlo, *Super Profits and Crisis* 115-163), while the tax rates for corporations and the rich were steadily lowered (IRS, "Corporation Income Tax Brackets and Rates"). So much so that by the 1980s "more than three-fourths of all federal income taxes were withheld from wages and salaries" (Perlo 58-59), and "the ratio of average CEO pay to the average pay of a production (i.e., non-management) worker was 431-to-1" in 2004, following "a peak of 525-to-1" in 2001 (Sahadi, "CEO Pay"). "In this period of general growth" as Michel Beaud argues, "inequality on a world scale increased" (*A History of Capitalism 1500-2000*, 217).

Far from being years of harmony and common prosperity in which class ceased to be a determining factor of social life, the Long Boom of the postwar years was a time, as H. W. Prentis, the former president of the National Association of Manufacturers (the organization of conservative big business) put it, of the "ominous rise of class consciousness" (Fones-Wolf, *Selling Free Enterprise* 43). Contrary to the dominant narratives, these were years of class antagonism, strikes, and pauperization of the working class (Rayback, *A History of American Labor* 387-413; Swados, "The Myth of the Happy Worker"; Webber and Rigby, *The Golden Age Illusion: Rethinking Postwar Capitalism).*

In the official representations of the Long Boom, modifications in the phenomenology of exploitation—namely, cultural adjustments in the way surplus labor is extracted from workers so they experience their own exploitation differently—are depicted as radical changes in the structures of capitalism. But the structures of capitalism have not changed since the rise of industrial capitalism and remain the same today. They cannot change because capital is accumulation of surplus labor: this is the grounding structure of capitalism, and without it and structures derived from it, capitalism cannot survive. But during the Long Boom (mostly because of the shortage of labor), capitalism found it necessary in order to increase profits to became worker-friendly in its cultural behavior. It therefore used "new" management techniques that modified the phenomenology of its labor practices. For example, it included workers in some decision-making processes. The participation of workers (e.g., the Toyota production regime), however, was actually an "affective" strategy for workers to use their own experience, knowledge, and emotions to plan the most efficient way to be exploited.

"The goal of the postwar participation program was to 'make workers feel they are participating' without restructuring work or the line of authority within the shop" (Fones-Wolf, *Selling Free Enterprise* 76). In other words, workers' participation was a ruse of management to "get workers to accept what management wants them to accept but to make them feel they made or helped to make the decision" (76). But in the cultural representation of "new" capitalism, the participation of workers was deployed as a mark to prove not only that capitalism was supportive of the freedom of individual workers but that individual freedom was achievable only through the free market.

The Long Boom was not, to put it more directly, an instance of transclass capitalism. It was a period of fleeting prosperity achieved by the increasing exploitation of workers in the U.S. and by more sustained exploitation of the workers of the global South. The exploitation of the workers of the South was "legalized" through the "new" anti-labor arrangements that were first imposed on the world through the Bretton Woods agreements (1944). The Bretton Woods agreements set the basic frame for the development of the postwar global financial regime and institutions: "The International Monetary Fund," "The International Bank for Reconstruction and Development" ("the World Bank"), and "the General Agreement on Tariffs and Trade" (the "World Trade Organization").

However, as the cost of domestic labor grew and the rate of profit fell, the provisions of Bretton Woods proved inadequate for capital. They were thus gradually replaced by new trade arrangements, starting in the 1970s, which were formulated under the market and economic theories now collectively known as "Neoliberalism." The Bretton Woods agreements and Neoliberalism pitted the workers of the North against the workers of the South by setting up transnational arrangements that increased the power of corporations, made the travel of capital across national boundaries easier and immigration more difficult, and deregulated banking and employment. With complete disregard for the environmental situation, working conditions, or even wage level, transnational capital was set free to force as much surplus labor out of workers as was physically possible.

Our interpretation of the Long Boom—as an integral part of the history of capitalism shaped by class struggles and not as a break with them—is criticized by the cultural turn on the grounds that this depicts capitalism as an essentialist, centered institution that is constantly advancing toward equality. Continuity readings are said to be unhelpful because they give capitalism a logocentric stability and in doing so make intervention impossible. Ernesto Laclau and Chantal Mouffe call this (illusion of) stability the "permanence of [an] egalitarian imaginary" (*Hegemony and Socialist Strategy* 160), which simply re-centers and re-constructs capitalism as a foundational system. Capitalism, accordingly, should be read in terms of its unstable identity, which is the site of intervention and change. Change, in other words, should be from within the system.

The Long Boom, which is itself regarded as a break within capitalism, is seen as bringing about another break (post-Fordism) within that break, and as a result, "Today it is not only as a seller of labour-power that the individual is subordinated to capital, but also through his or her incorporation into a multitude of other social relations: culture, free time, illness, education, sex, and even death" (*Hegemony and Socialist Strategy* 161). Super (mass) production replaces old relations (the effects of the social relations of production) with new relations based on "commodity relations" (161). The Long Boom, for the cultural turn, is the discontinuous sublime: it opens up the unrepresentable (difference) within capitalism at the level of social relations. Capitalism ("as we knew it") becomes other than itself: the excess of its materiality turns it into a discursive regime and transforms social relations grounded in production into cultural relations of commodity consumption. Consequently, it rearticulates its logic from class determination to indeterminacies of meanings (lifestyles). During the Long Boom, capitalist social relations are unmoored from labor/production, and in their difference from themselves, they produce a new capitalism beyond itself. In the "new" post-class capitalism, "New Social Movements"—urban, ecological, feminist and anti-racist struggles—take the place of "workers' struggles, considered as 'class' struggles" (*Hegemony and Socialist Strategy* 159; Gorz, *Farewell to the Working Class*).

The Long Boom, in other words, is seen as the discontinuity of the excessive within capitalism and where a "new series of social relations" outside the relations of production emerge. Capitalism consequently loses its coherence as a unified economic system and becomes a nomadic plurality of anti-essentialist, heterogeneous, and indeterminate cultural practices which are not "outside" capitalism but are difference within it. This is the difference that fissures the Long Boom and produces "post-Fordism." The cultural turn, however, has reservations about Fordism and post-Fordism as economic and social theories put forth by the "regulation school," because they, too, are seen as centering and systematizing theories that marginalize the indeterminate discursivity of capitalism and, by imposing closure on the social, represent it as an objective totality. Nevertheless, the cultural turn relies on some of the conclusions of "regulation theory" in its discussion of postwar capitalism [Laclau and Mouffe, *Hegemony and Socialist Strategy* 159-193; Gibson-Graham, *The End of Capitalism (as we knew it)* 148-173].

As regulation theory develops, it not only distances itself from class analysis but also forgets it, and in its forgetfulness transcodes the economic as cultural. This is another way of saying its materiality is without materialism. The underlying logic of regulation theory—what makes it appealing to the cultural turn—is overdetermination, namely, "neither politics nor ideologies 'reflect' economic forces, but ideological-politico-economic 'configurations' exist either as stable configurations or configurations of crisis" (Lipietz, "From Althusserianism to 'Regulation Theory'" 99). One of the major consequences of regulation theory for the cultural turn is that contradictions of capital are no longer seen as "structures" but as "unstable tensions" (100). This is a not very subtle way of rewriting class, shifting from a structure of conflicts into an open-ended process without antagonism.

The attack on capitalism as a continuous but varied history of class struggles is represented as an epistemological questioning. Like all epistemologies, this too has its roots in class interests. Remaking capitalism as a set of discontinuous practices and criticizing the continuity of class structures, together, make it impossible to understand class as a relation of property. Class is turned into an indeterminate class process that is the effect of a plurality of practices, most of which are said to be cultural rather than economic. This view of class, which gives an active role to "representation" (language) in understanding class, is perhaps the most popular theory of the Marxist Left in the U.S. and is widely disseminated through the writings of Richard Wolff, Stephen Resnick, and their co-thinkers, such as J. K. Gibson-Graham, with whom they have collectively edited such anthologies as *Re/Presenting Class: Essays in Postmodern Marxism* and *Class and Its Others*. We have already discussed the main features of class as a process grounded in capitalism as a discontinuity of breaks and fissures, but it is worth emphasizing that the effect of class as process is to redirect politics away from revolutionary politics aimed at ending class toward a reformative one based on providing for "class diversity" (Gibson-Graham, *The End of Capitalism* 52). This tendency is grounded in the radical democratic maxim that "the revolutionary task of replacing capitalism now seems outmoded and unrealistic" (263), and therefore, one has to accept and work within the system of wage-labor.

The notion of excess that underlies theories of capitalism as discontinuities, and class as unstable processes, reaches its orgiastic and melancholic bliss in Scott Lash and John Urry's *The End of Organized Capitalism*. The end of "organized capitalism," which they see as the beginning of "dis-organized capitalism," is actually the continuity of capital after the falling rate of profit has led to the collapse of the Bretton Woods agreements and abandoning a fixed rate of exchange by the United States in 1973. For Lash and Urry "dis-organized capitalism" is the trope of a new freedom for the subject of labor by means of new information technologies and knowledge capitalism. As liberal Left theorists, however, they do have some reservations, which they express by calling these changes "exhilarating...yet disturbing" (*Economies of Signs and Space* 31). They are disturbing because the end of "organized" capital for them is also the beginning of the end of the liberal subject and an emptying of the social from its meaning. However, they argue that dis-organized capitalism displaces the old restricting "structures" with flows and enables new aesthetic agency and nomadic networks of meanings. It opens up a new era of high-tech yet old-styled labor arrangements that are characterized by the small-size business firms and workshops of early liberal capitalism. These new wired and "smart" small workshops actually look back to medieval crafts-work and are a form of cultural anti-industrial post-industrialization—something that Arthur J. Penty hinted at in 1922 (*Post-Industrialism*). Instead of producing standardized goods, these smart workshops attend to the taste, desires, and aesthetic singularities of customers.

The excess and exhaustion of the Long Boom shifts capitalism not simply from inflexible standardized Fordist mass production to the post-Fordist flexible production but much more significantly, Lash and Urry argue, from "flexibility to reflexivity" (*Economies of Signs and Space* 120-123). "Reflexive" capitalism is the regime of the singular in which the individual "employee" (the actuality of worker or laborer recedes into the background) acquires the opportunity for self expression, as in the old, small, liberal, 19th century enterprises with their echo of medieval crafts. Reflexive production allows the employee to "make decisions" and put more time into the design aspects of production which has shorter runs. Reflexivity means individualization, which leads to a greater transformation of the workplace, namely, displacing the old Taylorist management style in favor of "shopfloor epistemology" (122), in which the individual employee is not circumscribed by structural constraints. In the reflexive workplace, freedom is not freedom from labor ("necessity" as Marx calls it) but from the protocols of labor: "how" labor is done not "why."

Reflexivity is the new outside of class; it is the space of autonomy for the post-class subject of new high-tech capitalism. This reflexive subject, however, has already lost its material freedom (from necessity) to capitalism. He/she has no control over his/her labor. The only site of freedom (reflexivity) is the aesthetic corner of culture—what Lash and Urry retrieve by going back to the culture of old-style 19th-century liberal capitalism: "a cosmopolitan spatial heterotopia, the modernity of Baudelaire, Simmel, and Benjamin" (32). The future for them is outside history in the self-reflexive closure of the singularity of high-tech flows.

The "reflexive accumulation" that Lash and Urry theorize is a dis-organized space in which culture penetrates economy and aesthetics permeates "both consumption and production" (*Economies of Signs and Space* 60, 61). The service sector emerges as a "third force" and abolishes the binary of classes—"capital" and "labor." The service sector, in other words, is the post-class in-between-ness that puts in question the volatility of the concept of exploitation as the outcome of the wage-labor system. The end of class, for Lash and Urry, does not end transformative politics. On the contrary, it opens up new spaces for politics without ideology because "contemporary developments do not produce a straightforward dominant ideology" since "ideologies are characteristic of modernity." In postmodern new times, "It is the global networks of communication and information that are crucial" (306), and the expansion of the scope of the symbolic increases the site of pluralistic social change (307). Social transformation in dis-organized capitalism, in other words, is the effect of image, affect, and a cosmopolitan aesthetic openness toward the heterogeneous and the divergent (308).

The end of class theory that underlies Lash and Urry's writings is more rigorously theorized in "risk society theory" in which the social relations of production are replaced by the cultural relations of hazards, as in Ulrich Beck, *Risk Society,* and Anthony Giddens, *Runaway World.* The agent of this transformation, as in all post-class theories, is technology. According to Beck, new technologies have produced a new global society of risks (the Chernobyl syndrome) in which class is marginalized by risk—the hazards of new post-Boom economies (9) affect the poor and the rich alike, as do all other environmental hazards. This means the division of the social into owners and workers is no longer relevant to the risk society.

Risk society theory, in other words, flattens the social and places the rich and the poor on the same level, obscuring the fact that the poor live in countries and neighborhoods that are radically more prone to "risks." Their living space is becoming the site for the toxic waste of the affluent. Not only is class erased from social life but even the old liberal ideal of equality is dismissed as an outdated residue of (non-reflexive) modernity and its industrial class society. Any idea or practice that does not support existing social relations is dismissed as outdated and old—interestingly this is also the formula by which capitalists compete with each other to market their goods. Old, often very old, ideas are given an unfamiliar representation and are then marketed as new. In the "new" social, for example, individual safety and not equality is now the norm of social justice in what Beck argues is "reflexive society" and a new stage in capitalism. But the "individual" is the oldest of all old subjects in capitalist cultural politics and its canonization took place over two centuries ago (e.g., Adam Smith's *The Wealth of Nations*). The historiography of capitalism in risk theory is based on the movement of capital from premodernity to modernity and then to reflexivity.

In the name of freedom of the subject ("reflexivity"), social theories of "reflexivity" legitimate the rule of the market in the form of freedom of choice in consumption. The reflexive subject is represented as consuming not because he needs something—in other words, instrumentally—but aesthetically, because he desires it. In desiring, the subject chooses in situations that are, according to post-theory, inherently undecidable, and thus there is no basis for choice. In choosing/deciding the subject becomes an ethical subject. The ethical subject becomes a substitute for the free subject. Free subjectivity is a social relation attained only after freedom from necessity when humans have transcended private property through a "complete return of man to himself as a social (i.e., human) being" (Marx, *Economic and Philosophic Manuscripts of 1844* 296). By obscuring the material basis of individuality in labor activities (social relations), theories of post-Fordism, dis-organized capitalism, risk society, mediatic capitalism, globalization, etc., legitimate the triumph of capital over labor by valorizing the spiritual, affective, and aesthetic through which they rewrite the alienation of labor as the reflexivity of a new indeterminate subjectivity, a body without organs—a difference before differences.

The image of the body without regulations is disseminated widely in contemporary cultural theory and produces a climate of exuberance for Neoliberal economics with a Deleuzian ecstasy about a market unbounded by norms. Neoliberal capitalism is mostly represented in the cultural vocabularies of values such as individualism, liberty, choice, and competition—a competition without discord, regulations, and barriers. Bill Gates, for example, represents Neoliberalism as a "friction free" capitalism (*The Road Ahead* 180-207).

Neoliberalism is the class "philosophy" of postwar capitalism. Although it has its roots in the Bretton Woods agreements of 1944, it only became an active force in transnational capitalism after the fall of the rate of profit in the early 1970s and the end of a fixed rate of currency exchange by the U.S., which led to the collapse of the Bretton Woods agreements. Neoliberalism helped to (temporarily) increase the rate of profits by using such international financial institutions as the IMF and the World Bank to change international labor and finance laws and thus make the cheap labor of the South available to capitalists of the

North. It further provided the discursive means for transferring wealth from the South to the North by imposing loans on poor countries.

There are two major components to the class theory of Neoliberalism: a market macro-philosophy that serves as a model for a new society and a micro-pragmatics of labor relations. Neoliberal labor relations are formulated in terms of a quasi-ethics of employment that is actually a calculus of profit and has reshaped the labor relations of capital to increase profits. The core of its labor relations is based on replacing continuing employment with "contract" work and continually substituting short-term contracts for long-term contracts; it subjects each part of a transaction to competition ("efficiency") for different contracts. It outsources tasks and holds competitions for particular tasks within a firm, what some call "insourcing." It increases flexible and casual work, changes the pension and health care arrangements, and reduces work safety practices. The end result is that "the absolute reign of flexibility is established, with employees being hired on fixed-term contracts or on a temporary basis, and repeated corporate restructurings and, within the firm itself, competition among autonomous divisions as well as among teams forced to perform multiple functions" (Bourdieu, "The Essence of Neoliberalism").

Cultural turn writings have normalized these labor practices through such concepts as singularity and contingency. The collaboration is so close here that, as we have seen, *The Economist* magazine comments, "Post-modernism and 'neo-liberal' free-market economics," which had developed independently of each other, point "in much the same direction" ("Post-modernism Is the New Black"). The postwar process of demolishing collective structures (class) and collectivities, which we have already discussed, eventually led under Neoliberalism to the "individualization of salaries and of careers as a function of individual competence" (Bourdieu, "The Essence of Neoliberalism") and is replicated in the post-ethics of the singular: "[D]o not consider me 'one of you,' don't 'count me in,' I want to keep my freedom, always: this for me, is the condition not only for being singular and other, but also for entering into relation with the singularity and alterity of others" (Derrida and Ferraris, *A Taste for the Secret* 27). Derrida's contribution to the logic of Neoliberalism goes beyond the idea of singularity. It includes, for example, his emphatic writings on contingency (*The Ear of the Other*; *The Gift of Death*) which provide Neoliberal management with the theoretical cover to represent "labor" and continuous work (secure jobs) as an absolute (metaphysics) that needs to be deconstructed into the flexibility and contingencies of short-term contracts. In other words, like all other social practices, labor relations are assumed to be a discourse, a matter of "language," but the question of language "has never simply been one problem among others" (Derrida, *Of Grammatology* 6). In language the "absolute" (labor) loses its authority and becomes "contingent"—neither necessary nor impossible. It is an in-between-ness: the situation in which the short-term contract places the subject of labor between having a job and losing it. The laboring subject remains constantly "uncertain" and thus becomes acquiescent. The contingent also serves the Neoliberal manager as the philosophy of responsibility and allows him to put the worker in a situation of increasing competition with others (act responsibly in reducing costs); this makes the working day a moment by moment fear of being fired and renders the subject more and more accommodating. Class consciousness is turned into company consciousness under "the silent compulsion of economic relations [which] sets the seal on the domination of the capitalist over the worker" (Marx, *Capital* I, 899).

The macro-philosophy of Neoliberalism grounds itself in classical and neoclassical economic theories, from Adam Smith and even Marx to the Marginalist neo-classical versions developed by Alfred Marshall and William Stanley Jevons. But it is not in any serious sense philosophically coherent and fails to be a consistent political theory as well. It is a practical (patched-up) ideology. It reduces economics from a scientific project to affective speculation (Chang, *Globalization, Economic Development and the Role of the State*; Dumenil and Levy, *Capital Resurgent: Roots of the Neoliberal Revolution*). As a political theory, it is a disjointed set of slogans. While it advocates a limited role for the state when it comes to regulating the market, it also assumes the presence of a very strong state in its demands for state protection of the individual right to private property. Philosophically and politically, Neoliberalism is a hodgepodge of practices and ideas from the Austrian school of economics, Milton Friedman's monetarism, and Jude Wanniski's supply-side economics to conservative tax-cut programs.

The core of Neoliberalism is articulated in the "Statement of Aims" of the Mont Pelerin Society issued on April 10, 1947. The main purpose of the group was to discredit a planned economy, which at the time was gaining support in the U.S. However, the society itself explained its goals in grand cultural vocabularies of death and renewal of civilizations:

> After World War II,...when many of the values of Western civilization were imperiled, 36 scholars, mostly economists, with some historians and philosophers, were invited by Professor Friedrich von Hayek to meet at Mont Pelerin, near Montreux, Switzerland, to discuss the state and the possible fate of liberalism...in thinking and practice. (http://www.montpelerin.org/aboutmps.html)

The underlying logic of Neoliberalism is that

> the position of the individual and the voluntary group are progressively undermined by extensions of arbitrary power... these developments have been fostered by the growth of a view of history which denies all absolute moral standards...[and] by a decline of belief in private property and the competitive market.... (http://www.montpelerin.org//mpsGoals.cfm)

These abstractions are an alibi for justifying Neoliberalism's practical goals which are above all to give free rein to capital but confine labor. It thus seeks to free the market from all state regulations and then to install the norms of the market as the norms of society in general—the social as the deregulated plurality of all competing against all. The fact that such a theory of society-as-market demolishes all forms of social solidarity and collectivity is not a source of concern; it is, as we have already argued, a stated goal. Recall Margaret Thatcher's words: "There is no such thing as society. There are individual men and women, and there are families" ("Interview"). Putting capital accumulation at the center means not only deregulation of the social but also the reduction of all social services—from heath care and schools to public transportation and social security. The Neoliberal utopia is where all public services are privatized and what is most profitable for capital is turned into a new ethics.

This, of course, is not simply a local goal but a global policy by which Neoliberalism has managed—through such institutions as the IMF and World Bank—to rewrite the financial laws on an international scale and, in doing so, restrict the rights of workers (anti-unionism), open up the banks and markets of the South to the capitalists of the North ("free trade"), and, while removing all obstacles from the path of capital, limit the movements of humans so that workers are kept in the low-wage regions of the South. Consequently, through the IMF and World Bank, Neoliberalism has rewritten the priorities of the South so that all public spending on social services is reduced and public sectors are privatized. The collective subject of labor is thus isolated as monadic subjects of consumption, desire, and a private aesthetic. Neoliberalism is the most aggressive form of contemporary capitalism and has produced the most epistemologically aggressive cultural theories—what we have called "post" theories such as poststructuralism, postcolonialism, postmodernism—to make class disappear from contemporary debates and analyses. These theories have translated class into difference and dispersed class antagonism into cultural values where questions of wage labor are displaced by questions of abortion, same sex marriage, stem-cell research, and the right to bear arms.

BINARIES (AGAIN)

Neoliberalism and its representational technologies have made the exploitation of workers of the South not only acceptable but also ethical by portraying it as a substantial help from the North, as an act of compassion by corporations who exploit the poor in the service of humanity, providing them with jobs and wages in order to lift them up from their poverty. The class binary of the propertied and propertyless, in other words, is reconciled by compassionate exploitation. Such a moral reconciliation is effective but naïve and fragile. In place of this simplistic moralism, the cultural turn puts forth a rigorous epistemological critique that, instead of merely reconciling binaries of the rich and poor, makes the concept of the binary itself epistemologically questionable and, in doing so, renders the very idea of opposition a residue of a dated metaphysics.

It has become an interpretive imperative in contemporary cultural theory, as we have already indicated, to read binaries as effects of a certain totalizing thinking and an urge to presence. They are thus dispersed through difference in order to open up a space for singularity and its heterogeneity. It is now routinely assumed that, as Nietzsche declares, "there are no oppositions, except in the customary exaggeration of popular or metaphysical interpretations, and that a mistake in reasoning lies at the root of this antithesis" (*Human, All Too Human* 12). For "post" thinkers, this "mistake in reasoning" is not a conceptual forgetfulness or a failure of logic, but rather an exercise of power in which, echoing Foucault's critique of the construction of "madness" in the West, "the plenitude of one becomes the lack of the other" as Toby Miller and Geoffrey Lawrence put it ("Globalization and Culture" 492).

Anti-binarism has become canonic thinking in cultural theory mostly because of the influence of such writers as Heidegger, Derrida, Foucault, Lyotard, Deleuze, and Guattari. What has especially popularized anti-binarism and made it the common sense of cultural theory are the annotations on texts by these writers and the application of their interpretive strategies to diverse reading projects in the work of such second-generation poststructuralists as Gayatri Chakravorty Spivak, Judith Butler, Homi Bhabha, Michael Hardt, and Antonio Negri.

Of course, anti-binarism as a means for obscuring class relations is not limited to the interpretive strategies of poststructuralism. Deploying Lacan's theory of "The Real," Slavoj Zizek, for example, argues that class as a historical reality—namely, "existing social groups" in opposition, such as "bourgeois" against "proletariat"—is an impossibility because the binary is suspended by the emergence of a third term "which does not 'fit' this opposition (lumpenproletariat, etc.)" ("Class Struggle or Postmodernism?" 132). The "third term" turns the binary into a plurality and renders class as a form of difference. This difference, which can never be overcome, is the excess of "the Real" and its incommensurability with "the Symbolic" (social reality). Lacan-Zizek's "the Real" is itself a class construct. By separating reality from the Real, it obscures wage-labor in desire—the lack which is itself another version of the blankness that we discussed in our analysis of abstract expressionism. Like blankness, "the Real" is the emptiness that contains all, a (Hegelian) space "whose spiritual aroma is religion."

Canonic anti-binarism is based on a textualization of the inside/outside (Derrida, *Of Grammatology* 30-65) that makes the "binary" a discourse of power in which "one of the two terms governs the other" and is therefore "a violent hierarchy" (Derrida, *Positions* 41). Textualizing ("deconstructing") cultural representations, as we have already suggested, is a double move by which what is seen as the subordinating relation of power is overturned. Thus conditions are prepared for "the irruptive emergence of a new 'concept,' a concept that can no longer be, and never could be, included in the previous regime" (42). Seeming opposites—speech and writing, for instance—actually rely on each other for their identity. Speech is not an original entity with an autonomous identity. Its seeming self-sameness is an identity effect because it is the result of its excluding from itself its self-difference and objectifying it in its outside as writing, which also is an instance of self-difference. Consequently, it becomes clear that speech and writing are not opposites but versions of difference. Opposites are not different from each other but are different within themselves and what they represent as their opposite is their own self-difference, which they have to absent from themselves in order to become self-present. However, this difference is not foundational; it never congeals into the ground of their being which would allow them to have an essence of their own:

> What is written as *différance*, then, will be the playing movement that "produces"—by means of something that is not simply an activity—these differences, these effects of difference. This does not mean that the *différance* that produces differences is somehow before them, in a simple and unmodified—indifferent—present. *Différance* is the non-full, non-simple, structured and differentiating origin of differences. Thus, the name "origin" no longer suits it. (Derrida, "Différance" 11)

The stated goal of anti-binary criticism is to develop a nuanced and subtle understanding of cultural meanings and halt the violence of binary totalizing by dis-closing the repressed differences and "other"-ness, which Levinas calls the place of the ethical (*Otherwise Than Being: Or Beyond Essence*). To do this, it de-layers the binaries, showing their underlying metaphysics through such reading strategies as Heidegger's "destruction" (*The Basic Problems of Phenomenology*) and Derrida's "deconstruction" ("Letter to a Japanese Friend"). The goal of a criticism of binaries, in other words, is said to be freeing the margins and their differences.

The anti-binarism in the cultural turn rewrites the historical materialist theory of class as a "simple opposition of dominant and dominated" (Derrida, *Specters of Marx* 55). It claims that such a class theory, like all binaries, obtains its analytic authority ("presence") by transposing the difference within class onto a binary of "outside" and "inside," thus establishing the antagonistic "proletariat" and "bourgeois." Rewriting the opposition "between" classes as a difference "within" them, the cultural turn destabilizes the truth of class as the social relations of labor, turning it into a playfulness of meanings without end. If the two terms of the binary are at odds with themselves and are thus indeterminate and not coherent, as such a reading claims, then they cannot be the ground for any coherent opposition (which is a difference "from"). To put it differently, if "proletariat" and "bourgeois" are uncertain (because of their self-difference), they cannot be in a relation of opposition to each other but are simply two versions of difference.

We have already discussed Derrida's theory of class at some length. However, given the enormous effect his class theory has had on cultural theory, we need to return to his theory here even though we may say again some of what we have said before. Any repetition, however, should not be too disconcerting since his views on this and related subjects are repeated over and over in almost every book on contemporary cultural theory.

Within this anti-binary self-difference, Derrida situates the materialist theory of class as a theory of the "identity and the self-identity of a social class" (*Specters of Marx* 55). Class is therefore a "problematic" category both theoretically and historically: theoretically because of "the insufficiently 'differentiated' nature of the concept of class as it has been 'inherited,'" specifically "the principle of identification of social class, and the idea that a social class is what it is, homogeneous, present and identical to itself as 'ultimate support'" ("Marx & Sons" 237). Historically, such a notion of class, according to Derrida, is unable to deal with the "new realities of techno-scientifico-capitalist 'modernity' of world society" (239). To be an effective category for social analysis today, he argues, class has to be inscribed with "a certain difference from itself, a certain heterogeneity in a social force" (237). To do this, he retheorizes the "economic" and turns it into an "aneconomics" of difference which includes not only "productivity" but also "a certain unproductiveness" ("Politics and Friendship" 205).

What is offered by Derrida as a means for "differentiating" class in order to make it "a much more subtle instrument' (203) turns class from a materialist concept that is deployed to analyze the structures of social antagonism over the appropriation of surplus labor under capitalism into a cultural poetics of difference. Derrida's familiar response to such critiques of his text has always been the same, namely, that he has been misunderstood. He states that his critique of class is not intended to demolish it but to "underscore" that it is

> 'problematic,' which does not mean either false or outmoded or inoperative or insignificant, but rather susceptible of transformation and critical re-elaboration, in a situation in which a certain capitalist modernity 'ruins' the most sensitive defining criterion of class (for example—but a great deal more needs to be said about this, for everything is hanging in the balance here—the concept of labor, worker, proletariat, mode of production, etc.). ("Marx & Sons" 236)

But he never does say more about this nor does he offer any argument to support his claims. He is, of course too subtle to say that class is "passé" (236) or that it is "irrelevant" (236). Such vulgarities would place him among right-wing theorists. He says that he is a man of the Left: "I vote Socialist" ("Politics and Friendship" 212). He wants to "complicate" class from the Left, but his "complications" actually destroy class as a materialist category of social analysis.

What he calls "complication" is a move by which what he writes in the center of his text is cancelled by its margins. In the center of his texts, he emphasizes, for instance, that class is "indispensable" (204). On the margins, however, he rewrites class as a trope of a generalized conflict ("Marx & Sons" 239) and subtly reads "economy" as "general economy," thus obscuring the material relations of property (class) by the cultural relations of non-productivity ("Politics and Friendship" 205). In the margins of the *Specters of Marx*, Derrida continues his argument (from "Politics and Friendship" 204) that capitalism has changed from its earlier industrial (19th and early 20th century) form into what in "Marx & Sons" he calls "techno-scientifico-capitalist modernity" (239). It is telling that Derrida, who has put in question not only the idea of progress and history as fictions of metaphysics and promises of "presence," uses history to erode the materiality of class in the name of "complicating" it to deal with the new capitalism which is the effect of the differential deployment of *tekhnē*, of techno-science or tele-technology. It obliges us more than ever to think the virtualization of space and time, the possibility of virtual events whose movement and speed prohibit us more than ever (more and otherwise than ever, for this is not absolutely and thoroughly new) from opposing presence to its representation, 'real time' to 'deferred time,' effectivity to its simulacrum, the living to the non-living, in short, the living to the living-dead of its ghosts. It obliges us to think, from there, another space for democracy. For democracy-to-come and thus for justice. (*Specters of Marx* 169)

Within this context of change and historical transformation, Derrida offers his theory of the "New International," which

> refers to a profound transformation, projected over a long term, of international law, of its concepts, and its field of intervention.... It is a link of affinity, suffering, and hope, a still discrete, almost secret link, as it was around 1848, but more and more visible, we have more than one sign of it. It is an untimely link, without status, without title, and without name, barely public even if it is not clandestine, without contract, "out of joint," without coordination, without party, without country, without national community (International before, across, and beyond any national determination), without co-citizenship, without common belonging to a class. (*Specters of Marx* 84, 85)

The "without's" here are supposed to mark the radical anti-essentialism of Derrida's "New International." However, in its structures and features it is, like the space mapped by Michael Hardt and Antonio Negri in *Empire*, a site of liberal constitution, citizenship, and human rights. The "without's" do not change its essentialist liberalism and its social metaphysics, they simply turn it into a hyperliberalism that obscures its essentialist foundation through excess. By proposing affect ("affinity, suffering, and hope") as the axes of association in the "New International" Derrida clouds the actual material relations of the social, which are constructed by labor and capital, and displaces freedom from necessity by freedom as human rights, which are in the end nothing more than the right to hold property and the legal protection that comes with it. Human rights in the "New International," co-exist with the dominant class structures and the property regime.

The inhabitants of the "New International" are cosmopolitan citizens of a global civil society that masks the international division of labor and its class relations in a generalized humanity. The cosmopolitan, in his absolute singularity, wanders across the word in secret connections with other singulars in the ecstasies of being "without" ("without title, and without name,...without coordination, without party, without country, without national community,...without co-citizenship, without common belonging to a class," 85) that mark his nomadic (anti-essentialist) and rebellious, anti-normative subjectivity. This is the stuff of which new populist business management theories are made. These theories construct the "new" bold global manager as a subject who makes decisions in the face of the undecidability of the market and forges a new ethics of organizing without organization (e.g., "Unglued Organizations," "Deconstructing the Corporation," "Farewell Vertical Integration, Welcome Networks" in Tom Peters's *Liberation Management*). The "New International" is the board room of global capitalism-to-come where the hard material conditions of international labor relations are obscured in utopian liberal fantasies.

Critics such as Tom Lewis point out that the "New International" is the space of the bourgeois utopia that Marx and Engels call "'true' socialism" ("The Politics of 'Hauntology' in Derrida's *Specters of Marx*" 146-153) and that its main concern is with the "'most reasonable' social order and not the needs of a particular class and a particular time" (Marx and Engels, *The German Ideology* 455). Aijaz Ahmad writes that the "New International" is the site of "anti-politics" ("Reconciling Derrida: 'Specters of Marx' and Deconstructive Politics" 104). To these and other critics, Derrida responds with anger, claiming that when he says the "New International" is "without common belonging to a class" it does not mean that he has abandoned class and class struggle. To interpret him otherwise, he claims, is a sign (and here he gives a version of the standard answer that he and his friends routinely give to all who critique him) that all oppositional critiques of him are based on shallow, "hurried and somewhat global readings" ("Marx & Sons" 239) and are "crude and demagogically polemical" (241) misinterpretations. Polemically he opposes polemic.

The "correct" interpretation is "simply, another dimension of analysis and political commitment, one that cuts across social differences and oppositions of social forces (what one used to call, simplifying, 'classes')" ("Marx & Sons" 239). The "New International," in other words, is grounded in the assumption that there are social dimensions "outside" specific classes and that the social is an assemblage of hybrid relations ("across social differences and oppositions"). These hybrid relations work outside the structural antagonisms over the appropriation of surplus labor and, by placing "bosses alongside workers" (Lewis, "The Politics of Hauntology" 149), diffuse class conflict in heterogeneity and difference. Derrida's commitment to class, it becomes clear, is a means for undercutting it by turning it into an indeterminate space that exists side by side with other contingent dimensions of the social and is thus one of many social meanings.

In its materialist sense, class is formed at the point of production: "The relations of production in their totality constitute what is called the social relations" (Marx, *Wage-Labour and Capital* 29). There is nothing outside these relations, which are constituted under capitalism (within which the architecture of the "New International" is set) by the private ownership of the means of production. To open up a parallel space and claim that it cuts across classes is to say that social relations are autonomous of class and are effects of cultural conflicts that are independent of property relations (what forms class relations).

Derrida's extra-class theory (of "another dimension") undercuts the logic of class by proposing that social logic is contingent and there are no dimensions that are prior or primary to others: "All that depends, *at every instant*," every "*singular* situation" is different (239). The theory of "another dimension" of the social constructs the social as a detotalized assemblage of contingencies, indeterminacies, and singularities. Difference and heterogeneity are the places of "hospitality" in the democracy-to-come (*Politics of Friendship* 104), which is a mystical space "without" class but not classless, a hyperdemocracy where excess of meanings turn it into a democracy of the indeterminate ("to-come") and the undecidable which is "the condition of decision wherever decision cannot be deduced from an existing body of knowledge…as it would be by a calculating machine" ("Marx & Sons" 240). Unlike existing democracies—which lack "messianicity *without* messianism" ("Marx & Sons" 251) and exclude the right to refuse rights and which also act in-differently according to the principle of "equality" that leaves out the "singular"—the democracy-to-come is the home of difference. It is a refusal of "presence" and the binaries on which such a presence is structured; it keeps open the undecidable and thus responsibility which is an activating of ethics. It is a secret (*Specters of Marx* 85) whose secrecy can never be represented in language; it is always singular and, like a secret, sacred.

The ideological role of the sacred (democracy-to-come) is to make all critiques of the worldly (existing democracies) irrelevant and beside the point; the democracy-to-come is a resecuring of democracy-as-is, putting it beyond question. Democracy-as-is is the arena of capital's exploitation of labor. The workers, in Derrida's narrative, will have to wait for justice-to-come. Democracy-to-come is a deferral of class struggles to make sure that the revolution never arrives. Here and now, in existing democracies, Derrida deconstructs binaries by representing them as part of the metaphysics of presence and thus makes speaking about class as the oppositional relations of labor and capital part of a discredited discourse of logocentrism.

However, fundamental binaries are not effects of an epistemological misreading, a closure of meanings, or discursive power relations. They are caused by the exploitation of the labor of workers by owners. Binaries are effects of the binary of labor and capital—they are constitutive of capitalism itself. As such, they reproduce themselves in all cultural practices and discourses, including Derrida's deconstruction of binaries and our own critique of it.

BINARIES AND PRIVATE PROPERTY

Binaries (man/woman, white/black, suburb/inner city, etc.) are reproductions in the cultural sphere of the material labor divisions that, at the point of production, divides people according to their relation to labor into workers and owners: into those who own nothing but their own labor and those who own the means of production by which they exploit the labor of workers. Private property, to put it more directly, is the cause of the cultural and social binaries that permeate everyday life (education, health, housing, etc.). But the historical materiality of these binaries and the fact that they are the results of the institution of private property are obscured by being naturalized through cultural representations that construct the binaries as effects of, for example, biology, intelligence, national character, or other features of "human nature" or equally unchangeable aspects of life. In more advanced social discourses, in which such concepts as "human nature" have lost conceptual credibility, the more abstract languages of philosophy argue that binaries, as we have discussed, are part of a metaphysics of the will to truth that, in a quest for presence and a centering certitude, constructs an "inside" which contains truth only by attributing its absence to an "outside" (Derrida, *Of Grammatology* 36-65).

Metaphysics, however, does not produce binaries. Binaries produce metaphysics in order to use the abstract discourses of Being to obscure their origin in the materiality of the relations of labor. A critique of metaphysics, as is customary in contemporary cultural theory, does not abolish binaries nor does it change their material effects on the every day. It merely represses them in cultural representations. But the material relations of labor, which produced binaries in the first place, return the repressed over and over again to daily life and its social institutions, and each time do so in new and different forms. Unless relations of labor are changed, binaries will continue to shape the logic and practices of contemporary social life, and its cultural representations.

There are no binaries as indexes of power in pre-class egalitarian societies because there is no private property in these societies. Differences in pre-class foraging societies are differences without privilege. These societies are based on equality of labor in production, universal access to material resources, and are structured along non-hierarchical social relations, which means their cultures are free from "binaries."

The two binaries that are often used as examples that binaries are actually power relations and not neutral are binaries of politics (especially decision making over the distribution of resources) and gender. In her extensive research into pre-class egalitarian societies, especially the Montagnais-Naskapi of Canada, Eleanor Burke Leacock has argued that in such societies "leadership" (a power hierarchy) "as we conceive it is not only 'weak' or 'incipient,' as is commonly stated, but irrelevant" (*Myths of Male Dominance* 138). Decisions in these societies are "freely arrived at, within and among multifamily units" (139). This political structure is itself the outcome of material equality, namely, the equality of all at the point of production.

> In egalitarian band society, food and other necessities were produced or manufactured by all able-bodied adults and were directly distributed by their producers.... It is common knowledge that there was no differential access to resources through private land ownership and no specialization of labor beyond that by sex, hence no market system to intervene in the direct relationship between production and distribution....
>
> The basic principle of egalitarian band society was that people made decisions about the activities for which they were responsible. Consensus was reached within whatever group would be carrying out a collective activity.... Men and women, when defined as interest groups according to the sexual division of labor, arbitrated or acted upon differences in 'public' ways, such as when women would hold council...to consider the problem of a lazy man.... (*Myths of Male Dominance* 139-40)

Gender relations, which are the other main zone of binary conflicts in bourgeois analytics, are based on equality in pre-class societies which have not developed the institution of private property. Leacock argues that among hunter-gatherers the myth of male dominance is just that, a myth *(Myths of Male Dominance)*. In "Women's Status in Egalitarian Society" and other essays, she relies on both her vast field research and historical analysis to examine how women's status in egalitarian society is "inseparable from the analysis of egalitarian social-economic structure as a whole" (*Myths of Male Dominance* 133). She then demonstrates the material basis of gender equality in pre-class societies and argues that "there were no economic and social liabilities that bound women to be more sensitive to men's needs and feelings than vice versa" (140). What has made gender the space of binaries is, of course, the division of labor. Leacock writes that there is no clear division of labor in an egalitarian society: "When necessary, the women helped with hunting, and if a woman was busy elsewhere, a man would readily look after the children" (37). Gender becomes a point of struggle over power because of the undermining of "women's autonomy and privatization of their social and economic roles" with the "breaking up of the egalitarian and collective social forms that are anathema to capitalist exploitation" (315). In other words, as she argues in "Relations of Production in Band Society," when "male dominance" arises "in otherwise egalitarian societies," it is "a function of changing relations of production reinforced by missionary teachings, legal systems, and European models" of capitalism (167).

All the research that finds egalitarian societies free from private property—and thus from the privileging of binaries—are seen as direct threats to the very ontology of capitalism and have been the subject of controversy if not outright dismissal. Nonetheless there is an unbroken chain of research and writings on this matter that consistently has proven the absence of private property and lack of corresponding binaries that naturalize hierarchies of power in pre-class societies (Zavarzadeh, *The Totality and Post*). These include writers with very different perspectives from the early work of Lewis Henry Morgan who called these societies beyond "property career" (*Ancient Society* 561) to the recent research of such scholars as Christopher Boehm who writes from a very different politico-ethical perspective and with an emphasis on language and other symbolic practices and maps out the egalitarianism of early societies—as in the "vigilant sharing of (Large-Game) meat"—and its evolution (*Hierarchy in the Forest* 191-193).

Morgan argues that early societies were based on "liberty, equality and fraternity" (*Ancient Society* 562) and describes the social life of both ancient societies and native Americans as "communism in living" (*Ancient Society* 454). Marx describes these egalitarian social formations as "primitive communism" (*Capital* III, 831). The "primitive communism" of hunter-gatherers is rendered inconsequential in contemporary cultural theory by portraying them as barely surviving their miserable and poverty-ridden life until the invention of agriculture and the emergence of private property and a ruling elite. This is itself a class interpretation. However, in discussing pre-class egalitarian societies one has always to be aware of Eleanor Leacock's warning:

> Archeological and ethnographic data on pre-class societies and societies where class relations were developed independently of colonial relations established by the powers of Europe and Asia are spotty and ambiguous. Archeological data on all but the broad outlines of socio-economic organization are generally suggestive, not conclusive, and to find records of a non-literate society means, of course, that it has already come into contact with, and hence been in some way affected by, the relations of commodity production." ("Introduction" 58)

The "broad outlines" of research on the social organization of pre-agricultural foraging societies indicate that the rise of binaries in social life is the effect of the emergence of private property. This leads to the formation of antagonistic social classes and the installing of a state by those who have appropriated the surplus labor in order to repress this antagonism and protect their own material interests. The development of forces of production, in other words, leads to the social division of labor which is both a "necessary phase in economic development" and also "a refined and civilized method of exploitation" (Marx, *Capital* I, 486). The surplus labor produced by these developments in labor practices is appropriated by a few as their own private property. Binaries are the effects of this two-tier economic system: the owners of the means of production and workers. This binary division, which is reproduced in all aspects of social and cultural life, is normalized as the effects, for example, of the inherent biological features of individuals (e.g., intelligence), their character traits (tendency toward hard work or laziness), their personal choices, or the like.

Modern scientific research on foraging societies demystifies these norms. It has its transformative moment in the "Man the Hunter" conference in Chicago (1966) and the publication of the discussions in *Man the Hunter*, edited by Richard Lee and Irven DeVore (1968). Richard Lee's own writings have shaped more recent inquiries (as in the special issue of *Anthropologica* on the "Politics and Practices in Critical Anthropology: The Work of Richard B. Lee" in 2003), and have provided the analytical structures for investigations of pre-class societies by focusing on the everyday life of the foraging people of the !Kung San of the Kalahari (Southern African "bushmen").

Lee's writings concentrate on the people who call themselves "Ju/'hoansi" but are also named "!Kung" and are a part of the "San" group. His research is conceptually innovative both in its local analysis of !Kung San practices as well as in its global conclusions about dominant views on "human nature," which have been made part of the cultural common sense of the West through, for instance, the philosophical writings of Hobbes, Locke, Rousseau, and others. Hobbes's theories, which naturalize hierarchies and inequalities, are essentially justifications of social life under early modern capitalism. His main argument is that "war" is the general condition of social life without structured rankings of power. In the absence of a "common power to keep them all in awe," therefore, the war was "of every man, against every man' (*Leviathan* 185) because he believed, "every man is Enemy to every man" (186). Peace, for Hobbes, is negative: the effect of subjugation to power. He contends that outside (Western) culture, there is raw nature, "no arts; no letters; no society," only "continual fear, and danger of violent death." Hobbes writes that the "Life of man," outside the culture of the West, is "solitary, poor, nasty, brutish and short" (186).

However, through his meticulous research and finely detailed analyses, Lee demonstrates the ideological work of Hobbes's writings. Not only is !Kung San social life free from structural social contradictions, poverty, and competition, but they also live what is basically a form of "primitive communism"—words, Lee writes, that marked "a simple concept" and "yet the very words evoke uneasiness and embarrassment" ("Reflections on Primitive Communism" 252). The !Kung San people's "primitive communism" is structured to give all people equal access to food resources, lakes, beaches, animals, and plants. But their equality is not simply a matter of the distribution of life-sustaining materials. The only true test of any egalitarian ("communist") society is whether there is equality in production practices (labor). Lee demonstrates how in foraging societies all adults equally participate in production of foods and other goods. In foraging "primitive communism," Lee argues, all primary life resources are communal property.

To point to one of the issues that is the subject of intense controversies on the matter of inequality and binaries, Lee's research showed that far from being poor, hungry, and living a life of absolute misery, hunting-gathering societies were balanced societies both ecologically and in terms of their food and diet. These societies were, in Marshall Sahlins' words, the "Original Affluent Society" ("Notes on the Original Affluent Society" 85-92; *Stone Age Economics*). To mention another controversial issue, Lee himself demonstrates that the San diet is extremely nutritious, and through close analysis of the daily diet, he concludes that it shows how women were equally active in producing food and other life matters and that !Kung San social life was centered on gender equality. This discovery leads Lee to rewrite the "hunter-gatherers" as "gatherer-hunters" in order to foreground what mainstream research had obscured: the equality of the female "gatherer" with the male in the "primitive communism" of the !Kung San.

Lee is interested in the "big questions." Thus, for him, the gathering-hunting mode of life among the !Kung San of the Kalahari exceeds its specific local importance. He questions the Boasian particularism that has dominated anthropology for so long and reads the foraging mode of life as part of a larger evolutionary history of humans. "Foraging," he writes in his groundbreaking book, *The !Kung San: Men, Women, and Work in a Foraging Society*, "was the way of life that prevailed during an important period of human history" (433). And he argues that the contemporary foragers "offer clues to the nature of this way of life." This is important for Lee because by understanding "the adaptations of the past we can better understand the present and the basic human material that produced them both" (433). However, he never regards contemporary foraging people as "fossils" of an earlier time but as socially dynamic and actively changing societies. His approach to history is dialectical not static.

Lee's work is of great significance in understanding binaries. He analyzes various aspects of the cultural life and social organizations of the !Kung San and examines the underlying logic of egalitarianism, which he argues marks not only the life of !Kung gatherer-hunters but is essentially typical of all pre-class societies. He argues that all the cultural and social practices of the !Kung San of the Kalahari are effects of the "foraging mode of production" ("Politics, Sexual and Non-Sexual, in Egalitarian Society" 51-53; "Is there a Foraging Mode of Production?"). Central to this mode of production is "a lack of wealth accumulation and the social differentiation that accompanies it" ("Politics, Sexual and Non-Sexual, in Egalitarian Society" 51). Land ownership, for example, is not individual but vested in "a collective of k'ausi, both male and female." But this group ownership is not absolute: it does not limit the resources of the land to those who actually reside on it. Other people from other localities can use the land since the principle of reciprocity and not absolute ownership shapes the social relations of all hunter-gatherers. Consequently, "an individual may utilize the food resources of several waterholes" as long as whatever is gathered and hunted is shared with others.

The lack (or existence) of private property in pre-agricultural societies has been a fiercely contested issue in the cultural and social sciences. Commenting on some of these debates, which became particularly intense after the "Man the Hunter" conference in Chicago (1966), Harold Demsetz wrote: "The question of private ownership of land among aboriginals…has been one of the intellectual battlegrounds in the attempt to assess the 'true nature' of man unconstrained by the 'artificialities' of civilization" ("Towards a Theory of Property Rights" 350). The reason that theory and history of private property are contested with such seriousness and passion is because, in bourgeois representations, private property is constitutive of the very identity of being human (Pryor, "What Does It Mean to Be Human? A Comparison of Primate Economies").

The idea of a society without binaries of the propertied and propertyless, namely an egalitarian society, has been under constant attack since the mid-20th century in part because any theory of society and its social organizations in the past (in)directly implies theories for the future. The translation of binaries, which are effects of private ownership, into categories of a metaphysics of presence in the cultural turn is part of this theory of the future. The cultural turn rewrites free enterprise and the social relations it produces (and for whose protection the Taft-Hartley Act of 1947 was crafted) as a question of epistemology. As in all metaphysics, it therefore obscures the fact that social institutions such as private property (congealed alienated labor) are historical and thus always in transformation.

The existence of a pre-class egalitarian society without a two-tier economy, and the social and cultural binaries that they produce, points to the historical possibility of a socialist society free from all binaries which are always effects of private property—class relations.

Part 2
Tracing Class

3

Class Is

Most Americans, when they are not thinking of themselves purely as individuals, regard themselves as part of the "middle class." Their evidence is that they own a car or two, have a mortgage on a house, go on vacation, entertain themselves at home with DVD players and Xbox video games, have iPhones and medical insurance, and send their children to college. The reality is that their cars and houses are actually owned by the banks, their vacations are often paid for with credit cards, their health care is rationed by HMOs, and their children's education is also financed by the banks, to whom they owe many thousands of dollars when they graduate. But this does not seem to disturb their belief in the "evidence." Like the realities of Disneyland, their favorite escape park, evidence looks more real when it is faked. On the other side of the faked realities, the fact is that the middle class is an ideological illusion and not an economic reality.

Even by the norms of conventional stratification, class polarization is the reality. In a special series on class in America, the *New York Times* reports an "extraordinary jump in income inequality. The after-tax income of the top 1 percent of American households jumped 139 percent, to more than $700,000, from 1979 to 2001...and the income of the poorest fifth rose only 9 percent" (Correspondents of the *New York Times*, *Class Matters* 19).

The middle-class lifestyle quickly collapses under the reality of economic pressures. Following the dot.com crash, for example, high-tech consultants and managers, who used to earn more than $100,000 a year, suddenly lost their jobs and discovered that their middle-class lifestyle had completely disappeared. Former owners of homes and stock portfolios found themselves sleeping in homeless shelters and "rubbing elbows with society's castaways—the mentally ill, drug addicts and other hard-luck cases" where, as one former high-tech worker explained, "We're all equal here" (Davis, "Dot-Com Bust Creating More Homeless").

The myth of the middle class is invented to obscure the fact that "we" (black or white, man or woman, gay or straight, etc.) are all wage-workers, and, therefore, "we" are "all equal here" because, as Marx puts it, "middle and transitional" levels of social differences "always conceal the boundaries" of classes (Marx, *Capital* III, 1025). The middle-class illusion blurring the sharp class lines that actually divide contemporary society into "workers" and "owners" gives relative ideological stability to capitalism which is always in one or another form of crisis. Whether it is the crisis of unemployment, inflation, overproduction, or war, the crisis is ultimately and always a class crisis (Harman, *Explaining the Crisis*). The idea of the middle class, in other words, is a social anesthetic. It numbs the mind to the social contradictions and dulls the pain of daily economic struggles for subsistence. The line that separates the bottom from the middle class is more a psychocultural effect than a material actuality.

The majority of people are convinced—mostly by the media but also by their education, their church, and the spectacle of shopping malls—that there are no classes in America. Everybody is equal. What shapes a person's life is her own personal hard work, ambitions, and dreams. Class, in the common view, is an old-world, mostly European, social hang-up that has no place in the new world of entrepreneurship.

But even when obstinate social reality forces people to acknowledge that there may be classes in America, Americans believe all classes are shades of one huge middle class that includes everyone. Class differences are merely shades of style and taste within the same (omni) middle class. In other words, there is a one-class classlessness in America. This is the same as saying there are no classes in America. The one-class classlessness idea is part of the larger cultural work to convince Americans that there is no longer a working class in America because economic changes have transformed the source of wealth from labor to knowledge and created a "new economy" that is creating a "post-capitalist" society. One of the main features of this new society is said to be that "Marx's 'proletarian' [becomes] 'bourgeois'" (Drucker, *Post-Capitalist Society* 39).

This is, of course, a recycling of the old theories of *embourgeoisement* (the working class moving up into the middle class) and is aimed at concealing the actual *proletarianization* of the so-called middle class. The *embourgeoisement* theory is based on the "new wealth" of the working class (their houses, cars, flat-screen TVs). It is grounded on a not so subtle turning away from class as a social structure—indicating the relations of people to ownership of the means of production—toward class as an inventory of objects and income. Focusing on the objects people own turns class into an empty, ahistorical concept since what a class "owns" is a historical index not an absolute or static list. What is owned exclusively by the privileged class at one time (a car or a computer, for example) will necessarily become a common possession of all classes as social production changes. But the ownership of these objects by other classes does not change their social structural relations.

The working class still has to sell its labor power to the owning class. Even on the basis of an inventory theory of class, the owning class now owns different exclusive objects that are out of reach of the working class because, as we have suggested, the inventory of products is historical. More and more people now drive luxury cars, such as Mercedes or BMWs, but these cars are no longer marks of belonging to the upper class, rather they are part of the mass marketing of luxury. In response the owning class has "new badges of high-end consumption…the nation's richest are spending their money on personal services," such as "personal chefs"; what matters, says Dalton Conley, is not whether "someone has a flat-screen TV…[but] the control they have over other people's labor, those who are serving them" (Steinhauer, "When the Joneses Wear Jeans" 136). The owning class, in short, owns the value of other people's labor. Everyone else—the middle class or, rather, those who have to work for a wage—owns only objects. Even then, middle-class ownership is precarious and unstable. Nearly everything that is owned—from computers to lawnmowers to decent houses in good school districts—is purchased on credit and financed by debt. Americans "now owe about $750 billion in revolving debt" (Steinhauer 141). The indebtedness of most Americans, or what two debt specialists, Elizabeth Warren and Amelia Warren Tyagi, call "middle-class distress" is so severe that they predict that by the end of the decade "nearly one of every seven families with children" will declare "itself flat broke" and file for bankruptcy (*The Two-Income Trap* 6).

What is significant in understanding class is that, in spite of changes in the inventory of objects owned by various people, one group of people—regardless of how many televisions they have or where they go on vacation—continues to be exploited by the other. The rate of exploitation has increased. CEO compensation (which is actually "profit" disguised as "salary") in 1990 was about 85 times more than the average worker's salary. In the first years of the 21st century, it is ranging from 475 to 525 times more (*Business Week*, April 17, 2000; "Executive Pay Watch" http://www.Aflcio.org/paywatch/ceopay.html).

The social differences that separate people from each other, most Americans believe, have nothing to do with class. They are part of people's own individuality. "It has become an unspoken cultural axiom: anything less than financial well-being is a person's own fault" (Lang, "Behind the Prosperity: Working People in Trouble"). Poverty is not seen as part of the working of the market but as caused by the culture of poverty. Individuality is a convenient cover-up for social inequalities. Even though Americans every single day come face to face with the brutal realities of huge economic disparities that contradict their cultural belief in equality, they feel quite nervous thinking about themselves in terms of class. There is something vaguely sinister and even anti-American about class.

People fear class because class makes people confront the actuality that social disparities are not individualistic—that is, exceptional or accidental—but are instead built into capitalism itself. Social differences are systemic, not eccentric. Class makes people acknowledge that the affluence of the few is the direct result of the wage labor of the many, who live in dull and depressing houses and apartments, have unhealthy diets, send their children to mediocre and dilapidated schools that lack basic educational facilities, and survive on hope.

Class critique links the plight of the poor to the comforts of the rich. It displays the harsh clarity of the exploitation of people by people. It shows how Americans' belief in equality, democratic fairness, and economic justice is an ideological story told to preserve the interests of the ruling class. The reality of class divisions in America delegitimates not only capitalism but also the State and the State institutions protecting capitalism (e.g., the tax system, the military, schools, and courts). Class, therefore, has to be discredited or at least marginal-

Chapter 3

ized in social discourses. Since the objective economics of class differences cannot be denied, this reality is mystified and converted into cultural values. The mass media obscure the economics of class by translating class into cultural status, pride, prestige, and lifestyle.

Class is an indication of the social relations of property. But in such books as *Class*, a bestseller by Paul Fussell, class is twisted into such habits and behavior as having a sense of elegance, a refined taste in wine, or an educated accent: "Regardless of the money you've inherited," according to Fussell, "your social class is still most clearly visible when you say things" (175). Class is distorted into "classy." If class is simply a matter of elegance, taste, and good manners, then anyone—rich or poor—can acquire them. Class, in the mass media, has nothing to do with property; it is a question of cultural sophistication. In Paul Fussell's book, people are differentiated, therefore, not by their economic access but by their politics (34) or more clearly by their taste, manners, style, and even their body weight: "It's the three prole classes that get fat" (48). Other writers have obscured class by talking about such things as the "digital divide" (Norris, et al., ed., *Digital Divide: Civic Engagement, Information Poverty, and the Internet Worldwide*). In translating the economic realities of class into cultural prestige, capitalism deploys not only the mass media, which it owns, but it also recruits elite cultural and social critics and academics who go much further and, as part of their services to capital, for example, deconstruct the very concept of class in their cultural analyses (Woodiwiss, "Deconstructing Class," Laclau, "Deconstructing Classes" 296-301).

In its various forms, such as feminism, queer theory, cultural studies, and film criticism, contemporary cultural theory, which is seen by many as the threshold of progressive thinking, actually takes a mostly conservative approach to class. It inverts the relation of culture and its labor base and represents culture itself as an autonomous agency of social change. Social change in contemporary cultural critique is a trope for putting "representation" under erasure and raising questions about the relation of language to reality. The inversion of the relation of culture (values) and labor (class) takes place by arguing that materialist theories of culture such as Marxism are based on a theory of adequation in which language is seen as faithfully and accurately reflecting reality. Marxist class analysis is then viewed as based on an "essentialist" notion of class as if class (which is seen as a language effect) is in any way an approximation of reality and capable of explaining social inequalities. If class is a concept, then as a concept de Man claims, it is merely a "metaphor" (*Allegories of Reading* 135-159). Therefore, class analysis is considered simply a form of writing (at best a description) and not an explanation. Class signifiers, in other words, do not have fixed signifieds (bourgeoisie/proletariat) since they are always in "play" and, therefore, are orphan signs with no decidable referents. Derrida, de Man, and other textualists argue that "classes," as Chris Jenks puts it, are "metaphors for particular language games and forms of discourse" (*Culture*, 74). Michel Foucault, whose work has influenced cultural critique even more than Derrida and de Man, goes so far as to deny the possibility of the exploited (powerless) and exploiters (powerful): "There is no binary...opposition between rulers and ruled at the root of power relations" (*History of Sexuality* I, 94). Whether it is through deconstructing binaries (outside/inside) and "textualizing" the relation of language and reality in Derrida (*Of Grammatology* 27-73) or by means of power analytics (Foucault, *History of Sexuality* I, 92-102), the two classes (workers/owners) are turned into in-between hybrids (the "middle class") in which the relation of labor and capital, exploited, and exploitation are rendered ambiguous and undecidable. The political economy of exploitation is thus turned into a hermeneutics of in-between-ness.

Both the mass media and cultural theorists conclude that the social differences of cybercapitalism are too complex to be analyzed by class. "Class," as Pakulski and Waters declare, is "dead" (*The Death of Class*). People's lives, in advanced capitalism, are no longer shaped by their work (production) but by their lifestyle and taste and consumption, according to David Brooks in his bestseller, *Bobos in Paradise*, which is an updating of Fussell's narrative. Class as an economic category is neutralized by such cultural reversals and turned into matters of refinement, subtlety, graciousness, urbanity, and a connoisseurship of the delectable. As an expression of "taste and lifestyle," this neutered class is actually seen as adding to the diversity and richness of social life instead of being a social problem of inequality that needs to be eliminated.

The focus on consumption as an index of freedom and equality makes the source of social inequalities unclear. According to these views, two persons who choose to buy the same jacket at Macy's, for example, are equal because of their seemingly equal access to goods and services. Equal consumption makes them equal. To many cultural critics this means everybody is now middle class or "we are all classless nowadays" because our identity is formed in the social relations of shopping. Shopping equality now means social equality. What is left out of this consuming logic is the material reality. If two persons buy the same jacket at Macy's, but one has to work five hours to pay for the jacket and the other can pay for it with only a half an hour of work, they are hardly equal. Equality is a question of production not consumption because value is produced by labor. But the labor theory of value is rejected by mainstream economics, which is obsessed with "supply and demand"—what Mandel calls the "psychological and individual aspects of the problem" (*An Introduction to Marxist Economic Theory* 22).

Nearly all contemporary debates on class deny that labor is the source of value and that the social relations of labor determine one's class. In his defense of capitalism, Weber has said the rise of capitalism is related to cultural values and not labor (*The Protestant Ethic and the "Spirit" of Capitalism*) and has extended this theory to legitimate the idea of the middle class by marginalizing the two-class theory, which shows the brutal aggression of capitalism over the accumulation of profit. Weber claims that class derives not from one's place in labor relations (production) but from one's life chances in the market (distribution).

But the market simply distributes the already available wealth. The question of class is how wealth is produced and not how it is distributed. The stock market may seem to produce wealth, but it is really just redistributing the wealth produced by the labor of the workers. This is readily demonstrated by the collapse of all the dot.com speculation based on "paper profits" rather than the actual production of wealth by the workers. It is, however, telling that "distribution" has now become one of the most popular theories on the Left for containing class antagonisms and social inequality (Fraser, *Justice Interruptus: Critical Reflections on the "Postsocialist" Condition,* and Fraser et al., *Redistribution or Recognition?*). The existence of capitalism depends on its ability to accumulate profit. But profit does not come from buying low and selling high (market relations). The real source of profit is human labor power—not technology. The ideological illusion of the middle class covers up this truth: what Marx called, "the innermost secret" and the "hidden foundation" of the entire society in the "direct relation between the owners of the conditions of production and the direct producers" (*Capital* III, 927).

Human labor is a commodity which has the peculiar property that its use is a source of new value (Marx, *Capital* I, 270-280). The worker not only produces the equivalent of her own wages but also a "surplus labor" for which she is not paid. "Surplus value"—not trade nor technology nor knowledge—is what produces profit. The lower the cost of labor, the higher the profit. This is why capitalists move all over the world to find the cheapest labor power possible. Globalization is a corporate theory that conceals the mechanism of profit. If technology or knowledge were, as many believe, the source of profit, there would be no need for Nike to go to Pakistan or for IBM to make its computers in Thailand.

The class question is the question of what is the relation to labor power. Those who have to sell their labor power to earn a living—the producers of profit—are part of one class. Those who purchase human labor and take the profit away from labor are part of another. There is no third class—there is no middle class. The middle class has no material base: it is a makeshift class that receives handouts from capitalists in the form of a salary that is actually a fraction of the surplus labor. The middle class, in short, is given a little more of the share of wealth produced by labor in the form of a salary that provides for greater consumption and more cultural status, thus enabling it to separate itself from the "crude" working class and align itself politically and culturally with the ruling class.

The middle class is a fraction of the working class—one that is culturally segregated from the body of workers in order to provide a social buffer zone against class antagonisms. Members of the middle class, however, are on shaky ground since the cultural features that distinguish them from the other workers are too fragile to provide a stable place. Like the high-tech workers who have lost their high incomes and now their homes, the middle class is always only one paycheck away from collapsing back into the underclass. Without the middle class, the rigid clarity of the social division of owners and workers becomes clear. Then capitalism will be seen for what it actually is: a social regime in which the relatively few who own capital exploit the labor of the many. The middle class blurs the lines of this brutal division of people.

Absorbing the extremes into a moderating middle is done mostly through the proliferation of pseudo-choices that make no real difference but give the chooser a unique identity that separates her from others in her class position. Driving a Volvo instead of a Chevy truck gives the two drivers a cultural image that masks the fact that they are both wage-earners.

What people need is not more cultural identities but equal economic access. As long as people believe in the myth of the middle class, they continue to think that they can work hard and get ahead in life. The majority cannot, and the few who do, do it by pushing others behind. Capitalism is a zero-sum game. Not everyone can be a winner; there have to be losers. The middle class uses cultural games of consumption and pride to blur the harsh realities of losing. The historical role of the middle class now is to recognize that it is not a distinct social class from the workers and to see how it lives on the handouts from the capitalists—handouts made from the exploitation of workers.

The middle class needs to abandon its cultural identity games and stand in solidarity with the workers to make history by making society free from class inequalities—free from classes of any kind. The middle class is invented for one purpose only: to "increase the social security and power of the upper ten thousand" (Marx, *Theories of Surplus-Value* II, 573).

4

Abu Ghraib and Class Erotics

I

The romance novel *The Ruby* is ostensibly a tale of love, intimacy, and caring. However, the author, Ann Maxwell, directly addresses its heroine and its implied reader in a dramatic scene, instructing them "to stop thinking like a good little civilian.... The law is for little old ladies who worry about burglars or for salary slaves whose flashy cars get stolen. You're in a different world now, a world where it's power against power, and law has got sweet fuck all to do with it" (125).

Through the erotic vocabularies of intimacy, caring, love, and desire, women's romances make the class aggression, carnage, and atrocities of capitalism seem normal and even dangerously desirable. They naturalize the class violence of global capital as acts of duty, compassion, and, above all, love. Abu Ghraib is an extension of the distorted fantasies in romances and an effect of capital's aggression against "the other" concealed by these fantasies. Neither accidental nor an exception, the tortures and atrocities are part of the structures of imperialism and militarism that are integral to capitalism in its appropriation of the labor and resources of others.

The controversies over Abu Ghraib have focused mostly on whether these were the acts of rogue soldiers or part of an established policy originating with Rumsfeld, Cheney, and others. Neither theory can explain the logic of torture at Abu Ghraib and elsewhere and why it continues. Even the congressional ban on torture, as the *New York Times* notes, actually provides legal protection for continuing torture (Dec. 16, 2005), and may be bypassed altogether by the President as indicated in his "signing statement" when he signed the bill into law (*The Boston Globe*, Jan. 4, 2006). The violence, repression, and sexual displacement at Abu Ghraib are not haphazard but are symptoms, we argue, of the class structure manifested in the culture of capitalism.

Class divisions of labor and property are global: imperialism and its military dynamics, as Lenin argued, are "the highest state of capitalism" because they are essential to maintaining profit and the exploitation of labor (*Imperialism, the Highest Stage of Capitalism*). Capitalism legalizes systemic class violence as necessary to keep "law and order" and protect the "American way of life," but it is merely a code for protecting private property. The torture and brutalities at Abu Ghraib are thus repetitions and not exceptions in the class relations under capitalism.

Class violence is largely justified through the cultural products, such as women's romances, normalizing it and making it part of the affective structures of the every day. Through fantasies of love, these romances produce a form of cultural common sense that reconciles readers to the anxieties, isolation, fragmentation, and estrangement produced by the violence of daily exploitation. Women's romances, to put it differently, are cultural crisis managers for capital.

Approving of this role, romance writer Diana Palmer argues that romances are healthy "daydreams" that "enable people to step back from problems that threaten to be overwhelming.... I produce fantasy," she says, "for people who need a one-hour escape from reality" ("Let Me Tell You about My Readers" 157). My readers, she says,

> represent the hard-working labor force. They are women who spend eight grueling hours a day in a garment factory, in front of a classroom, or behind a desk. Most of them are married and have children. Some are divorced or widowed. These hard-working women leave their jobs at the end of the day and pick up their children at day-care centers. They go home to a house that needs cleaning, to dishes that need washing, to meals that have to be prepared.... Romance novels allow these women...to live in luxury and even, sometimes, in decadence. The novels allow them to escape the normal cares and woes of life by returning in dreams to a time less filled with responsibilities.... (155-56)

Women's romances hold a contradictory place in culture. Represented as trivial literature, they are largely invisible to critical attention. However, they are embraced in the common sense as spaces of caring, intimacy, and erotic pleasures, and interpreted by their defenders as texts of transgression and vehicles of guilty pleasure—part of a "resistance literature" of women.

We read them otherwise. At the same time, we recognize that they fulfill a genuine affective need. Marx criticizes religion as an "inverted world consciousness" ("Contribution to the Critique of Hegel's Philosophy of Law: Introduction," *Collected Works* III, 175). While it is, he says, "an *expression* of real suffering," it only offers an "*illusory* happiness." Thus, he argues, "The call to abandon their illusions about their condition is a *call to abandon a condition which requires illusions*" (175-76). Women's romances are both articulations of the cultural imaginary of capital that normalizes the "condition which requires illusions" and a complex illusory expression of women's genuine need to overcome the alienation, self-estrangement, and hardship capital produces. The materialist critique of women's romances is a critique of this imaginary as part of the struggle to change the conditions requiring these illusions.

II

"Love" is fundamentally a social relation among people. But under capitalism, the ideology fetishizing the commodity-market changes this social relation among people into a "fantastic relation between things" (Marx, *Capital* I, 165). Women's romances are both commodities for consumption and one of the most influential cultural products of capital; according to statistics of the Romance Writers of America for 2005, there are about 64.6 million romance readers in the U.S. ("Romance Writers of America's 2005 Market Research Study").

Romances show intimately how narratives of love under capitalism are actually narratives of property and its protection by violence—whether in the name of the law or renegade justice. The erotics of property is perhaps most explicit in Elizabeth Lowell's many novels (also published under the name Ann Maxwell) in which the struggle for ownership of the prized possession fuses the sensuous desires of body and precious objects (gold, diamonds, rubies, pearls, etc.) with global economics: for example, the crisis of the free market in China (*Tell Me No Lies*, 1986, reprint 1992, 1996, 2001, 2006; *Jade Island*, 1998, 1999) and the new Russia (*Amber Beach*, 1997, 1998), as well as the international diamond trade (*Death Is Forever*, 2004; reprint of her Ann Maxwell work, *The Diamond Tiger*, 1992, 1999).

Women's romances produce a cultural unconscious that transcodes the violence involved in the accumulation and protection of capital *into acts of love and aggressive caring* necessary for the security of the self, safety of the family, love of country, and guarding civilization. In one of Silhouette's new "Bombshell" romances, for instance, a secret "black ops" woman's unit is "elated" at "their night's work on the oil field [killing terrorists]...bodies lay everywhere...the oilfield and its income restored" to allied control. "Sure, she was motivated by larger ideals...but at the end of the day, it all came down to protecting the people she knew and loved" (Dees, *Medusa Project*, 282-83). By inverting the everyday class-violence of capital into the compassionate acts of dedicated heroes, who protect their loved ones by wreaking violence and inflicting retributive justice on the enemies of freedom and property, romances expand the cultural tolerance for violence and aggression.

Culture, as we argue throughout this book, is an extension of material social relations. In saying this, we are obviously opposing mainstream cultural views that insist that "culture" is an autonomous realm of post-materiality, values, and spirituality—what Herbert Marcuse calls "affirmative culture." From this dominant point of view, women's romances are seen as self-fashioning acts of desire that produce their own history rather than being affected by history. Similarly, the events at Abu Ghraib are also seen as trajectories of (sadistic) desire and acts of (perverse) pleasure that express *individual* affects and not the historical relations of injustice between capital and labor. The two—capital and labor—are viewed as "different" and singular events that have nothing to do with each other. For affirmative culture, reading the two together, in terms of the impact one has on the other, is seen as a reductive interpretation. However, in materialist cultural critique, as in science, it is precisely *in the reductive* that the underlying abstract structures of practices and phenomena are stripped away from the cultural discourses that obscure them and are shown in *their rigid clarity* (Steven Weinberg, "Two Cheers for Reductionism").

III

Women's romances are vital acts for affirmative culture: they dissolve the material injustices of empire in the discursive spiritualization called love. But how do they do so? How do they turn the war on terrorism, the brutality of Abu Ghraib, and the violations of Guantanamo into the intimate pleasures of protection? One of the main functions of the capitalist class logic is to isolate each part of our daily lives and, for example, put a cultural gap between women's romances and Abu Ghraib. Consequently we do not realize how the pleasure we take in reading romances prepares us to be shocked by the atrocities at Abu Ghraib (and therefore assert our identity as a moral person), at the same time teaching us to concede that torturing the other is necessary for the safety and well-being of our loved ones and ourselves. This class logic generates a fantasy of retribution and conceals the reality that "torture," as nearly every expert declares, "doesn't work," and may, in fact, put us in more peril.

This split cultural consciousness—that both relates and obscures the relation between women's romances and the atrocities in Abu Ghraib—is produced by the capitalist rule of efficiency, articulated in the code of *whatever it takes to get the job done*. This code gives violence an aura of idealism and sacrifice by representing its aggressions as a principle of protection, giving it the urgency of maintaining law and order for the good of the community. The actual goal is, of course, the protection of the property of the privileged few.

"Whatever it takes" is the stock-in-trade of espionage tales, military novels, and crime thrillers and the backbone of masculine culture. To say that this code is constitutive of the underlying structure of narratives in women's romances may seem contradictory, since they are commonly seen as the very opposite of the administrative reason of efficiency and pragmatic violence of "whatever it takes." But the nurturing pleasures in romances are simply the class doubles of capitalist violence. It is through these pleasures that capital reduces the social tensions produced by its actual exploitative practices and situates people in a zone of the emotions, affects, and desires.

Romances are imaginary scripts for the necessity of violence. It is not surprising, therefore, that nearly all the elements of the current wars in Iraq and Afghanistan—torture, eroticized violence, deploying mercenaries (privatization of the military), disregard for basic human rights, transgressions of recognized ethics in humane conduct, humiliation of the enemy—are part of the narratives of various romances. Two examples, a dozen years apart, demonstrate how widespread this logic is in romances. In her *Dancing on the Wind* (1994), a Regency era romance, Mary Jo Putney writes:

'Horrified,' Kit said, 'You mean torture?' Lucien looked at her. 'If that's what it takes to find your sister'.... She had always thought of herself as a civilized woman, but apparently she was not, for she found herself seriously considering Lucien's suggestion. (307)

Such validation of torture is further actualized and eroticized in Sherilyn Kenyon's novella, "'Captivated' by You" (*Born to Be BAD*, 2005), part of her series featuring a "shadow antiterrorism agency" known as "BAD"—the "Bureau of American Defense" (243)—and "made up" of a "motley, often illegal bunch" (250). The story focuses on using sexual "bondage and dominance" to capture and interrogate a terrorist but not before spending most of the narrative in erotic, sadomasochistic games between the hero and heroine operatives in their sexual "'training' sessions" (253, 349). The actual torture and interrogation of the terrorist is represented in the form of ironic sexual games as the male agent poses as a transvestite dominatrix, "Latex Bettie," and gets the terrorist "along with a full confession" by "wield[ing] a mean whip. He had Bender spilling more guts than a kosher butcher" (360). Torture is not only eroticized here, it is also made playful and ironic—so much so that the brutality of "a mean whip" is easily overlooked.

Violence in many romances is often inordinate and excessive. In Putney's *Dancing on the Wind*, for example, the violent killing in the novel gets so out of hand that the hero feels the need to justify the carnage by saying "what happened tonight was justice not slaughter."

But when is killing "justice not slaughter"? Romances direct readers to produce the preferred responses through several strategies. The first authorizes preemptive and retributive violence in the name of protecting "one's own"—one's family, property, or nation—against any perceived threats. In *The Ruby* (1995), Ann Maxwell's hero says, "taking care of her meant being more ruthless and murderous than the people who were stalking her" (340). Masculinity is fundamentally tied to possession and protection—a real man protects his own and ruthlessly does "whatever it takes" to do so. But the ideology of protection and retribution is not enough to distinguish "justice" from "slaughter." As one Navy SEAL worries in Suzanne Brockmann's *Flashpoint*: "'it still felt like slaughter'...the truth was, Jimmy had seen too much death, too much bad for the alleged sake of good" (309).

Why are these narratives written, and why are they written the way they are? The philosophical incoherence in women's romances—professing adherence to civilized codes but actually ignoring them—is part of the structure of all ideological practices. In *All the Queen's Men* (1999), Linda Howard's hero, "the CIA's legendary Black Ops specialist," fighting for democracy and free civilized society, openly declares that he is not bound by civilized conventions: "I'll do whatever's necessary.... I don't put limitations on what I'm willing to do to get a job done" (274). In *Flashpoint* (2004), Suzanne Brockmann's hero, another soldier of civilization, goes so far as to promise to carry out a revenge beheading in order to free his lover. Catherine Coulter's series of "FBI thriller" romances invariably end with "slaughter," not with the civilized justice of due process. In her *The Target* (1998, reprint 1999), for example, the villain is assassinated, after he is in legal custody, by the heroine's crime-boss father, whom the heroine absolves because "You tried to protect family" (377).

In the name of protection, then, romance novels disregard the rules of the civilized world coded into laws and revert back to the old logic of retribution. This is the same reversion that underwrites the logic of Alberto Gonzales's 2002 "Memorandum for the President." Gonzales declares the "Geneva Convention on Prisoners of War," whose violation the Red Cross says is "tantamount to torture," to be "obsolete" and "quaint." He treats such laws as bureaucratic impediments to real justice—that is, to retribution (January 25, 2002, reprinted in *The Torture Papers,* ed. Karen J. Greenberg and Joshua L. Dratel, 118-121).

Romances develop a pedagogy of violence that teaches readers lessons they take into daily life where they make judgments about war and peace, terrorism, democracy and the uses of force. It normalizes violence as the only way to "get things done" for the protection of self and civilization. Therefore, when the Chairman of Delta Airlines, says that he would do "whatever it takes to cut costs by one million" (*BBC World News,* May 19, 2005), everyone seems to think that he is, in fact, doing the right thing.

"Whatever it takes" is a class code for deploying violence in the interest of the ruling elite, but it has acquired a culturally reassuring aspect through popular culture. "Whatever it takes," for the Delta chairman, is unlikely to mean cutting the multimillion-dollar salaries and bonuses of the top executives, but it definitely will mean downsizing and firing employees; cutting salaries and benefits and pensions. In terms of the war on terrorism, "whatever it takes" commonly rules out negotiation, and it certainly excludes any redistribution of wealth or significant anti-poverty programs, no matter how many have argued that terrorism has its roots in global inequalities.

To contain the ethical dilemmas and (ideo)logical inconsistencies in these romances, the pedagogy of violence invokes another strategy of legitimation. It tries to justify violence against the "other" by always representing the enemy as excessively brutal, morally and ethically depraved, and frequently also sexually perverted. In contrast, the hero is always represented as fundamentally good and "capable of surprising tenderness" and caring (Maxwell, *The Ruby* 177). In her essay, "Love Conquers All," romance writer Elizabeth Lowell argues that the "classic romance warrior-heroes...do not enjoy destruction. Ultimately they use their strength, their intelligence, and their discipline to defend rather than exploit those who are weaker than they" (92). No matter how brutal are the hero's own actions, they are always redeemed by what is represented as his caring, tender ruthlessness in the act of protection, as opposed to the enemy's extreme depravity. To maintain this binary, romance novels represent the "enemy" as engaging in almost every imaginable perversion and cruelty from the trafficking of children, pederasty, sadomasochism, gang-rape, and mutilation to mass murder, serial killings, hijackings, and beheadings. In Brockmann's *Flashpoint,* for example, the warlord, terrorists, and gun dealers in Brockmann's imaginary "Kazbekistan" (a generic "hotbed of terrorist activity") are represented as sexually "debasing" and physically brutalizing one of the (American) heroines, including "carving their initials into her skin" (240-41).

Women's romances eroticize and normalize this inverted fantasy—rampant in popular culture and thus part of the common sense of the troops—in which the enemy is the embodiment of perversity and cruelty, and therefore, the soldier-hero has every right to torture him in order to get the job done, which is caring for America and Americans. Abu Ghraib is an extension of, not an exception to, the distorted fantasies in romances and an effect of the class violence concealed by these fantasies.

Many romance readers commonly "forget" these graphic scenes of violence. This is because popular culture encourages a process of *selective inattention* to what is read. In reading selectively, readers skip pages or avert their eyes from unpleasant scenes out of boredom or to avoid distress, especially when the violence becomes excessive. But before turning their attention away, they cannot help but notice what it is that they do not want to see. While readers differ over what they attend to and when they turn away (even differing from themselves in what they see and what they skip in each reading), they are all taught the same cultural lesson by popular culture: to look away, to disregard what is beyond the boundaries of tolerance, and to be actively inattentive to brutality

Violence in women's romances is eroticized and made acceptable as part of an ethics of intimacy. Representations of cruelty, assault, and carnage all occur in close proximity to representations of sensuousness and sexuality. In Linda Howard's *Mr. Perfect*, the heroine is nearly strangled to death. But in the narrative the therapy for her damaged throat is said to be hot sex. Howard writes, "she might wake up in terror, but she went back to sleep with every muscle limp from an overdose of pleasure" (*Mr. Perfect* 397). The link between violence and sexual pleasure is even greater when we recognize how much of the psychic tension, thrills, and stimulation of the senses in popular narratives are generated by violence. Violence is the main source of excitation, tension, emotional intensification, and sensual stimulation in popular culture. Reader's imaginations are saturated and penetrated by violence—which is all the more impactful since we engage it in those moments of relaxation and escape when we suspend our critical thinking.

Popular culture is a *narcosis of violence*—simultaneously eroticizing it and desensitizing the reader to aggression. The pleasures of women's romances are not innocent "guilty pleasures" that simply assert the power of women. Popular pleasures fulfill a necessary social function: they teach how to make sense of and actively disregard the violence of daily life, including how to misrecognize the reality of torture.

IV

Capitalism has always represented itself as a superior form of social life. It claims that, unlike socialism with its planned economy, the economics of the free market and democracy offer people an equal chance in their economic life; equality before the law, and freedom of expression in their social life. In other words, capitalism's legitimacy depends on its promise of freedom and equality of all people both economically and politically. However, capitalism cannot remain capitalist and at the same time maintain its promises of equality and freedom for all because the survival of capitalism depends on constantly increasing its profits, and increasing profits is impossible without the exploitation of some people by others. Capitalism, in short, is based on class divisions that it maintains, in large part, through violence. Popular cultural forms like romances normalize violence, making it the idiom of daily life and numbing people to its destructive consequences.

In Abu Ghraib the enemy is portrayed as an unyielding and depraved person, just as villains are in romances. He is seen as holding the secret that will save the lives of loved ones. His silence therefore has to be broken by whatever means necessary—"by whatever it takes." Romances prepare the reader to accept as necessary the strategies of violence deployed in implementing "whatever it takes" against the other, who only has be *named* as a threat.

The International Red Cross reports that "70-90 per cent of the persons deprived of their liberty in Iraq had been arrested by mistake" as reporter Mark Danner points out. Danner comments on the Abu Ghraib photos and asks us to

> consider the naked body wearing only the black hood, hands clasped above his head: Pfc Lynndie England, grinning back at the camera, pointing to his genitals with her right hand, flashing a thumbs up with her left. This body belongs to Hayder Sabbar Abd, a thirty-four-year old Shiite from Nasiriya.... Mr. Abd says, 'he was never interrogated, and never charged with a crime.' 'The truth is,' he told...*The New York Times,* 'we were not terrorists. We were not insurgents. We were just ordinary people.' (*Torture and Truth* 3)

Women's romances provide the cultural logic for the scenarios that are acted out at Abu Ghraib and in the photos we have all seen. Women's romances and the atrocities at Abu Ghraib may seem to be part of two different worlds—one the world of textuality, of love and intimacy, the other the real world of war and aggression—but they are part of the same fundamental class logic in which culture legitimates the violence needed for exploitation.

Culture is not the articulation of an autonomous imagination. It is an extension of labor relations, and moralizing about popular culture or the crimes at Abu Ghraib will not change culture. In the struggle for social change, the task of cultural critique is to contribute to developing a consciousness of totality that can grasp the class relations in their specificity. Only changing the relations of labor and capital will change reality.

5
Class and 9/11

One of the signs of the collapse of contemporary U.S. education is the interpretation the majority of Americans make of the "event" that is now marked by the cultural sign of "9/11." For many, the "event" is proof that "they hate us." The only way, in other words, most Americans brought up in the U.S. educational system can make sense of the "event" is affective. Any attempt to introduce even a mildly analytical "why" ("Why do you think 'they' hate Americans?") is seen as the height of emotional crudeness and intellectual vulgarity if not outright anti-Americanism.

Having reduced the "event" to a trauma, the reaction to the trauma has been also traumatic. In the days following the "event," waves of violence by ordinary people, the FBI, the police, the INS, the local militia, and neighborhood vigilantes were unleashed towards the "other" and those who looked the "same" as the "other." With a sentimental and equally violent patriotism, the U.S. flag has been used to more decisively sort the world out into lovers and haters of "our way of life." U.S. pedagogy has so paralyzed people's critique-al consciousness, most are now helpless witnesses to the emergence of a national security state ("The Patriot Act") and the preemptive class aggressions of the empire.

The teach-ins and forums which were held about the "event" were only slightly more layered expressions of the affective. Most were sessions in talking trauma which, following the trauma theory popular in many cultural circles, dissolved history into the unrepresentable affect (Felman, *The Juridical Unconscious: Trials and Traumas in the Twentieth Century*; Lyotard, *The Differend*; LaCapra, *Writing History, Writing Trauma*; Caruth, ed., *Trauma: Explorations in Memory*). The teach-ins became occasions for displacing an analytical grasp of history by an ecumenical sentimentality for the suffering.

Michael Berube's essay, "Ignorance Is a Luxury We Cannot Afford" (published in *The Chronicle of Higher Education* a few weeks after "9/11"), is exemplary of the lessons in empathy to avoid the analytical. It is rhetorically a masterful lesson in the erasure of all traces of thinking about the "event" in part because it preemptively announces itself as an intervention in ignorance. After describing how he had shelved "the course assignments" in his classes to devote "most of the rest of the week...to a discussion of [students'] reactions to the attack," he narrates a range of readings of the "event" and concludes that the "most troubling" analyses of the "event" were from the political left, some of which were coming uncomfortably close to justifying the indiscriminate slaughter of innocents. Many students immediately connected the attack to various American operations in the Middle East, and I wanted them to be very careful about how they made those connections. Of course, I said, of course the attacks must be placed in the broader context of the history of U.S. foreign policy in Asia and the Middle East. But any analysis that did not start from a position of solidarity with, and compassion for, the victims, their families, and the extraordinary rescue workers in New York and Washington was an analysis not worth time and attention. (B-5)

What Berube's teaching seeks is moral clarity, which has become the conservative touchstone in reading the "event" (Bennett, *Why We Fight: Moral Clarity and the War on Terrorism*), and not analytical critique. Berube quickly moves to block by "clarification" any attempt at such a critique by saturating the session with details (what he calls "background information"): "Very well, some students replied, but what does it mean to 'place the attacks in the broader context of U.S. foreign policy'? Here, not surprisingly, what my students wanted and needed most was basic background information" (B-5).

What follows, in the name of curing ignorance, are stories about U.S. foreign policy but no conceptual analysis:

Was it true, they asked, that the CIA once financed and trained bin Laden? Well, yes, I said, but at the time, in the 1980s, we financed just about anyone who showed up and offered to drive the Soviets out of Afghanistan. No, we didn't have the same kind of relationship to bin Laden that we had to Noriega or Pinochet or the Shah or Somoza or any of the other dictators we'd propped up in the course of waging the cold war. (B-5)

The story in contemporary pedagogy (which has opportunistically concluded, for the most part, that knowledge is a story and all concepts are tropes) performs an essential ideological task. It offers a non-explanatory explanation and thus constructs an "enlightened false consciousness" in the classroom (to use the term by Sloterdijk in his *Critique of Cynical Reason* 5-6). Teaching through stories produces knowingness without knowing and consequently cultivates a savvy cynicism about ideas, analysis, and explanation. It rejects causal explanations (in fact it dismisses the very idea of "cause-effect") and puts in its place vaguely plotted details that hint at moving but have no analytical yield: the pleasures of stories replace the critique.

This is important because no account of the "event" can forget the CIA. However, most accounts of the "event" evoke the CIA in order to obscure its role by telling CIA stories of high intrigue in exotic lands and thus divert attention from the other CIA whose role is crucial in understanding the "event." The CIA that is openly discussed and critiqued to obtain radical credentials for the storyteller is, as Berube's tale demonstrates, a political agency of the U.S. Government. The other CIA—the one that is covered up by these narrative details—is only officially a political agency of the State. In practice, it is the gendarme of American capitalism: it is an economic rather than a political outfit.

Berube's lesson obscures this CIA which is an extension of U.S. corporations and whose task is to wage a clandestine class war against the working people of the world in order to keep the world safe for U.S. investments. In his teaching of the "event," there is no hint that the CIA's actions might be symptoms of the systematic aggression of market forces against the workers and that the "event" might be an outcome of global capitalism. The CIA becomes a story-machine producing absorbing narratives that circle around personalities, places, and actions but lead nowhere. They build an illusion of knowing. Analysis of the economic role of the CIA (which produces material knowledge of global relations) is obstructed by details that have no analytical effect. Why, for instance, did the CIA fight to drive the Soviets out of Afghanistan? Berube's "waging the cold war" seems to imply that the dynamics of the conflict is "ideology." The U.S. and the Soviets simply had two different "political" systems and cultures. Thus, in Berube's version of history, it is natural that the CIA wanted to drive the Soviets out of Afghanistan and increase the U.S.'s sphere of political and cultural "power" in the region. The conflict between the Soviet Union and the United States, in other words, is a clash of ideas.

Underling his pedagogy, in other words, is a view of history as an expansionism of "power" (as in Hardt and Negri's *Empire*) and as conflicts of "ideologies" (as Fukuyama argues in his *The End of History and the Last Man*). It is based on the notion that discourse and ideas shape the world since, ultimately, history itself is the discursive journey of the "Soul" toward a cultural and spiritual resolution of material contradictions. This theory mystifies history by replacing class (labor) with ideas and discourse, and consequently produces world history as a "clash of civilizations" (Huntington, *The Clash of Civilizations and the Remaking of the World Order*) and rewrites the world in the interests of Euroamerican capitalism. According to the "clash" theory (which is the most popular interpretive axis of "9/11"), people do what they do because of their "culture" and not because they exploit the labor of others (so they can live in comfort), or because their labor is exploited by others (and therefore they live in abject poverty). "9/11," in other words, is seen as an instance of the clash of civilizations: culture (that is, values, language, religion, the affective, etc.) did it. "They" hate "our" way of life ("Their values clash with Our values"). Since values are viewed as transhistorical, the clash is considered spiritual, not material.

But culture didn't do it. Contrary to contemporary dogma (codified, for example, by Stuart Hall in his "The Centrality of Culture"), culture is not autonomous; it is the bearer of economic interests. Cultural values are inversive: they are a spiritualization of material interests. Culture cannot solve the contradictions that develop at the point of production; it merely suspends them. Material contradictions can only be solved materially, namely through class struggles that would end the global regime of wage labor. "9/11" is an unfolding of material contradictions—not a clash of civilizations. If teaching the "event" does not at least raise the possibility of a class understanding of it, then teaching is not pedagogy—it is ideology.

To be more precise: the CIA fought the Soviets (and then the Taliban) because U.S. capitalism needs to turn Afghanistan into a "new silk road." The conquest of Afghanistan, in other words, was planned long before the "event," and its goal was neither liberation of the Afghan people nor what the CIA calls "democratization." It was simply aimed at turning the country into a huge pipeline station. In his testimony before the "House Committee on International Relations Subcommittee on Asia and the Pacific" on February 12, 1998 (three years before "9/11"), John J. Maresca, the vice-president for international relations of Unocal Corporation, stated that

> The Caspian region contains tremendous untapped hydrocarbon reserves, much of them located in the Caspian Sea basin itself. Proven natural gas reserves within Azerbaijan, Uzbekistan, Turkmenistan and Kazakhstan equal more than 236 trillion cubic feet. The region's total oil reserves may reach more than 60 billion barrels of oil—enough to service Europe's oil needs for 11 years. Some estimates are as high as 200 billion barrels. In 1995, the region was producing only 870,000 barrels per day (44 million tons per year [Mt/y]). ("DOCUMENT: A New Silk Road: Proposed Petroleum Pipeline in Afghanistan" 29)

The problem for U.S. capital has been how to get the energy to the market. The safest and most profitable way to get the energy to the West, Maresca testified, was to build "a commercial corridor, a 'new' Silk Road" through Afghanistan (35). "Developing cost-effective, profitable and efficient export routes for Central Asia," according to Maresca, is a "significant and intertwined" convergence for "U.S. commercial interests and U.S. foreign policy" (35). Afghanistan had to be liberated because, as Maresca explained to Congress, oil and gas consortiums "cannot begin construction until an internationally recognized Afghanistan government is in place" (34-35). In short, Afghanistan was liberated to "build the 'new' Silk Road" and not because of a "clash of civilizations."

Teaching that brings up the "event" in the classroom has a pedagogical responsibility to at least raise these issues. To limit "knowledge" to "background information" and then substitute CIA stories for conceptual analysis of material causes is not curing ignorance but legitimating it. Attributing the causes of the "event" to culture obscures the world's class relations and conceals the fact that their "hatred" is not the effect of an immanent evil in their religion or language or values but the result of the brutal exploitation of capital that has torn apart "their" way of life to build new silk roads all over their world. The silk road always and ultimately leads to "events." To blame other cultures, as Berube does when he refers to "searing images of cheering Palestinian children," is to let capitalism off the hook. It is a practice that produces a false consciousness in students so that they make sense of the material world through spiritualistic values that marginalize the actual struggles over the surplus labor of the "other"—it is the others' surplus that makes their own lives comfortable. This is not curing ignorance; it is the corporate pedagogy of a flag-waving nationalism.

The pedagogy of affect piles up details and warns students against attempting to relate them structurally because any structural analysis will be a causal explanation, and all causal explanations, students are told, are reductive. Teaching thus becomes a pursuit of floating details—a version of games in popular culture. Students "seem" to know but have no knowledge. This is exactly the kind of education capital requires for its new workforce: workers who are educated but nonthinking; skilled at detailed jobs but unable to grasp the totality of the system—energetic localists, ignorant globalists.

This pedagogy provides instruction not in knowledge but in savviness—a knowing that knows what it knows is an illusion but is undeluded about that illusion; it integrates the illusion, thereby making itself immune to critique. Savviness is "enlightened false consciousness": a consciousness that knows it is false, but its "falseness is already reflexively buffered" (Sloterdijk, *Critique of Cynical Reason* 5). The effect of this reflexive falseness is that "one knows the falsehood very well, one is well aware of the particular interest hidden behind an ideological universality, but one still does not renounce it" (Zizek, *The Sublime Object of Ideology* 29).

What a pedagogy of savviness teaches is knowing with a "wink." In fact, the wink places such knowledge on the borderlines of what Sloterdijk calls "kynicism" (217-218)—absorbing the falseness through an ironic, tongue-in-cheek pedagogy that completely abolishes the conceptual for the pleasures of the story. The story is represented as liberating the concrete of daily life from the conceptual totalitarianism of abstractions. (We are using "totalitarian" and "totalitarianism" here in their sanctioned "liberal" senses because we do not have the space for a critique of liberal vocabularies and their concealed economic assumptions). Totalitarian and its derivations, however, have always been used by liberals to guarantee "liberal-democratic hegemony, dismissing the Leftist critique of liberal democracy as the obverse, the 'twin' of the Rightist Fascist dictatorship" (Zizek, *Did Somebody Say Totalitarianism?* 3). Story-pedagogy consequently becomes lessons in politics as desire, affect, and unsurpassable experience, as in the writings of Marjorie Garber (*Symptoms of Culture*), Nestor Garcia Canclini (*Consumers and Citizens*), and Eve Kosofsky Sedgwick (*Touching Feeling: Affect, Pedagogy, Performativity*).

These pedagogues theorize desire, the affective, trauma, feelings, and experience—which are all effects of class relations—as if they were spontaneous reality. They deploy the affective in teaching in order to outlaw lessons in the conceptual analysis of social totality, which is aimed at producing class consciousness in the student (the future worker). The classroom is constituted as the scene of desire where the student is interpellated as the subject of his affects, and these affects, in their assumed inimitability, ascribe to him an imaginary, matchless individuality. The un-said exceptionality of affect in the classroom of desire becomes an ideological alibi for the negation of collectivity grounded in objective class interests. The student is taught to "wage a war on totality" by activating "the differences," and in "the honor of the name," identify with himself as an unsurpassable singularity that exceeds all representations (Lyotard, *The Postmodern Condition* 82). In contrast, the pedagogy of totality is the negation of the negation.

Berube's stories of a political CIA are narratives of capitalist desire aimed at fragmenting the internationalism of class connectedness among working people by dehistoricizing and localizing affects (suffering of the same and cheering of the other). However, the "event" has a history and, as an objective materiality, cannot be understood without placing it in the world-historical class struggles. But in the classroom of "enlightened false consciousness" constituted by desire, class has no place. Any explanation of the "event" as a moment in the unfolding of the international class struggles—as a moment in which "two great classes" (the rich and the poor) are finally "directly facing each other" (Marx and Engels, *Manifesto of the Communist Party* 41)—is suspended in silence.

To put class back into teaching of the "event" is to move beyond dissipating history through trauma and anecdotes of affect. It puts an end to teaching saviness, which masquerades as a cure for ignorance. The pedagogy of totality teaches the abstract relations that structure concrete material reality and is not distracted by the details of appearances because "abstractions reflect nature more deeply, truly and *completely*" (Lenin, "Conspectus of Hegel's Book *The Science of Logic*" 171) and bring the student closer to grasping social totality: "the relations of production in their totality" (Marx, *Wage-Labour and Capital* 29). Social totality is thus constituted by class antagonism, and therefore its unity is a "unity of opposites" (Lenin, "On the Question of Dialectics" 359-360). The hostility to conceptual analysis and particularly to class critique in contemporary pedagogy goes well beyond the teach-ins on the "event." It is a fundamental dogma of "radical" bourgeois pedagogy, which commonly wipes out class from teaching on the grounds that class is part of a totalizing politics. To be so totally opposed to totalizing is, of course, itself a totalization. But totalizing in opposing totalization does not seem to bother anti-totalizing pedagogues because the issue, ultimately, is really not epistemological (totalizing) but economic (class). In contemporary pedagogy, totalizing is an epistemological cover for the class cleansing of pedagogy.

The pedagogy of affect is always and ultimately a ruse for pragmatism, which is, as the writings of Richard Rorty demonstrate (*Achieving Our Country*), an apologetics for what actually "is"—the dominant system of wage labor. Pragmatism deploys the affective to naturalize the existing social relations of property by teaching affect as the only site in which the "hopes and aspirations" of the subject of learning can be fulfilled: a site in which class is "dead" and desire is sovereign (see for example, Brooks, "The Triumph of Hope over Self-Interest"; Pakulski and Waters, *The Death of Class*; and Gallop, "The Teacher's Breasts"). Sovereignty, however, is not the sovereignty of the individual of affect but of consumption, which is eroticized to interpellate her as the individual of affect. "Ideologically, we see the same contradiction in the fact that the bourgeoisie endowed the individual with an unprecedented importance, but at the same time that same individuality was annihilated by the economic conditions to which it was subjected, by the reification created by commodity production" (Lukacs, *History and Class Consciousness* 62).

6

Eating Class

Diets are class food. The class politics of the Atkins and Ornish diets, from which such other well-known diets as the "Zone," "South Beach," and "Sonoma" diets derive, have proven to be especially divisive. Posing as a neutral agent, the government took it upon itself a few years ago—in an almost Hegelian scenario of the relation between the State and Civil Society—to do an "impartial" study of the two and put an end to the class strife that is acting itself out in the antagonism over food.

The conflict indicates that diet, like everything else in social life and in spite of what people like to believe, is determined not by what people desire but by the limits and conditions imposed on them by the social class in which they live their lives. This is quite an un-American thing to say, but people eat their class and not their food! Food preferences are shaped by what one can afford to choose. Free choice is always determined by what one is not free to do. Pierre Bourdieu's extensive study of class differences in France documents the class differences in taste, showing how "the opposition between the tastes of luxury (or freedom) and the tastes of necessity…are the product of material conditions of existence defined by distance from necessity, by the freedoms or facilities stemming from possession of capital." People, Bourdieu argues, "have a taste for what they are anyway condemned to….Taste is…a forced choice, produced by conditions of existence which rule out all alternatives as mere daydreams and leave no choice but the taste for the necessary" (*Distinction* 177-78).

By class we do not mean "lifestyle"—that is, how people seem to themselves and others—or their manners of consumption, where they shop, what accent they have, where they live, or what kind of car they drive. These are effects of class. These cultural signs are manufactured to signal levels of cultural prestige, or lack of it: a sort of social pecking order. These signs belong to cultural semiotics and not class, which depends on people's position in the social relations of production: the "owning" and not the "pecking" order of society. What divides people into classes and determines what they eat is whether they sell their labor power to earn a living or purchase other people's labor power and make a profit from it by not paying them for the "surplus labor" they extract from them.

The antagonism between the Atkins and Ornish diets and the politics that has divided their followers are class politics appearing as personal preferences and tastes in food, health, and the aesthetics of the body.

The Atkins diet is essentially a proletarian diet: meat, eggs, and other high protein sources along with forbidden "fats," especially butter and cream. This is real food, according to Atkins, not the "invented, fake food," as he calls it, of "our sophisticated, modern lifestyle" (Atkins 21, 27).

Meat is the food of the working people. It is not only socially and culturally associated with the proletariat, but it is also materially a food of necessity for that class which relies on the raw energy of its body for subsistence. In order to withstand the sheer physical demands of their jobs, working people need a substantive food—something that can support their bodies in the daily beating it takes from hard work. Protein promotes muscle building, and moderate to high protein, meat diets (like Atkins) are shown to avoid the muscle loss caused by high-carbohydrate, low-fat diets (Graves 91-92).

In telling the story of his recovery from his automobile accident, Stephen King highlights the class basis of "meat." Referring to his marriage, he writes that he and his wife came from similar working-class backgrounds, "we both ate meat; we were both political Democrats" ("On Impact").

Atkins claims his diet is "a dream diet—luxurious, sane, healthy" (17). What it is, is a worker's diet that is highly satiating without requiring any special work, attention, or calculation—unlike the elaborately complex Ornish diet which is a full-time avocation in itself. All the Atkins's dieter needs to do is avoid nearly all carbohydrates and eat only "pure proteins" and "pure fats," as much as you want, and, Atkins says, experience rapid weight loss without ever feeling hungry. A typical dieter, for example, eats "ham and eggs for breakfast, tuna fish for lunch, and chicken, pork chops, or steak for dinner" (12).

The Atkins diet is proletarian not only in its substance but also in its style and framing assumptions. It is written in a "realistic," straightforward style, free from all indirection. It is highly suspicious of bourgeois indulgences, refinements, cultural elegance, and what Atkins criticizes as the "exotic" (22).

When questioned about some of the inelegant consequences of his diet (such as "bad breath" from ketosis), Atkins laughs at the bourgeois mind-set that puts such refined considerations ahead of the strong, healthy body his implied audience needs to earn a living. This privileging of the interpersonal is an extension of the bourgeois lifestyle—what Atkins likes to call "our sophisticated, modern lifestyle"—that has made "low-fat, high-carbohydrate," diets the dominant "fad" diet according to Atkins. This dominance (like the dominance of the bourgeoisie) is undeserved, he argues, because in spite of such dominance, this diet "hasn't...done a thing to take pounds off" (9). Whereas his diet is, he says, "*the* human diet raised to its healthiest pitch and stripped of the 20th century food inventions" (22)—that is, stripped of all those bourgeois food refinements. It is *not* the idle diet of the idle ruling class.

The strict, low-fat, mostly vegetarian Ornish diet, in contrast, is above all a diet for those with the time and commitment to devote to it because "when you eat, you are feeding more than just your body" (Ornish 69). As one health magazine puts it: "The doctor's 10 percent-fat meal plan may save your life, but who can stick with it?" The Ornish diet is an inclusive "life-choice program." It entails comprehensive food and lifestyle changes that are difficult to maintain without the help of support groups and weeklong retreats. Eating becomes a full-time leisure activity because the dieter requires frequent "grazing," since with the low-fat, high-carbohydrate diet "you get hungry sooner [and] feel full faster" (25). Eating, for Ornish, becomes "a form of meditation," what he calls, "a way of eating with awareness" (73) of self in the world. In other words, eating is a gaze into one's soul: a Zen moment in which a single bite becomes "exquisitely satisfying," but only if "you really pay attention" (71). Every Ornish meal is an extended Proustian moment: a bourgeois ecstasy of the senses.

In his book, *My Life in the Middle Ages*, James Atlas describes how his upper-middle-class parents, with their "fanatical adherence to the nutritional theories of Dr. Dean Ornish," were "obsessively vigilant about their diets, removing the skin from chicken with surgical precision, reducing salt and butter intake, maintaining what my father liked to call a 'a thin edge of hunger'" (5).

In its substance the Ornish diet is elegant, colorful, variegated, and highly pleasurable. It is, a recuperation of what Atkins excludes from eating: the absolute "exotic" (Atkins 22), the romantic space within which the bourgeois lives a fantasy life. The recipes, which are created by some of the top gourmet chefs in the country, from Chez Panisse to Lutece, are an extended romance with food, a sumptuous cornucopia of textures, smells, and tastes to stimulate the senses from "black pepper polenta" (Ornish 277) to a "succulent truffled potato stew" (191).

These variations of texture, taste and color are aimed at making sure that the eater is never bored. Atkins, on the other hand, addresses the class that cannot afford to be bored with food or anything else in life, and is instead contemptuous of boredom as a dietary consideration.

Ornish, who is highly conscious of the desire of his bourgeois audience to pamper itself and enjoy an opulent variety, offers a "spectrum of choices," what he calls an "amazing graze" (25) of constant nibbling, with such focused attention on the refinements of taste, that each bite is "heaven." In sharp difference, Atkins's claims for an amazing no-hunger weight loss (Atkins 62-64) are based on meals of such substance they offer long-lasting satiety. One diet offers assurances of constant sensuous consumption, the other a pledge for the absence of want and hunger.

Under the alienating conditions of wage-labor, Marx writes, "man (the worker) only feels himself freely active in his animal functions—eating, drinking, procreating" (*Economic and Philosophic Manuscripts of 1844*, 275). This is the class contradiction of diets: they restrict one of the few arenas of "freedom" for "estranged labor" under capital. Of course, such "free" activity is not free since all the physical functions from food to sex have become intensively commodified, and the worker increasingly has to exchange wages in order to "freely" fufill her physical functions. But eating is still largely considered to be outside work (i.e., part of leisure); as Marx notes, "the worker only feels himself outside his work and in his work feels outside himself" (274). Eating, thus, is one of the main compensations for the alienating pressures of work and estranged life under capitalism, and highly fatty foods are perhaps the most satiating for most people and thus the most coveted. They signify "richness" in taste and sensation. The Ornish diet is beginning to fall off in popularity not only because the extravagance of time, labor, and resources it requires are not affordable for most people, but also because it is perceived as an extreme deprivation. While some research supports the effectivity of very low-fat diets in lowering heart disease as well as breast and prostrate cancer, such fat-restricted diets—for all their "exotic" variety of foods—have a high dropout rate. They deny the pleasurable "freedom" of "rich" sensuous indulgence. This is another reason why the much more reductive Atkins diet, with its elimination of nearly all fruits, vegetables, and grains, has continued to have many adherents, in spite of the health warnings—it is so fat-laden and functionally satisfying.

In their stark differences the two diets perform what Marx and Engels, in the *Manifesto of the Communist Party*, called the main feature of capitalist society, the simplification of class antagonism: "Society as a whole is more and more splitting up into two great hostile camps, into two great classes directly facing each other" (41). As with social class, the stark antagonism that separates Atkins and Ornish is now mediated by a series of intervening class fractions—the "middle classes"—hybrid diets that have replaced them in popularity. The "Zone Diet" (Sears) and the "South Beach Diet" (Agatston)—and their different variations, such as the "Sonoma Diet" (Guttersen)—are exemplary of this hybridity. They are actually "State" diets which, in their seemingly impartial midway, offer an eclectic combination of the two and silently reiterate the official government recommendations that give them legitimacy and institutional approval. The "Zone," "South Beach," and "Sonoma" are "reasonable" diets. They obscure the rigid class clarity of the Atkins and Ornish diets.

Regardless of their innumerable surface variations, all diets repeat, in their different food registers and combinations, the two fundamental divisions of society into the classes of workers and owners.

In eating food, we eat our class.

7

The Class Politics of "Values" and Stem-Cell Funding

I

The contemporary public debates over controversial issues such as abortion, school vouchers, the war on terrorism, corporate corruption, tax cuts, and the defense budget are usually phrased in the cultural idiom of values, ethics, character, integrity, safety, and the like. The recent debates over embryonic stem-cell research, for example, treat the issue almost exclusively as a matter of values. Those against it argue for the rights of the embryo: "A free and virtuous society," writes Pope John Paul II, "must reject practices that devalue and violate human life at any stage from conception until natural death." Opponents, in other words, use "values" to denounce the use of public funds for stem-cell research.

To the extent that science or even heath care enter this debate, they do so in terms of such cultural frames as bioethics and medical ethics which subordinate the objective and material findings of science to cultural values (Ruse and Pynes, eds., *The Stem Cell Controversy*, and Scott, *Stem Cell Now*). Similarly, those who argue that scientific research on the subject should be pursued ground their arguments in another version of cultural values. Their values are based on life after birth—healthy life free from such illness as Parkinson's disease, Alzheimer's, diabetes, and other afflictions. In other words, as the controversies over stem-cell research show, the cultural in contemporary social debates has become a discursive means for representing the material as spiritual: economic practices are culturalized and their role in shaping actual social life is blurred.

The value of cultural values, as we have discussed before, is that they are strategies of containment in what Herbert Marcuse calls "affirmative culture" (*Negations* 88-133). As instruments of affirmative culture, values lift the "spiritual world" out of "its social context" and thus make culture "a (false) collective noun and attribute (false) universality to it" (95). The "decisive characteristic" of affirmative culture is the assertion of a universally obligatory, eternally better and more valuable world that must be unconditionally affirmed: a world essentially different from the factual world of the daily struggle for existence, yet realizable by every individual for himself 'from within,' without any transformation of the state of fact. (95)

By controlling the emerging scientific discoveries in the name of values, culture "affirms and conceals the new conditions of social life" (96). The culture conflicts over stem-cell research are only ostensibly about life. They are actually class struggles over the material conditions of social living and how these conditions are organized to make access to social resources easy or restricted.

The power of values, whether conceived in high aesthetic terms (for instance, the Kantian "sublime") or in more everyday frames such as family values, derives from their being represented as the zone of affect and the personal and, therefore, of post-reason and post-historical primacies, which are seen as ends in themselves.

Under capitalism values are alienated from social life and have been relegated to autonomous zones of epistemological contemplation and the populist imaginary. This is because values, along with all social conditions of living, are distorted and inverted by a system founded on exchange values. To disalienate values, they need to be transvalued not by means of a Nietzschean meditation (*Beyond Good and Evil*) but through class struggles that will reverse the inverted material conditions of living by ending wage-labor. All values are derived from social labor, and as long as labor power is exchanged for wages, they are alienated from use-value and, therefore, appear to be independent. Contemporary cultural theory, following Baudrillard's notion that the system of value is ultimately produced by exchange value (*For a Critique of the Political Economy of the Sign* 130-142), regards use-value to be an "alibi" of exchange value and thus affirms exchange-value as practical reality. In spite of its formal critiques of commodity exchange, contemporary cultural theory legitimates wage-labor and the system of exchange-value through such evasive moves as retreating into a theory of the "gift" as a solution to contradictions of the system of exchange (Baudrillard 204-212; Derrida, *Given Time: I. Counterfeit Money*), or by epistemological musings on general economy (Bataille, *The Accursed Share*) and declaring use-value to be a metaphysical aftereffect.

In contemporary discourses, in other words, the materiality of values—as grounded in use-value—is obscured by spiritualizing it and idealistically placing it outside the capitalist system of exchange (as "gift" for example). Values are consequently treated as ends in themselves which is a cultural strategy for masking the historical relations of class and power and representing them as universal. Values are never ends in themselves: they are always constituted by their outside and serve the interests of that outside. Behind the spiritualization of values—which inscribe the outside in the inside and thus normalize social contradictions—class interests always "lurk in ambush" (Marx and Engels, *Manifesto of the Communist Party* 58).

II

The translation of stem-cell research into cultural matters is exemplary of the way the turn to culture converts the economic into the spiritual and makes the political economy of the every day, and the social relations that shape it, invisible. The social contestations over stem-cell research, like all social disputes, are not about values but about social labor and the appropriation of its surplus.

Science is itself the product of social labor: its emergence and advances are determined by whether social labor produces enough surplus to make available the time and resources necessary for training, developing skills, scientific inquiries, and experimentations. The "genius" scientist is an effect of this long social and historical preparation. The culture conflicts are over how the surplus of social labor should be spent, and furthermore who should benefit from such expenditure. These seemingly cultural issues are economic and class matters not only in terms of where the State should allocate public funds, but also in terms of who should benefit from the outcome of the scientific work that is funded—in short, who will have the "right" to market and thus profit from the new discoveries?

The values debate focuses on public funding, but public funding is itself the immediate form of surplus labor in conducting stem-cell research. (We are, of course, putting aside here, the fact that the possibility of stem-cell research itself is the result of a long historical preparation that is enabled by social surplus labor.) Those who use the excuse of the usefulness of stem-cell research for curing illnesses argue that public funding (the social surplus) should go to the private biotech and genetic research industries. In other words, they want to socialize the *cost* of new research (funding it through people's taxes) but privatize its *profits*. The new procedures/medicines that will be developed will then be patented by these companies and sold at a high profit back to the people who have provided the funding (through their taxes) for these discoveries.

The opponents of public funding for stem-cell research deploy another version of the universal "value of life" argument. Invoking the value of life (before birth), they seek to block the transfer of public funds to these industries and instead favor the use of public funds to support projects in defense, national security, and intelligence industries, with whom the pro-life movement has close ideological ties. The Bush administration, for instance, from the 2000 presidential campaign up through the president's veto of stem-cell research legislation has ardently opposed public funding or support for activities and industries that the pro-life movement considers abortion related (e.g., not only stem-cell research but also the "Plan B" morning-after pill), while at the same time strongly supporting energy and defense industries—from oil companies and the development of a national missile defense system to the Iraq War.

The values war over embryonic stem-cell research, in other words, is an *intra*class war that is conducted to determine which segments of capital will be subsidized by the State. The cultural turn mystifies the material interests involved in these class conflicts and represents them as wars over ideas, beliefs, faith, and, in a word, values. Even though they are covered up by values, the actual material contradictions in these social contestations always break through the thick layers of cultural mediations and expose the class interests that lie behind the spiritual (values).

The seeming unity in the pro-life argument—which initially was cohesive in its opposition to embryonic stem-cell research—has been shattered by the change of "mind" of a number of strict pro-life conservatives who, in spite of their previous values arguments, have declared their ardent support for public funding of embryonic stem-cell research. To show that they are acting consistently and ethically have no "other" motives, they have re-interpreted "values" and adjusted them to their new position. Consequently, they have given a new meaning to the ethical: it is now "ethical" and also "compassionate" to support public funding of research on stem cells because such research would save the lives (after birth) of millions of people who suffer from such devastating illnesses as Alzheimer's, Parkinson's, and diabetes. Opposing stem-cell research, according to the re-description of the ethical, not only makes a person socially regressive, but also shows that one lacks a sense of morality and is incapable of a subtle understanding of the nuances of complex issues. In defense of their new position, the new conservative supporters of funding have listed their credentials as advocates of life (before birth) and their relentless anti-abortionist fights. They have then declared that their new support is based (as Orrin Hatch, Senator from Utah, puts it) on years of studying the subject and this has convinced them of the great life-saving potential of stem-cell research. Others, such as Senator Gordon Smith (from Oregon), and (before his death) Senator Strum Thurmond, have added personal life stories to show that their support is rooted in pain and compassion. Listening to Orrin Hatch's defense of his revised position on the funding of embryonic research is like listening to an extremely subtle or, as some reporters called it, "complicated" ("Wired News," August 9, 2001) theological argument, in which the (pro-life) definition of life itself is re-defined to justify government subsidies for research benefiting biotech corporations. Then Senate Majority Leader, Bill Frist, has been quite explicit about this redefinition of "pro-life" as now meaning the "value" of life "at all stages of development" in order to support legislation "increasing funding for research" on stem cells (Frist, "Meeting Stem Cells' Promise—Ethically" A19). The new believers in public funding of embryonic stem-cell research have inverted the orthodox position on values and done so not because of some immanent transformation in values but because of the outside of values—that is, economic factors.

This change of "mind" by pro-life conservative senators who set social policy has not been caused by ethical, political, personal factors, or a sudden flash of enlightenment owing to intellectual hard work. The ethical rhetoric and personal testimonials are all codes to justify the side they have now taken in the on-going class war over the appropriation of social surplus labor. The biotech industry stands to make huge profits from any scientific and medical breakthroughs into embryonic stem-cell research and has relentlessly lobbied for public funding for such research (Taylor-Corbett, "Embryo Research: Profit vs

Ethics?"; Pollack, "Stem Cell Bill Seen as a Qualified Boon for Research"). Government funding will not only reduce labor costs but will also lessen the financial risks of investing in this mostly uncharted territory. The biotech and pharmaceutical industries have already reaped huge profits from the results of publicly funded research into drugs for fighting AIDS and other illnesses. Public funding of stem-cell research is another thinly disguised State subsidy for the biotech/pharmaceutical industries. Pro-pharmaceutical/biotech conservatives now want these subsidies and justify them as life-saving and ethical because their own economic interests have changed (e.g., see Ismail and Morente, "Capital Hill Stem-Cell Backers Received Health Industry Dollars").

The owning class, of course, is not economically monolithic and its various class fractions have different objective economic interests: class struggles are not limited to the struggles between classes but extend to conflicts within classes. The *intra*class battles among owners determine which class fraction gets the largest part of the social surplus labor. The split among pro-life conservatives is not the outcome of changing minds but of taking a material position in this *intra*class war. This *intra*class division over distribution of public funds (the social surplus) is being played out in conflicts at all levels of the "State" over public funding: not only between branches of government—Senate support and presidential veto (Stolberg, "First Bush Veto Maintains Limits on Stem Cell Use")—but also between Federal and "local" states, as California and other states use their taxes to fund embryonic stem-cell research following the presidential veto (Rudoren, "Stem Cell Work Gets States' Aid after Bush Veto"; Bellomo, *The Stem Cell Divide*). Public funds that go to stem-cell research subsidize the biotech/pharmaceutical industries, reducing the money available, for example, to the defense industry, the energy industry, or the airline industry. To make sure that its economic interests are secured, the biotech industries has given the (new) advocates of public funding for stem-cell research more than $4 million in contributions over just three election cycles (Ismail and Morente, "Capital Hill Stem-Cell Backers Received Health Industry Dollars").

The values argument, accordingly, has shifted to re-evaluate the previously de-valued and re-institute it as a "true" value. This shift is rooted not, as it represents itself, in spirituality but in the logic of profit. The cultural turn turns profit into a cultural value not simply to obscure how values are manufactured to suit the ruling economic interests but, more importantly, to divert attention away from the larger economic contradictions. In particular it suppresses awareness of the fundamental contradiction hidden in the conservatives' support for subsidies of private industries—how such subsidies implicitly demystify the myth of the "free market." The free market is always represented in the values argument as an example of human freedom—as a repository of cultural values, such as liberty, freedom of the individual, free choice, and self-determination, to name only a few. However, the free market, in the debates over stem-cell research, is a *simulation*: its free-ness is a free-effect manufactured by State subsidies. The cultural values that are drawn from this simulacra of freedom, in turn, become themselves simulations of a spirituality that is itself a simulation of faith (in the "free market"). The spiritual—in short the values of freedom of the individual, freedom of enterprise, freedom of choice—is seen as exceeding all materialist explanations. But it turns out, the spiritual is just cover for the economic. The anti-abortion position that propels the crusade against stem-cell research is such a cover-value. As we discuss in another chapter, it is a "value" manufactured to control wages in the market by providing a reserve army of workers for capital.

8

Abortion Is a Class Matter

Abortion is neither exclusively a gender question, as in the liberal-feminist insistence on "reproductive rights," nor is it simply what pro-life advocates, in their moralizing stance, call the universal "sanctity of life."

Both pro-choice and pro-life positions are fraught with class contradictions. "Rights" feminists have shown little serious interest in the rights of women of color, who do most of their domestic work. Pro-life women have few moral qualms about supporting militarism and the defense industries, whose main task is to make more efficient machines for slaughtering humans. They have enthusiastically backed imperialist invasions by the U.S. in Iraq and Afghanistan as well as the daily slaughter of the Palestinians by Israel's military. Some of the most ardent supporters of Israel's occupation of Palestine and the invasion of Lebanon are American pro-life groups who, for example, organize group trips to Israel to help its economy, which is collapsing because of lack of access to cheap Palestinian labor. Much of the opposition to the Likud Party in Israel and support for the new centrist Kadima Party has been a reaction against the ways in which the Likud Party has often put ideology before economics. Its frequent closing of the borders and other restrictions have deprived Israeli industries of easy access to cheap Palestinian labor. One of the implicit promises of the new "forward-looking" Kadima Party to Israeli capitalists is that it will produce a new situation, and will change the status quo to make the Palestinian labor force once again available to them.

The pro-choice and pro-life ideologies are, in the end, based on a rather discredited bourgeois notion of (human) "rights"—one that is an ideological device giving the illusion of equality for all and that uses the legalistic discourse of equality before the law to obscure the material gap between unequal classes.

Pro-choice feminists have formulated the question of abortion as primarily a matter of individual freedom: a woman's reproductive rights. Using a progressive-sounding rhetoric, they have actually reaffirmed the existing social relations, which privilege the individual, and substituted the legalism of "rights" for economic equality. Consequently, they have produced a populist imaginary that fantasizes that reproductive rights are autonomous from the social relations of production. In other words, they do not regard freedom from wage labor to be the condition for the emancipation of women. They simply want to reform capitalism by opening up more high-paying positions for women and to succeed economically within the existing system of wage-labor. They are not interested in transforming wage-labor; they simply want to have a better life within it. For pro-choice feminists, in other words, abortion is a personal issue, and since for them the personal is political, their politics are personal and wrapped up in identity.

The pro-life movement is also an ardent supporter of wage-labor and the so-called free market and entrepreneurship. It appeals to the same principle of the "rights" of the individual, but it defines the individual, as we have indicated in our discussion of stem-cell research, as a legal being before birth. By retreating into the false abstraction of the sanctity of life and what Roland Barthes calls the "lyricism of birth" (*Mythologies* 102), the pro-life movement also covers up the gap between classes and represents all life as equal, erasing the profound material differences that affect the birth and health of the child, from access to prenatal care to the economic conditions that enable breast-feeding, particularly for working mothers (Ebert, *Ludic Feminism and After* 238-41). This equality of life is as empty as the equality in liberal rights.

In spite of their cultural conflicts, the pro-choice and the pro-life arguments are two related ideological modes addressing different class fractions. Using different discourses, they both support the ways in which capitalism secures the dominant productive processes. Anti-abortion activism is an activism on behalf of capital to more effectively control the supply of labor. It has the very real economic impact of increasing the reserve army of the unemployed and thus putting pressure on wages to constantly lower them. Anti-abortion activism is also economic in its use of cultural politics to displace class struggle. Through the rhetoric of rights and life, it converts class matters into cultural value questions.

The pro-choice movement is also a group ideology to control the supply of labor. It is composed, for the most part, of well-educated women and men from that class fraction that bourgeois stratification theorists call the upper-middle class. In advocating women's right to choose, it is also acting to preserve the privileges of this highly paid segment of the labor force.

It acts, in short, like a guild that protects the living standards of its members by putting strict conditions on membership and thereby securing a higher pay for its associates. The upper-middle class, thus, attempts to limit the supply of labor through family planning and abortion in order to promote the highest standard of living for its own class by appropriating a larger share of the social surplus labor. Specifically, women's right to reproductive self-determination—that is, a woman's right to decide when and how many children she will have—has the economic effect of providing a more flexible, educated, highly paid labor force.

The pro-choice campaign for the availability of family planning clinics, access to contraception, including the "morning after" or "plan B" pill, and distribution of condoms in schools helps reduce births. Reductions in the birth rate also bring down the cost of such social programs as welfare as well as medical costs and, therefore, increase, or at least preserve, the public resources available to the middle class for its own use through tax breaks and other devices for the transfer of wealth to this class. Abortion and reproductive control, in other words, are means through which the upper-middle class assures the perpetuation of its own class privileges by limiting the available labor force. On a more immediate and personal level, by postponing childbirth or foregoing it altogether, upper-middle-class women are able to complete advanced education and take executive and professional positions within the dominant economic and power structures of capitalism.

Both movements, thus, act as ideological agents tied to the economic needs of capitalism. Pro-choice is a response to capital's demand for elite, highly trained knowledge workers, while the pro-life "values" agenda implements capital's need for easy access to an abundant cheap labor force. The contradictory directions of the two are symptoms of the structural class contradictions of capitalism itself.

The opposition, by right-wing groups, to birth-control and family planning programs throughout the world ends up recruiting a global reserve army of the unemployed for capital. Even if the poor have access to health insurance, most of the insurance policies available to them refuse to pay for contraceptives. However, it is ideologically interesting that these very same insurance policies will pay for Viagra and other lifestyle drugs for men, one of whose effects is increased reproductive activity, thus leading to larger families and a larger pool of workers. The effects of the pro-life opposition to abortion, as well as its overwhelming lack of support for any form of contraception (even as a means of reducing the need for abortions), fulfills the economic needs of monopoly capitalism under the alibi of family "values." Pro-life practices increase the labor reserve and, thereby, exert enormous pressure on wages, making sure they are always kept at an absolute minimum. As Engels puts it in his critique of Malthus, "the population is always pressing against the means of employment" ("Outline of a Critique of Political Economy" 438).

To say that the pro-life position is an enactment of capital's need for an abundant and cheap labor force may strike many as odd and counter-intuitive because the majority of pro-life advocates are from the working and lower-middle classes. One of the roles of the ruling ideology, however, is to convert the economic interests of the ruling class into cultural values—the "sanctity of life," "testing in schools," "family values," "law and order," "work ethics," "national security," anti-"gay marriage"—that can be embraced as extra-economic, "natural" values by the lower-middle and working classes. In fact, the hegemony of the ruling class is commonly obtained by appealing to cultural values that mask the economic interests of capital.

The lack of class consciousness among many working people—who all too often end up supporting the conservative agenda under the name of "values" and acting against their own objective class interests—shows the success of the dominant ideology in displacing the material with the cultural. Left cultural critique is complicit with the production of this false consciousness. But it has tried to obscure its own role in this process by engaging in lengthy theoretical debates to "prove" that there is no such thing as "false consciousness," and if there ever had been, it was a long, long time ago during the era of industrial capitalism

(Althusser, *Lenin and Philosophy* 127-186; Zizek, *The Sublime Object of Ideology*). Instead of offering analytical critiques of "values" politics, the Left has largely retreated into an affirmative narration of the dominant culture under the pretext that the culture of oppression is a hybrid. Thus, no matter how oppressive the dominant culture might look, it always contains, according to these critics, simultaneous lines of resistance and, therefore, a promise of liberation (Frow, *Cultural Studies and Cultural Value;* Butler, *Precarious Life: The Powers of Mourning and Violence*). The Left in the North has quite effectively commodified and marketed the "culture is resistance" myth (Duncombe, ed., *Cultural Resistance Reader*) to justify its own participation in capital's exploitation of labor. What the "post-al" Left—i.e., postmodern, poststructuralist, postcolonial, post-Marxist, post-, etc. (see Zavarzadeh's "Post-ality")—calls resistance is always a way of embracing capital through a cultural relay, such as consumption practices, (anti)abortion, sex work, tax cuts, as John Fiske's readings of culture demonstrate (*Understanding Popular Culture*).

Discussing pro-choice and pro-life values always involves, either directly or indirectly, questions of birth, birth rate, resources, and population. Population in itself, however, is not the issue (Foster, *Marx's Ecology: Materialism and Nature* 81-140). Class is the issue. As Engels puts it, population is "invented" by bourgeois economics in order to explain away the (class) crisis of capitalism which produces cycles of boom and bust, "over-production and slump" ("Outline of a Critique of Political Economy" 436). It is also used to represent the outcome of market "competition" as facts of nature and to treat these "facts" as themselves manifestations of divine providence. In his critique of Malthus, Engels argues that his theories are part of a "Christian economics" or "the economic expression" of a "religious dogma"—one that turns class differences into an inevitable theological order ("Outline of a Critique of Political Economy" 439).

Malthus claims that "population, when unchecked, increases in a geometrical ratio" while food, or what he calls "subsistence for man," increases only "in an arithmetical ratio" (*An Essay on the Principle of Population* 21). The inevitable natural imbalance between the two, he argues, causes poverty. "Pauperism," for Malthus, Marx writes, is "an *eternal law of nature*" ("Critical Marginal Notes on the Article 'The King of Prussia and Social Reform. By a Prussian'" 194). This, Marx argues, obscures the real cause which is not "nature" nor is it something that "workers have brought upon themselves by their own fault" but is instead "modern industry" (195) and its laws of profit. This is emphasized by Engels, who writes that, according to Malthus,

> the earth is perennially overpopulated, whence poverty, misery, distress, and immorality must prevail; that it is the lot, the eternal destiny of mankind, to exist in too great numbers, and therefore in diverse classes, of which some are rich, educated, and moral, and others more or less poor, distressed, ignorant, and immoral. (*The Condition of the Working-Class in England* 570)

Hunger and poverty are natural excesses, or as Foucault would call them, "events" ("Nietzsche, Genealogy, History" 154), that defy all rational explanations and social remedies based on them. This theological naturalism, as Engels points out, is "the keystone of the liberal system of free trade" ("Outline of a Critique of Political Economy" 437), which legitimates the existing social divisions of labor and its class relations through the free market—itself a galaxy of excesses of unexplainable "events" in "competition," according to bourgeois philosophy.

Malthus's argument for the naturalness of class is ultimately grounded in the super-natural, namely, divine intervention that produces the conditions—through the unevenness of the food supply and population—within which two classes, "a class of proprietors and a class of labourers must necessarily exist" (98). Class divisions, and with them poverty and hunger, according to Malthus, therefore have to be accepted as facts of nature. But, hunger is not, as Robert Owen explains in his critique of Malthus, the result of a "deficiency in Nature's stores," but of "man's laws" (Foster, *Marx's Ecology* 108). Poverty is caused by lack of access to food which is determined by one's class position and not by lack of food itself.

Locating Malthus's theory and the problem of population, in general, in political economy, Engels argues that while Malthus was right in stating that "there is always a surplus population," he is wrong in thinking that "there are more people on hand than can be maintained from the available resources of subsistence"(*The Condition of the Working-Class in England* 380). Malthus, according to Engels,

> confuse(s) means of subsistence with [means of] employment. That population is always pressing on the means of employment—that the number of people produced depends on the number of people who can be employed—in short, that production of labour-power has been regulated so far by the law of competition and is therefore also exposed to periodic crises and fluctuations. ("Outline of a Critique of Political Economy" 438)

Population, in other words, is a class matter. Surplus population is used as a reserve army of capital to maintain low wages and high profits, or as Marx writes:

> the greater pressure that the reserve by its competition exerts on the employed workers forces them to submit to over-work and subjects them to dictates of capital. The condemnation of one part of the working class to enforced idleness by the over-work of the other, and *vice versa*, becomes a means for enriching the individual capitalists. (*Capital* I, 789)

By representing the question of (anti)abortion as a matter of rights, ethics and abstract life, pro-choice and pro-life theories conceal the class politics of abortion and its role in naturalizing capitalism. Both pro-choice and pro-life treat the (anti)abortion question as a local issue, effectively isolating it from the relation of capital and labor that actually shapes "ethics" and "rights."

The (anti)abortion issue is not a reproductive issue in itself. It is about controlling the labor force within different class fractions. (Anti)abortion, to put it differently, is always a production matter. What is at stake is economic equality. Democracy is not merely a matter of legislated individual "rights." Rather in its most fundamental sense it is an economic issue: freedom from necessity, namely, the satisfaction of the needs of all people by socializing the means of production and ending the commodification of human labor and the class system that it produces. Both pro-choice and pro-life movements embrace wage labor, and the only question for each of them is how best to ensure legal "rights" within that system.

(Anti)abortion is not simply a reproductive rights/right-to-life question and therefore its solution involves what Engels, in his *The Origin of the Family, Private Property, and the State* (182), calls the "first precondition for the emancipation of women": opening up a space for women in "public industry"—that is, equality in social labor beyond privatization—and consequently the elimination of the "individual family...[as] the economic unit of society." This is another way of saying that the solution to (anti)abortion requires reorganizing a new society free from private ownership of the means of production. Reproduction is always an effect of production.

9
E-Education as a Class Technology

E-education is represented in the media and other cultural outlets as a form of teaching that is not only innovative but is also politically progressive. The development of online courses and Internet universities is considered to be a new educational force that will empower people and change society by educating everyone, thereby removing existing social inequalities and remaking the world as an inclusive democracy.

This view of e-education—which downplays the role of the economic in bringing about social justice and instead makes culture (in this case, education) an independent forceful agent of social change—is very dear to big business. As usual, what serves the interests of big business is validated by culture as the new, groundbreaking cutting edge of social reality. E-education is no exception. It is said to be part of what N. Katherine Hayles, in her discussion of cyberwritings, calls the "zesty, contentious, and rapidly transforming medial ecology of the new millennium" (*Writing Machines* 7).

In spite of the exuberance with which e-education is embraced by cyber-academics and techno-evangelicals (such as the editors of *Wired* and writers of such books as Alexander's *Digital Democracy* and Trippi's *The Revolution Will Not Be Televised: Democracy, the Internet, and the Overthrow of Everything*), it is ultimately not about education or democracy in any serious sense. It is part of a cultural politics that obscures class relations by representing *economic* inequalities as *information* differences—a digital divide—and seeks the cure for differences not outside but within capitalism. This, by the way, is one reason that business oligarchs are providing "free" access to the internet for poor schools and give laptops to children (the future labor force) in the Third World.

E-education is not a pedagogy; it is a class technology.

Nothing in contemporary cultural politics makes this more clear than the way the underlying technologies of e-education are legitimated as a new historical force by cultural theory. Unlike the writers of *Wired* and other cyber-rebels, contemporary cultural theory, for the most part, has been skeptical about the claims of online communications because of their implicit guarantee of "complete instantaneous information," as Bill Gates describes it in his *The Road Ahead*, that provides the communications ground for a "friction-free capitalism" (180-207). The Internet and e-education, according to contemporary theory, claim an immediacy, transparency, and plenitude, which Jacques Derrida, in his essay "*Différance*," critiques as presence-Truth (*Margins of Philosophy* 3-27).

For Derrida, who has set the framework for critiquing the immediacy of truth in recent theory, "presence" is the promise of an unmediated and, therefore, authentic and reliable meaning ("truth") that can never be fulfilled because what seems to be immediate is always already mediated and, therefore, lacks directness and simultaneity, which are seen as qualities of truth. E-communication, for example, far from being instantaneous, direct truth (of a message), is actually a layered fiction that tells us more about writing than truth. Gates's frictionlessness, in other words, is made up of frictions because it, like all communication, is punctuated by enumerable relays and spacing of mediations. It is a simulacra of the frictionless, an absent presence.

The questioning of presence underlies Derrida's critique of such opponents of capitalism as Marxism. For Derrida the main Marxist concepts, such as "class" and "class struggle," which claim to explain how material conditions act as the dynamics of education and society, are fictions. They are missing presences that share the fate of all writing, which is self-difference, and therefore are marked by an inability to refer to reality (e.g., economic inequality) outside language. Marx's *Capital* is like Joyce's *Ulysses*; it consists of what Paul de Man calls, "allegories of reading"—self-referential metaphors on the unreadability of texts and not explanatory concepts. According to de Man, all concepts such as class are tropes in disguise (*Allegories of Reading* 245, 135-159).

According to Derrida, as we have already discussed, class is a fiction of presence: "the idea that a social class is what it is, homogeneous, present and identical to itself" ("Marx and Sons" 237), belongs, he says, "to another time" ("Politics and Friendship" 204). "Any sentence," he emphasizes, "in which 'social class' appeared was a problematic sentence for me" (204).

Derrida, in other words, uses the logic of "presence" to criticize the anti-capitalist notions of class and class struggle that underlie education. But when it comes to e-technologies, which involve the very same claims that he attributes to the Marxist theory of class, namely, the promise of presence—what Gates calls "complete, instantaneous information," Derrida abandons his critique of presence. To put it differently, he has long argued for the opacity of the text and its constitutive representationality, which puts it at odds with speech and its metaphysics of immediate, non-representational "presence." However, in an accommodation of cybercapitalism, he speaks in his later writings about a mode of presence (the ineffable) in e-texts: "The figure of text 'processed' on a computer is like a phantom to the extent that it is less bodily, more 'spiritual,' more ethereal. There is something like a disincarnation of text in this" (*Paper Machine* 30). Text (self-difference) becomes less textual and more responsive to cybercapitalism, which maintains that it is driven by a new immaterial labor—the figure for a new spiritual capitalism and a new materialism without materiality.

E-technology has not only spiritualized the text but has also become, according to Derrida, the new dynamics of history. Having previously criticized the concept of class because it embodied determinism, Derrida becomes a technological determinist in his later writings and affirms the principles of knowledge capitalism and the end of labor. In his *Archive Fever*, for example, he writes:

> in what way has the whole of this field been determined by a state of the technology of communication and of archivization? One can dream or speculate about the geo-techno-logical shocks which would have made the landscape of the psychoanalytic archive unrecognizable for the past century if, to limit myself to these indications, Freud, his contemporaries, collaborators and immediate disciples, instead of writing thousands of letters by hand, had had access to MCI or AT&T telephonic credit cards, portable tape recorders, computers, printers, faxes, televisions, teleconferences and above all E-mail....electronic mail...is on the way to transforming the entire public and private space of humanity.... (*Archive Fever* 16, 17)

As we said at the outset, privileging e-education is not simply privileging a pedagogy but a political theory in which material labor is marginalized and culture is said to shape the social. Derrida confirms this view, which is at the heart of capitalist cultural politics, by stating that e-mail (culture) changes not only such social relations as the "juridical and...political" but, most importantly, "property rights" (17). What is represented as a cultural innovation is really a new way of affirming existing property relations. E-education does not change the social relations; instead, as we will argue, it hardens them.

In proposing e-technologies as the driving force determining history, Derrida not only contradicts his previous views, which deconstructed causality and determinism into the aleatory and indeterminable play of the sign (*Signeponge/Signsponge* 54, 92, 116), but also actively argues for what is basically a new technological determinism. He forgets his own writings, which have opposed the claims of all theories of communication based on presence, and justifies e-mail and its "quasi-instantaneous" quality (*Archive Fever* 16) by what is basically a theological argument. E-mail, he says, is an exception, an excess to the grand laws of logocentricity and presence that he has used to critique metaphysics because it is not "technique" in the "ordinary and limited sense of the term" (17). In other words, responding to the new demands of capital, Derrida defends, in an (ideo)logical turning around, what he has always critiqued. By appealing to the "extraordinary," the excess of the normal, which borders on the super-natural, becomes a rationalization of e-mail. Theory becomes theology and like theology seeks an explanation of the material in the super-material.

It is important to keep in mind that what we have called "contradictions" in Derrida's writings and his interpretive inconsistencies are not signs of his philosophical shallowness or thoughtlessness. Like all logical discrepancies, these contradictions and inconsistencies are effects of class contradictions. The class character of Derrida's new technologism becomes clear in his argument for knowledge capitalism and the end of labor. E-technologies, according to Derrida, have put an end to the division of labor. This division, which Marx thought was fundamental to capitalism, Derrida finds is "untenable today" because e-technology has turned all workers "into 'intellectuals,'" (*Paper Machine* 37). But the actual practices of global capitalism show that far from workers becoming "intellectuals," knowledge capitalism separates knowledge from labor and pits one against the other. Derrida's ecstasy over e–technologies covers up this increasing gap.

What is lost in the arguments made by both Derrida and Bill Gates is that machines, cyber or otherwise, are social. They reproduce the prevailing social relations. They do not change them. But the myth of technology as agent of social change is renewed by each generation, which of course has its own version of the myth. These mythologies—that technologies of print, radio, television, and now the Internet will radically change education, establish equality and thus transform the social structures of production—have been powerful cultural forces. But no such radical change by technology has so far taken place. Social changes are the results of labor relations; they are only administered by technology. Education is not changed by technology but is the effect of class relations that have essentially remained the same over the centuries: relations in which "Freeman and slave, patrician and plebian, lord and serf, guild-master and journeyman, in a word, oppressor and oppressed stood in constant opposition to one another, carried on an uninterrupted, now hidden, now open fight..." (Marx and Engels, *Manifesto of the Communist Party* 41).

In spite of the introduction of ever newer technologies, the prevailing class relations have determined the basic structures of education. Education remains a means for training the new labor force and not an agent for human freedom. Education not only teaches the technical skills that the workforce needs, but, perhaps more importantly, it also educates them in "consciousness skills" through which they subscribe to the ruling class values and concede that the way things are—is the way they ought to be. In other words, in class societies education reproduces the existing social relations; it educates the workforce to "look upon the requirements of [the capitalist] mode of production as self-evident natural laws" (Marx, *Capital* I, 899).

Social inequalities are not caused by a lack of education and therefore cannot be changed by education and educational technologies. Inequalities are the outcome of transformations of social surplus labor into private capital and thus are structured into wage-labor relations. Within the existing labor relations, it does not matter how well-educated people are since, in the end, they will have to sell their labor to earn a living. How they live and think is determined by the laws of motion of capital which demand the least expensive workforce. The social division of labor and not pedagogy is the index of (in)equality. Equality is the effect not of education but the collective freedom from necessity. True, education makes a difference in the lifestyles of individuals (the educated may live better, eat better, dress nicer, drive more expensive cars, for example) but only within the existing inequalities. The educated live better only by conceding to these collective inequalities. Education has become an individualistic "solution" to a collective social problem—the exploitation of wage-labor. In exchange for a more comfortable lifestyle, the educated accepts the existing economic injustice, and a segment of the educated even becomes a militant supporter of capital by providing theoretical concepts to justify it. Through education capital creates what Nikolai Bukharin and Evgeny Preobrazhensky call "'cultured' controllers of the working population" (*The ABC of Communism* 228).

Education, like all social practices, is part of class relations. As such, it has a contradictory and thus critical side that is produced by people becoming aware that their material interests conflict with those of the ruling classes and fighting it out. E-education obscures this critical potential by turning education into training in which "critique" is replaced by "skills" and an affirmation of the social division of labor on which the division of society is based. The social division of labor "converts the worker into a crippled monstrosity by furthering his particular skill as in a forcing-house, through the suppression of a whole world of productive drives and inclinations.... It...mutilates the worker, turning him into a fragment of himself" (Marx, *Capital* I, 481-82).

Training is part of the post-class curriculum of knowledge designed to de-educate people by educating them as sources of cheap labor for capital. E-education is not a new pedagogy for democracy. It is a new class technology for transforming people into less expensive commodities for merchants of human labor. To put it more bluntly, e-education turns human beings into highly efficient but cheap instruments of labor for capital.

The myth of e-education as a progressive agent of change is so common, in part, because when most people talk about the radical changes brought by e-education, they are really talking about the "content" of education and the way it is delivered. But education is not a matter of "delivery" of a pre-packaged "content." It is, to quote Marx again, the "development of human powers as an end in itself" (Marx, *Capital* III, 959). It is attained through a critique-al give-and-take that enables students to grasp not simply a disciplinary knowledge but the way knowledge relates to the social world and to the underlying structures of that world in its historical totality. In a sense education is learning how to connect the seemingly disparate spheres of the every day and the social world that frames it.

In the same way that contemporary cultural theory has displaced "labor" by "technology" in order to legitimate e-education in the interests of capital, it also justifies "training" through concepts and interpretations that marginalize education. In his essay, "Truth and Power," for instance, Michel Foucault dismisses the idea of critique-al education by declaring its most effective result, the "universal intellectual," outdated (126). The "universal intellectual" is the critique-al citizen who goes beyond concrete experiences and points to the abstract logic of capital that underlies the seemingly unrelated aspects of the alienated reality of wage-labor and explains how, for example, the "savage inequalities in school" (Kozol, *Savage Inequalities: Children in America's Schools*) are not an anomaly but the regulated outcome of certain tax policies, health-care regimes, access to food, pollution laws, state-sponsored spiritualism (faith-based subsidies), and those cultural theories that, in the name of "difference," "singularity," and "value," normalize them. The "universal intellectual" is the bearer of what Foucault ironically calls "the just-and-true-for all" (126) and almost mocks as the "consciousness/conscience" (126) of the collective. In place of the "universal intellectual," who provides concepts such as "class" and "critique" by which the social totality is brought into focus, Foucault puts what he calls the "specific intellectual" (126). "Specific intellectual" is actually a metaphor for the post-class "expert" (128) who is "trained" in specific skills. Foucault's "specific intellectual" is not passionate about objective truth (class) and social justice (classlessness), what Foucault dismisses as a "rhapsodist of the eternal." Instead, he is, above all, a "strategist" (129), a practical person who goes around "truth" (whatever it might be) to solve a problem. He knows, for example, how to work and improve the conditions in prisons (130). In other words, he is not interested in questioning the "truth" of laws (the coding of property rights), for whose transgression people are put in prison, but rather is interested in reforming the conditions of prisons, so that prisoners, for example, can "speak for themselves" ("Intellectuals and Power" 206). He accepts the laws and concedes to the sanctity of private property but also wants to make sure that those who violate it are treated humanely. He is a pragmatist, and, like all pragmatists, he works with what works within the system, namely, within the limits of the existing reality (of wage-labor) that is legitimated by the system and in turn legitimates the system. Education educates people to not be diverted by existing "laws" but instead to seek the logic that make those "laws" lawful. "Training," in contrast, teaches people to accept the "laws" as if they were derived from the body of objective reality itself and to adjust to them in the same way one adjusts to the weather.

E-education is the device for training experts. It represents the practicalities of living under class as the "real reality" and teaches the "skills" to get a job and to get along within it. Training, in other words, is the conversion of human labor into a ready-to-use commodity and the reduction of humans to their marketable values. Although it represents its interest in the practical as post-ideological, e-education, like all forms of education, does not simply teach content, in this case technical skills; it also teaches a way of looking at the world and living in it—what we call "consciousness skills." By this we mean the cultural values and attitudes (devotion to family, patriotism, dedication to hard work, mistrust of thinking and of big words, putting "mind before matter," etc.) that make sure the student—the future worker—goes along to get along with capital. E-education tutors students to see the social world in purely experiential terms and, in fact, warns them against such "abstractions" as truth, which in the underlying philosophy of Pragmatism is reduced to "those beliefs" that are "good to believe" (Rorty, "Solidarity or Objectivity?" 24). Training teaches people to develop a "commoditized apprehension of reality" (to use Michael Taussig's phrase from his study, *The Devil and Commodity Fetishism in South America* 10).

The reduction of education to training and critique to the pragmatics of getting along is a class matter. As classes have become more sharply divided and "society as a whole" is more and more "splitting up into two great hostile classes" (Marx and Engels, *Manifesto of the Communist Party* 42), education itself has also split along class lines. For the majority, it has become more and more a form of "training" and less and less a mode of critique-al understanding of the every day because modern capitalism needs increasingly more "new" experts, highly skilled workers, and proficient managers. E-education fulfills this demand in the least expensive way; it facilitates raising the ratio of surplus labor—getting more "productivity" out of working people's labor power.

In the contemporary class war, training, which is really a form of de-education, is culturally represented as the empowerment of people. This representation has been effective because the way triumphalist capital has treated labor (corporate downsizing, abrupt layoffs, abandoning of pension programs, cutting salaries and wages, reducing health-care benefits) has made parents focus in panic on one single issue: their children's prospects for getting and keeping a job. The cultural representations of e-education as innovative pedagogy count on this panic which is the effect of class blackmail. This supposed empowering (i.e., getting a job) is actually a life impoverishment because it merely teaches students the job skills capital needs in the short term and as these skills quickly become outdated, capital uses the deskilled workers to increase its reserve army of the unemployed through which it puts pressure on the workers to keep their wages low. The skills that training teaches, no matter how complex and sophisticated, do not make the workers irreplaceable. Instead, through the quantification and rationalization of skills in the curriculum, training makes workers more easily replaceable. Deskilling is not being without skills. Rather it is having skills that are quickly and easily replaceable: training is teaching replaceable skills. It is the educational strategy for reinforcing "The silent compulsion of economic relations" that "sets the seal on the domination of the capitalist over the worker" (Marx, *Capital* I, 899). "Training" turns "work" into the practice of replaceable skills and thus makes it the negation of the worker. The "trained" worker, therefore, "only feels himself outside his work, and in his work feels outside himself" (Marx, *Economic and Philosophic Manuscripts of 1844*, 274).

Education is not a matter of accumulating content but the effect of ongoing and rigorous encounters and critiques among teachers and students questioning the dominant assumptions and practices. It should be put beyond the sphere of commodification. Education is critique-al; training is functional—it is the delivery of already agreed-upon content. While e-education trains people to mind their own business—be practical—and make the best of the world as it is, critique-al education teaches students to struggle for new social arrangements, to question the world as it is. Education is an act of production, whereas training is essentially reproduction and consumption.

The Internet is an instrument of reproduction; it works in the sphere of circulation not production. In their enthusiasm for the Internet, educators and administrators confuse the tremendous power of the Internet in reproducing and disseminating content for its (lack of) ability to educate. Such a mistake is, of course, not personal or professional. Rather it is a historically necessary mistake—a class "insight" by capital that reaffirms class differences and, in doing so, reaffirms the privilege and power of one class over the other.

The existing class divisions are kept in place and sharpened by the mass of schools, community colleges, and universities that are appealing to the business hype about the Internet as the hot, new thing and, more and more, are deploying it to deliver educational content to their students. They do so, for the most part, to cut costs: they are usually universities that lack the financial resources to provide critique-al education for their students. In substituting the Internet for critique-al education, they are also reducing their students to information processors and practical implementers.

At the same time that mass universities are excited over the "hot" e-education and *distance* leaning, the elite schools, in their "cool," aristocratic aloofness emphasize *close* learning. As e-education further commodifies the consciousness of citizens and de-socializes learning by isolating students and confining their education to signs on their computer screens, the elite classroom acts as an active place of critique-al and cultural interaction. This face-to-face interaction is radically different from the detached cyber-interactions of distance learning in which a lonely student posts a functional question to another lonely student or to the overworked and equally isolated instructor who, in return, provides functional answers. There is no cultural or pedagogical space for critique in e-education; it is an entirely instrumental performance. Elite education separates itself from mass education by insisting on education in small classes as a critical space for educating knowledge producers.

The Internet, in other words, far from democratizing learning, sharpens class lines in society. Elite universities and schools will continue to educate their students through close-learning and dynamic, face-to-face critique-al encounters, while mass universities and schools will deploy e-education and distance learning in order to deliver low-cost content to their students. Cyberstudents are trained to have the necessary skills and information processing to function in the factories and e-enterprises owned and managed by those who are critique-ally educated in elite universities ("'cultured' controllers of the working population").

The Internet is not an educational tool. It is a tool in the class struggle over shaping the consciousness of the new workforce as instruments of labor. In a cost-effective manner, it delivers the content necessary to turn working-class students into performers of low and mid-level jobs for global capital. E-education is an annex of the free market: the cheaper the training, the lower the cost of labor for big business. It does nothing to educate people for a democracy with equal economic access for all. Instead, it reproduces the existing class relations with a vengeance.

10

Gender after Class

LUDIC FEMINISM

Contemporary feminism is a Ludic Feminism. It is largely indifferent to material practices under capitalism such as labor, which shapes the social structures of daily life. In theory and practice, feminism has fetishized difference and erased the question of exploitation, diffusing knowledge of the root conditions of women's realities in particularities of oppressions. It has embraced the cultural turn—the reification of culture as an autonomous zone of signifying practices—and put aside a transformative politics. So much so that it is little more than a painfully parodic linguistic game.

A new (Red) feminism is needed now: a feminism that clears out the undergrowth of bourgeois ideology which, by troping the concepts of class, history, theory, and labor, has limited the terms through which feminism understands the condition of women. Red Feminism is concerned not only with the "woman question" but even more about the "other" questions that construct the "woman question"—the issues of class and labor.

For all the family quarrels in Ludic Feminism, as institutionalized by post-theories (e.g., Benhabib, Butler, Cornell, and Fraser, *Feminist Contentions*; Butler, Laclau, and Zizek, *Contingency, Hegemony, Universality*), its ways of understanding gender and sexuality are strategies for bypassing questions of labor and capital—the social relations grounded in turning the labor power of the other into profit. Feminism now dwells, instead, on matters of cultural difference. In reclaiming a materialist knowledge, Red Feminism contests the cultural theory grounding Ludic Feminism. Specifically, it argues that language—discourse in its social circulations—is "practical consciousness" (as Marx and Engels write in *The German Ideology* 44) and that culture, far from being autonomous, is always and ultimately a social articulation of the material relations of production. Ludic Feminism localizes gender and sexuality in the name of honoring their differences and the specificities of their oppression. In doing so, it isolates them from history and reduces them to "events" in performativities, thus cleansing them of labor. For Red Feminism, the local, the specific, and the singular, namely the concrete, is always an "imagined concrete" and the result of "many determinations" and relations that "all form the members of a totality, distinctions within a unity. Production (labor relations) predominates not only over itself...but over the other moments as well" (Marx, *Grundrisse* 100-101, 99).

Ludic Feminism is gradually disappearing into the irrelevance of high-bourgeois caprice and humor interlaced with a defensive populism. It is turning into a Bakhtinian carnival in which playfulness, puns, and corporeal analogies are substituted for transformative arguments (Probyn, *Blush: Faces of Shame*), and the resignification of the world has taken the place of critique-al analysis for changing it (Gallop, *Anecdotal Theory*).

Globalization, to take one specific issue that has had a serious impact on the lives of women and their families around the world but especially in the global South, is understood in ludic theory as "a discourse, as the language of domination, a tightly scripted narrative of differential power" [Gibson-Graham, *The End of Capitalism (as we knew it)* 120]. The class contradictions of globalization are mystified in a "politics that offers a compressed temporality—traversing the distance from 'nowhere' to 'now here'" (Gibson-Graham, *A Postcapitalist Politics* xxi).

The consequences of reading globalization figurally have been disastrous for feminism. J. K. Gibson-Graham, for example, deploy Sharon Marcus's metaphors (in her "Fighting Bodies, Fighting Words") to compare globalization to rape (*The End of Capitalism* 120-147). "There are," Gibson-Graham write, "many obvious points of connection between the language of rape and the language of capitalist globalization," and they list by way of example such words as "penetration," "invasion," and "virgin territory" (124). Globalization, in their tropes, has the brutal force of the violence of rape and has become a discourse of power and oppression. Rape is understood not as domination but as a narrative (mis)representation of victimization and sexualization that can be resisted through resignification. Change, for them, is therefore changing representations—rewriting the script of rape/globalization. Thus resistance to capitalism involves reinscribing the "body of capitalism." Elaborating on Elizabeth Grosz's troping of the male body, they believe the power dynamics of globalization can be transformed by "differently conceiv(ing) of the body of capitalism, viewing it as open, as penetrable, as weeping or draining away instead of as hard and contained, penetrating and inevitably overpowering" (135). They thus rewrite "finance capital (or money)" as "the seminal fluid of capitalism" and as "a spectacle of bodily excess, a wet dream" (136), representing it as "unleashing uncontrollable gushes of capital that flow every which way, including self-destruction" (135-36).

These analogies, however, cannot explain material exploitation which is the root cause of globalization. Furthermore, this double move—treating rape as a matter of power relations and then turning power relations into linguistic associations—isolates rape from the social relations of production making it into a local gender question that is, for them, simply a matter of the performativity of language (123). Playing with these supplementary tropes, their analysis drifts further and further away from globalization as an objective reality of contemporary labor relations. It becomes not only a frivolous troping of globalization but also a trivialization of the fate of women and their sexuality under capitalism. The fight against globalization—the plundering of the labor of the other—turns into the question of "how might we get globalization to lose its erection" (127)? This turns out to be not that difficult because, in the interpretation of Lisa Disch who admires their arguments, their views of globalization amount to saying that "what we know as globalization is less a rape…than…mutual masturbation" (Deconstructing 'Capitalism'").

Gibson-Graham's general argument uses feminism as a pluralizing strategy to claim that capitalism is not the sole source of exploitation in the global world. Therefore, "the script of globalization," they write, "need not draw solely upon an image of the body of capitalism as hard, thrusting and powerful" (*The End of Capitalism* 138). Consequently the representation of the intervention of multinational corporations (MNC) in the economy of the host country, does not have to be read in terms of the standard script. They then ask the question which implies its own answer: "Could we not see MNC activity in Third World situation in a slightly different light, as perhaps sometimes unwittingly generative rather than merely destructive" (130)? In other words, their Ludic Feminism ends up as an apologist of multinational corporations and leads to the climax "that the economic 'rape' wrought by globalization in the Third World is a script with many different outcomes. In this case we might read the rape event as inducing a pregnancy" (131). The grand finale of their discursive analysis of globalization as rape is that exploitation is good for women:

> For some women involvement in capitalist exploitation has freed them from aspects of the exploitation associated with their household class positions and has given them a position from which to struggle with and redefine traditional gender roles. (132)

This is too painful to call it comical. The conclusion of their cutting-edge feminist "analysis" is identical to the liberal banalities that are written day in and day out in the pages of such house organs of global capitalism as *The New York Times* (the main site for the dissemination of Thomas Friedman's views on globalization). In his "In Praise of the Maligned Sweatshop," which we have already discussed, Nicholas D. Kristof writes that the sweatshops in Africa set up by capitalists from the North are, in fact, "opportunities," and he advises that "anyone who cares about fighting poverty should campaign in favor of sweatshops" (*The New York Times,* June 6, 2006, A-21) His argument is summed up by two sentences printed in bold font and foregrounded in his essay: "**What's worse than being exploited? Not being exploited**" (A-21).

Globalization, for both the liberal writer and the Ludic Feminist, is the same: Gibson-Graham see it "as liberating" a plurality of economic practices (139). Heterogeneity is what matters most. This view is indistinguishable—except in its corporeal metaphors—from the standard (very standard) neoliberal economic theory and its history in the North (David Harvey, *A Brief History of Neoliberalism*). Ludic Feminism, along with Neoliberals, declares that the "revolutionary task of replacing capitalism" is now "outmoded" (Gibson-Graham, *The End of Capitalism* 263), and the only way to change it is by theorizing capitalism "as fragmented" (263) and not as a totality that enjoys unity and singularity (251-262). Feminist politics is, for them, essentially a "language politics" (*A Postcapitalist Politics* 54-59). Ludic Feminism is an ally of the old idealism grounded in the fantasies of a "triumph over materialism" (George Gilder, *Microcosm* 371-383) and the new pop-management theories that derive from it (Tom Peters, *Liberation Management*). All their arguments are anchored in the rejection of totality in favor of a dispersed disorganization related by a network of metaphors (*Microcosm* 370-381) aimed at a new spiritualism in which capitalism itself is not a decided reality but a nomadic "fluid" (*The End of Capitalism* 135).

Red Feminism is, among other things, an argument that capitalism does not need the oppression of women, homophobia, or racism to survive. It needs labor—cheap labor. Thus, for feminism to be a serious force in the struggle against global capitalism, it needs to be grounded in the labor theory of value, in class as the global relations of property, rather than in the "local," community (Gibson-Graham *A Postcapitalist Politics* 79-99).

Gibson-Graham, of course, are not alone in being more interested in waging "war on totality" and to "activate the differences" (Lyotard, *The Postmodern Condition* 84) than in struggling against exploitation and for socialism.

Socialism presents a quandary for Ludic Feminists. They find they can neither reject nor accept it. In response to an interviewer who says he no longer knows "what it means...to say he...is a socialist," but that he "wouldn't take any pleasure in saying that [he is] not a socialist" either, Gayatri Chakravorty Spivak says she is not so much for socialism as she is not against it: "Like you," she says, "I would not like to call myself an antisocialist" (Spivak and Plotke, "A Dialogue on Democracy" 18). Yet both agree that socialism, in some of its most fundamental aspects, is "unacceptable" (17)—because of what they and Neoliberals regard to be its "statist orientation" and "narrowly economic focus" among other reasons. Their criticism is largely a defense of ludic individualism.

Gibson-Graham, Spivak, and many other Ludic Feminists have moved a long way from the struggle to end capitalism. In fact, contemporary feminism has reached an impasse in which, as Gibson-Graham's *A Postcapitalist Politics* clearly indicates, it cannot think the future of humanity outside of capitalism. The freedom of women is now considered possible only by embracing capitalism—by accepting and working within the system rather than transforming it. This is one of the more telling aspects of Gayatri Spivak's interview on transnational resistance. Not only does she seem to readily accept "capitalism with a small 'd' development" (5)—that is, indigenous, low growth capitalism in the Southern theater, a version of "subsistence perspective" (Mies and Shiva (*Ecofeminism*; Bennholdt-Thomsen and Mies, *The Subsistence Perspective*)—but she repeatedly suggests a form of "enlightened benevolent" giving on the part of capitalist countries of the North. In other words, the post-socialist feminist's argument finally collapses into the clichés of bourgeois ethics: the "unfinishable tug-of-war" between "taking and giving," which "relates to the ethical" (14). Global philanthropy, represented as ethics, becomes the social policy of transnational feminism not only for Spivak but also for many NGOs.

Even more common is the reification of market economy in which consumption becomes the main arena of change. There is something of a North/South divide, however, around the "politics of consumption." Consumption is used in contemporary feminism and the Left, generally, as a means for displacing production and class. However, class conditions determine consumption. This is quite clear in the different ways consumption is understood in the North and the South. In the North, where liberty not poverty is the primary question, consumption is related to desire; while in the South, liberation from consumption and a voluntary simplicity are represented as the urgent response to poverty. The call for freedom from consumption, which is little more than an ahistorical and moralistic slogan, is at the heart of Mies and Shiva's micropolitics. As Mies argues, "the only alternative" to the "unending growth and profit" of the "world market system" is "a deliberate and drastic change of lifestyle, a reduction of consumption and a radical change in the North's consumer patterns" (Mies and Shiva, *Ecofeminism* 62). The authors, however, are silent on class and production. What they say is, in the end, not very different from "Just say No." It does little, if anything, to radically intervene in the structures of exploitation of capitalism. Only in the most trivial sense does social change take place through consumption. Fundamental social transformation is always a change in production and its class relations.

Contemporary capitalism increasingly tries to secure its fundamental relations of profit by setting up a global civil society that is mapped out in terms of NGOs. These are used in many ways to secure the interests of global capitalism by displacing class and marginalizing production practices through entrepreneurship and the free market. It may be necessary to make a distinction here between transnational globalization and internationalism [Ebert, *Cultural Critique (with an attitude)*]. By emphasizing transnational globalization, Ludic Feminism legitimates a transnational order based on culture, at the center of which is consumption. This is globalization in which transnationality is marked by observing that, for example, a clerk in Hong Kong listens to the same music and enjoys the same jeans and "Gap clothes" as a teacher in Rumania or a teenager in London. This new civil society is based on consumption, and the connections that it makes are connections among objects of desire. It is a civil society of commodification. In opposition to this, internationalism is based on a world historical solidarity beyond the boundaries of nationality and consumption and founded upon class and production for freedom from necessity and the end to exploitation.

Red Feminism argues against the view of globalization as a market order and a regime of consumption and for internationalism: the solidarity of all workers of the world beyond national boundaries.

Ludic Feminism "wages war" not so much against the exploitation of people by capitalism but against repressing difference. In doing so, it is quite willing, as Spivak indicates, to form alliances with "capitalism with a small 'd' development" (Spivak and Plotke 5).

What is needed is not a new "global-girdling" consumptionist feminism, but a Red Feminism. Instead of alliances based on ethics, which is a reification of individualism and individual desire(ing), a materialist international collectivity committed to emancipating women and all oppressed people from need and the exploitation of their labor needs to be constructed.

RED FEMINISM

The cultural turn and its linguistic tendencies in feminism have isolated issues of gender and sexuality from their material conditions. Red Feminism is an argument that gender and sexuality cannot be fully understood outside class relations. However, Ludic Feminism has obscured class and its relation to gender and sexuality by treating "history," "agency," "modernity," "postmodernity," "essentialism," "theory," "labor" and the "concrete" as cultural effects and as (semi-) autonomous sites of resistance as part of its claim to being a transformative practice. Culture, however, is never independent of the social relations of production, and cultural resistance, in and of itself, is not capable of transforming these relations. The most effective way to undertake such a transformation is by class struggle, which brings about "root" changes through reorganizing the relations of labor and capital and puts an end to social class. All social differences, such as gender, are effects of class—the inequality of labor. Red feminism is bringing class back to feminism. However, to do this requires rematerializing what Ludic Feminism has culturalized. We begin with:

Theory

It has become a ritual for Ludic Feminism to dissociate itself from "theory" which it regards as an abstract concern with little relevance to the actualities of gender and sexuality. Theory, in ludic discourses, is elitist (masculinist) and utopian. More specifically theory is seen as an act of "totalizing" which is synonymous in ludic circles with "totalitarianism."

Judith Butler distances herself from theory by assuming the familiar pose of "ignorance." "Not knowing" has become the mark of genuine "knowing" in Ludic Feminism, following Lacan, Zizek, and others. Butler states that "I do not understand the notion of 'theory,' and am hardly interested in being cast as its defender..." ("Imitation and Gender Insubordination," 14). Jane Gallop goes further and devotes an entire book to refashioning theory into anecdote and turning concepts (the abstract) into tropes (the concrete) (*Anecdotal Theory*).

These ludic acts of distancing from theory are not only theoretical but are also effects of a theory of theory. They put in question the idea of theory as an explanatory critique of social totality and instead privilege theory as play and as playful readings of the play of differences in sexuality, gender, and texts of culture. Theory-as-play shifts the focus of analysis away from the material social relations of production to cultural representations. In a complex move, it quietly affirms the existing social relations of production through subtle and highly nuanced transgressive readings that put cultural norms in question. Material relations remain intact while cultural representations are textualized and their founding truth is shown to be a language effect and not objective reality (which, in the process of reading, is declared an objectivity effect).

Theory-as-play focuses not on gender relations as material social relations but on a critique of their representations. It shows how, for example, what is seen as natural gender and sexuality are performativities in/of language, and marks the incoherence of their seeming coherence by teasing out the working of tropes in these representations (Butler, *Antigone's Claim; Undoing Gender*).

Red feminism approaches theory as an explanatory critique. It is fundamentally different from theory-as-play in that theory-as-play is almost exclusively a critique of representation and, therefore, understands change as changing representations through, for example, re-signification (Butler), re-metaphorization (Cornell), and re-description (Rorty). In opposition to theory-as-play, theory-as-explanation argues that representation is always and ultimately determined by the relations of labor and capital. Social change that can transform gender relations is a matter of changing the relations of gender to class relations. For theory-as-play, culture is a linguistic chain—a staging of conflicting significations. Red feminism, in contrast, regards culture as always articulated by the social relations of production. Thus culture is where people become aware of their objective class interests and fight it out. Culture, as E. P. Thompson puts it, is a "way of *struggle*" not a chain of signification ("Long Revolution" 33). Meaning, which is the focus of Ludic Feminism, is not the trajectory of nomadic signs but a social relation.

Why theory matters.

Capitalist cultural politics produces a "spontaneous" daily consciousness that perceives the social world as an assemblage of fragmented, (semi-) autonomous practices, each with its own unique and different "cultural logic." This is the view privileged in ludic theory in the name of honoring "difference." Red Feminism demonstrates that the fragmentation of the social is an effect of the alienation of labor (Marx, *Economic and Philosophic Manuscripts of 1844*). Its normalization in ludic theory (as, for example, the "body without organs") is a response to capital's need to block any understanding of social totality that brings to the surface the fundamental contradictions of the capitalist regime, namely, the representation of the unequal exchange of wages for labor power as equal. This exchange—which is the ground of all capitalist institutions, from love to education, healthcare, imperialism, and power—is mystified through cultural difference, which is valorized in Ludic Feminism.

Red theory is necessary for transforming gender relations. It provides a knowledge of social totality by which gender is grasped as class and feminism itself is rearticulated as a materialist theory: "Without revolutionary theory, there can be no revolutionary movement. This idea cannot be insisted upon too strongly at a time when the fashionable preaching of opportunism goes hand in hand with an infatuation for the narrowest forms of practical activity" (Lenin, *What Is to Be Done?* 369). Ludic eclecticism—for example in Rita Felski's *Literature after Feminism*—is a popular form of this practical opportunism now.

Agency

Any mobilization of counterhegemonic agency requires that one first theorize "agency" itself. There is a tendency in Ludic Feminism to theorize agency in a pragmatic and local frame that is located in the specificity of situational actions. In other words, Ludic Feminism argues that all effective actions have a strong local dimension—at times it even claims that this locality is a form of materiality. However, while localizing the subject, it theorizes the subject in an unhistorical and idealist fashion. It somehow assumes that the subject, by the sheer power of its spontaneous experience, can undertake transformative action. In fact, the basis of its coalition politics is this idealist, but localized, subject: a subject that can enter into negotiation with other subjects and in a collaborationist mode bring about change. Change here is always a code word for opportunistic reform. This notion of agency—local, pragmatic, reformist, and coalitionist—predominates in Left Ludic Feminism.

To say it a different way: Ludic Feminism avoids the question of class, which is the only site of historical agency. It does so by first representing class as a dated view and then proposing, as an updated position, the subject of coalition located in identity politics. It multiplies the subject and regards this to be an emancipatory act: a feminist subject, an African American, a Latino, and a Queer subject, etc. These isolated subjects are all masquerading as subjects of agency. Red Feminism argues that a productive notion of agency has to be highly critique-al of such theories of agency which, in the final analysis, substitute life-style practices for class and then recognize this class-as-lifestyle as the main axis of human praxis.

This does not mean that sexuality, gender, or race are not sites of struggle, but rather they are not autonomous spaces. Sexuality becomes a marker of social differences only in a class society. Race is the historical site of racism under capitalism where the cheap labor of the slave, the colonized, and the racially different immigrant is the source of profit. In other words although race, gender, and sexuality are indeed spaces of historical agency and sites of social struggle—*they become so because of the divisions of labor and property relations (class)*. Therefore, in a world conquered by capital the *only* historical agent is the *other of capital*: the wage-laborer. Any counter-hegemonic agency or human praxis that does not center itself along this contradiction and this class antagonism will produce agency that might make the ludic writer feel empowered and enabled but will leave the existing social practices intact. To be very clear, the route to social transformation does not pass through coalition—it is firmly centered in revolution.

Identity Politics

Identity politics puts forth an identity without class—one shaped by nomadic meanings of desire and experience. It is a subjectivity that does not put pressure on or threaten the existing social relations of labor. Even when the question of labor cannot be avoided, for example, in discussions of feminism and anti-racist struggles, labor becomes mostly a question of jobs and employment, that is to say, of income (e.g., "equal pay"). But income, in-and-of-itself, does not determine the relation of the subject of labor to the conflictual structures of labor. Income, to be more precise, can be from profit or from wages.

When the question of labor has been dealt with in Ludic Feminism or anti-racism, it has, for the most part, been reduced to how to increase the income of the subject—even the issue of domestic labor has been largely understood in terms of "unpaid labor" and income for housework. Income is a matter of consumption; class is a question of production. Rarely has feminism or anti-racism struggled against the existing labor relations based on the hegemony of capital. The few exceptions have been those historical materialist feminists and anti-racists who have engaged the class constructions of gender, race, and sexuality. But this work, especially in feminism in the 1970s and 1980s, has been largely cut off by the rise of Ludic Feminism and Left identity politics.

Ludic theory grants autonomy or at least semi-autonomy to race, gender, and sexuality and regards each in terms of its own assumed immanent logic, which is untranslatable into any other logic. The question therefore becomes HOW gender works, HOW race works, HOW, in effect, the cultural logic operates? The material logic of these relations—the question WHY gender works the way it does—is made marginal.

There is no immanent logic of race, gender, and sexuality. There is only the single, inclusive logic of production that structures all. Most feminists, anti-racists, and queer theorists have been quick to dismiss such a materialist theory by saying that the logic of labor cannot explain desire in sexuality, oppression in racism, and inequality in gender relations. However, gender, sexuality, and race become social differences only and only when they become part of the social division of labor.

Racism, contrary to Foucauldian theory, is not simply a matter of asymmetrical power relations nor is gender nor is sexuality. Homophobia is not simply oppression—the exercise of power by heterosexuals over homosexuals. Gay bashing is the articulation of violence, that is to say, the effect of power, but power cannot be understood in its own terms without inquiring into its genealogy in relation to property. Contrary to ludic theory, power is not the effect of discourse nor is it simply the immanent condition of all relations. Power is the social and political manifestation of the ownership of the means of production. In other words, power is always generated at the point of production, and its effects should also be examined in connection to the relations of production. Racism is not simply oppression (the exercise of power by whites over blacks); sexism is not simply oppression (the exercise of power mostly by men over women). It is true that racism, sexism, and homophobia are *experienced* by the subject (e.g., African American, woman, lesbian) as effects of oppression and power. If we limit our inquiry to this experiential level, we will end up simply with ethnographies of power, which would be of very limited use. If, however, we move beyond regarding racism, sexism, and homophobia as simply effects of power to understand why power is derived from ownership of the means of production, then we will be able to theorize relations of class, gender, race, and sexuality in a more historical and transformative way.

Modernism/Postmodernism

Concepts of modernism/postmodernism and modernity/postmodernity are above all spaces of contradiction: they are concepts that have been used to come to terms with the history and shifts in cultures of capitalism. Modernity is the ensemble of all the conceptual strategies—from science to painting to music to sociology to psychoanalysis—used by the modernist subject to locate itself in the contradictions between wage-labor and capital. There are no ("modernist") styles in isolation from the historical unfolding of wage-labor and capital, from laissez-faire capitalism to monopoly capitalism.

To separate modernism from postmodernism or, for that matter, modernity from postmodernity may give the illusion of conceptual clarification and historical location, but it is eventually a species of what Marx and Engels in the *German Ideology* called "combating solely the phrases of this world" (30), that is, a politics of phrases. Postmodernity's various forms—in Jameson, in Lyotard, in Butler, in Zizek—are all continuations of the attempt to understand capitalism without class. All of them are based, as we have already suggested, on the assumption that capitalism has changed—that there has been a fundamental structural change, a "break" in capitalism demanding a new set of conceptual categories to understand the impact of capitalism on culture and society. The question of (post) modernity, however, is neither one of style nor of culture, because both style and culture are eventually the outcome of the primary contradictions of capitalism. Red Feminism supersedes the well-worn categories of modernity/postmodernity, modernism/postmodernism, and their rehearsal in Habermas, Eagleton, Jameson, and Butler, by returning to the main question. And the main question is mode of production. In place of positing that capitalism has changed, it is necessary to return to the basic issue: in what way has capitalism changed? Has the capitalism of modernity really been transformed into another capitalism (that of postmodernity)—what Jameson, borrowing Ernest Mandel's phrase, calls "late capitalism"? Or does capitalism remain the same regime of exploitation—in which capitalists extract surplus labor from wage-earners. What has changed, as we have already argued, is not the fundamental factor of property relations but the way that exploitation is articulated. Capitalist ontology remains the same; only its phenomenology has been modified. It is not exploitation that has been transformed—and this is the ONLY index of the structure of change—but rather the *form* of exploitation has changed. If this simple "fact" is recognized, then the whole debate about modernity/postmodernity, modernism/postmodernism turns out to be simply a politics of phrases.

In dealing with the question of history and the place of humans in history, the determining factor should not be modernity/postmodernity but rather what cuts through the modern and postmodern and places humans in their densely layered and complex history. *The relations of humans and history are the relations of labor.*

Referentiality

Ludic theory, as we have argued, does not break free from the referent; rather it substitutes new modes and forms of reference and referentiality for those notions of the referent that have lost their historical usefulness for capitalism. To be more clear, traditional theories of the relation between language and reality (which have been the core of common notions of the referent and referentiality) were based on what might be called a "Fordist" relation of correspondence between signifier and signified. This form of referentiality was more suitable for early industrial capitalism whose main features were Taylorism in management and the assembly line in production. However, with the emergence of cybertechonologies—which have brought with them new management techniques, such as plural organization and team management; substituted the post-Taylorist flexible workplace for the old Taylorist management, and opened up the labor force to women, African Americans, Latinos, and other marginalized groups—the mode of representation based on the adequation of signifier to signified has became historically irrelevant. One of the features of the new cybertechnologies is hypertextuality and pluralization of the sign. The sign—which in Fordist industrialism worked to a very large extent on mostly a single level—has became subject to various forms of doubling and self-referentiality, the effect of which is what Baudrillard calls "simulation" and "simulacra" (*Simulacra*).

The fact that signs have become plural and the relations between signifier and signified have become relations of relays within relays does not mean the referent is lost. The referent, in response to social relations, has become plural. A new Red theory of reference is needed. In reobtaining a more socially effective referent for language, we think the referent can be retheorized through *Capital*, specifically chapter 10 of volume I, in which Marx explicates labor in the working day. In brief, the discussion of the working day provides a very effective frame for establishing a theory of reference in which language is once again put in a relation of materiality to history in the form of labor. The new theory of reference thus should be based on a labor theory of language, which shows how meaning is a social relation.

"End of Ideology"

In Left ludic theory, especially in the work of Ernesto Laclau and Chantal Mouffe, ideology is seen as undergoing a "break." In their writings, Laclau and

Mouffe, through a heavy reliance on Lacan and Althusser, have erased the materialist theory of ideology articulated in Marx and Engels's *The German Ideology* and more emphatically reiterated in Marx's *Capital*. In order to dramatize the break, they have reduced the classical Marxist theory of ideology to a simple "false consciousness" and have represented Althusserian and post-Althusserian views as groundbreaking conceptual feats. Ideology after this "break" has become a generalized representation from which no one can escape and in which everyone is condemned to live their (social) life. One of the consequences of such a notion of ideology, of course, has been its erasure of the rigid clarity of class antagonisms.

Ideology has a very specific and materialist meaning in Red Feminism. In various chapters of *Capital* I, Marx explains the process by which the worker exchanges his/her labor-power for wages. In chapter 10, he explains the precise mechanism of the working day during which the worker produces the equivalent of his wages and also surplus labor. In chapter 6, he theorizes the difference between labor and labor-power and concludes that labor-power is that particular "commodity whose use-value possesses the peculiar property of being a source of value, whose actual consumption is therefore itself an objectification of labour, hence a creation of value" (270). The exchange, he concludes, between the capitalist and the worker, is an exchange of labor-power for wages. This exchange, as we have repeatedly stated, is represented in bourgeois theory as a free, unfettered, and equal exchange. In fact, at the end of chapter 6, Marx makes a point of dwelling on this "free-trader *vulgaris*" view of the exchange of wages for labor-power and concludes that it is anything but an equal exchange: it leaves the worker, Marx notes, "like someone who has brought his own hide to market and now has nothing else to expect but—a tanning" (280).

The Red Feminist concept of ideology seeks to account for the representations of this exchange as an equal and fair exchange. This is the core of the Red theory of ideology: how the relation between wage-labor and capital is represented as free and equal when it is anything but (it is "a tanning"). False consciousness is a concept by which a materialist understanding marks the consciousness that regards this exchange to be an exchange among equals conducted in freedom. It is a false consciousness because it explains the material by the cultural (e.g. legal discourse). It thus sees the exchange as unfettered and uncoerced when, in fact, as Marx himself argues, this exchange takes place under "the silent compulsion of economic relations"—a compulsion that "sets the seal on the domination of the capitalist over the worker" (Marx, *Capital* I, 899). False consciousness is the consciousness that accepts the exchange of wages for labor-power as equal.

Essentialism

Ludic Feminism puts essentialism and anti-essentialism at the center of contemporary gender theory. This move translates social struggle and its materialist understanding into epistemology. To translate social struggle—which is always over surplus labor—into epistemology is to reiterate a Hegelian move, at the core of which is the explanation of history by ideas rather than by labor. Therefore any materialist theory that insists on the primacy of labor over ideas, the primacy of materiality over spectrality, is bound to be seen by ludic theory as essentialist. To be essentialist it seems, therefore, becomes necessary if one believes that a cultural theory must be rooted in making sense of human labor. Cultural theory accounts for the way practice is mediated through innumerable cultural series. To insist that such an accounting should always already be anti-essentialist—that is, to always only deal with specific situationalist practices—is to reify micropolitics and to cut off the relation between micropolitics and its underlying global logic of production. To put it another way, the Ludic Feminist debate on essentialism/anti-essentialism is a debate that eventually aims at severing the relation between the local and the global by positing the global as an essentialist, totalizing abstraction. Doing so blurs class lines and puts in place of class itself a series of fragmented, seemingly autonomous identities (race, gender, sexuality)—it marginalizes human solidarity, which is based on collective labor practices.

The Intellectual

The genealogy of the new intellectual begins with Foucault's statement in his interview "Truth and Power," where he contests the notion of the universal intellectual with the idea of the specific intellectual. The specific intellectual, in contrast with the universal intellectual, is one who always works on the micro-level and produces specific knowledges. She does not suffer from the illusion of any grand narratives, such as human emancipation. For Foucault it is unethical to make such grand gestures when one can engage specific issues in specific contexts. In his conversation with Gilles Deleuze, Foucault elaborates on his idea of the intellectual and intellectual practice by stating that the function of such an intellectual is essentially to enable the oppressed to find their voices and to be able to speak for themselves ("Intellectuals and Power" in *Language, Counter-Memory, Practice* 205-217).

The notion of the specific intellectual has undergone a number of redescriptions in contemporary theory, and one of its more widely recognized forms is the idea of the new "public intellectual." Public intellectual is a person who is able to bridge the gap between academic disciplinary knowledge and larger public concerns. Both Foucault and contemporary theorists, who, in response to him, have focused on the public intellectual, are of course influenced by Gramsci and his notion of the role of the intellectual. The question of what constitutes an intellectual is not simply a matter of fixing an identity or prescribing a set of tasks (as Foucault, Gramsci, and contemporary theorists all do). The role of the intellectual is most clearly marked by the Marxist tradition in which the intellectual is the person whose work is aimed at producing a theoretical consciousness. Theoretical consciousness in Red Feminism draws on Lenin's argument and its restatement by Lukacs. Lenin regards this function—the production of a theoretical consciousness—to be so important that he writes, and we repeat his words again: "without revolutionary theory there can be no revolutionary movement. This idea cannot be insisted upon too strongly at a time when the fashionable preaching of opportunism goes hand in hand with an infatuation for the narrowest forms of practical activity" (*What Is to Be Done?*). Lenin eliminates the artificial difference between the worker and the theorist. He argues that the worker is a theorist. Gramsci, of course, echoes Lenin when he talks about the role of common sense and philosophers. It is useful to quote at some length from Lenin's statement in *What Is to Be Done?* because it clarifies the relation of the theorist and society, and the intellectual and the proletariat; it also sheds further light on the question of theory itself. Lenin writes:

> This does not mean, of course, that the workers have no part in creating a [socialist] ideology. They take part, however, not as workers but as socialist theoreticians, as Proudhons and Weitlings; in other words, they take part only when they are able, and to the extent that they are able, more or less, to acquire the knowledge of their age and develop that knowledge. But in order that working men [and women] may succeed in this more often, every effort must be made to raise the level of the consciousness of the workers in general; it is necessary that the workers do not confine themselves to the artificially restricted limits of 'literature for workers' but that they learn to an increasing degree to master general literature [i.e., theory]. It would be even truer to say 'are not confined,' instead of 'do not confine themselves,' because the workers themselves wish to read and do read all that is written for the intelligentsia, and only a few (bad) intellectuals believe that it is enough 'for workers' to be told a few things about factory conditions and to have repeated to them over and over again what has long been known. (384)

Invoking Lenin's concept of the theorist-intellectual here may seem quite counter-productive given the extreme antagonism of Ludic Feminism to Lenin. It is thus necessary to address the relation of feminists, sexual theorists, and Lenin. For bourgeois feminists, Lenin is the symbol of patriarchal oppression. This common antagonistic disdain for Lenin comes both from the widespread demonization of Lenin in bourgeois ideology and from a very basic and widely circulated misreading of Lenin by feminists—most notably of two of his letters to Inessa Armand (Lenin, *On the Emancipation of Women*). These letters are commonly taken as proof of Lenin's oppressive patriarchal and puritanical indifference to women's concerns and sexuality: specifically the issue of "freedom of love" and his critique of feminist intellectual work—Armand's proposed pamphlet for proletarian women on love, marriage, and the family. But such a reading of Lenin is quite ahistorical—it ignores the actual historical situation of Armand's work and Lenin's writing—and is blind to the fundamental erasure of class and bourgeois bias in feminism itself. Lenin is raising here the very basic question of class that feminists and sexual theorists, in nearly all their forms, have largely suppressed—what Lenin calls the "objective logic of class relations in affairs of love" (*On the Emancipation of Women* 39) as opposed to "subjectively" understanding "love" and sexuality as Armand and most feminists propose. Lenin critiques the notion of "freedom of love" by enumerating a series of materialist understandings of the concept against the prevalent bourgeois notions dominant in the "top-prominent classes" (38-39). He then argues that it will be the dominant bourgeois ideology that will prevail, resulting in misinterpretations of Armand's argument. In short he is not suppressing Armand's project but critique-ally supporting it and, through a patient pedagogy, attempting to help Armand protect her project from the reality of bourgeois distortions that will "tear out of it phrases...[to] misinterpret you" (42)—that is, misinterpret the class distinctions and objective class realities of the conditions of sexuality as well as misinterpret the material needs of proletariat women for *sexuality free from material constraints*, as opposed to bourgeois demands for the *exercise of desire free from moral constraints*. This is a distinction that continues to be lost on feminist and sexual theorists today, and the continued antagonism toward Lenin's patient, but critique-al, pedagogy says considerably more about feminist intellectuals' own inability to engage critique and the class limits of their own understanding than it does about Lenin.

Totality

In ludic theory, totality is either rejected in the name of pragmatism (which is sometimes called "practice") or equated with totalization. Pragmatism's operational definition of truth—"the true is the name of whatever proves itself to be good in the way of belief, and good, too, for definite, assignable reasons" (James, "What Pragmatism Means" 59)—makes it difficult to argue for a postcapitalist society that would be inclusive in its economic access and its political and cultural freedoms. In other words, a pragmatist approach to truth will return us back to a misrecognition of the relation of labor and capital. A pragmatist approach would have to say that such a relation is acceptable and truthful because, on the practical level, it works. It seems to us that any theorization of totality has to be very critique-al of such pragmatism and its various versions in ludic theory. The version of pragmatism that we just paraphrased is one developed most notably by Richard Rorty. But Lyotard also puts forth a version of pragmatist social theory in his *Just Gaming* and the *Differend*. Lyotard's social theory takes as its point of departure his closing statement in *The Postmodern Condition*: "Let us wage a war on totality; let us be witnesses to the unpresentable" (82). Lyotardian anti-totality social theory eventually leads to a notion of indeterminate judgment, that is to say, a judgment that is not based on any foundation of truth. This Lyotardian theory becomes the paradigm of ludic jurisprudence in which justice is separated from truth because truth is by definition a totalization, and justice has to attend to the "differend," the "unpresentable," and the untranslatable.

In contrast to a Rortyian anti-totality pragmatism and the Lyotardian "differend" (judgment without truth), a more productive way to deal with totality is found in Lukacs's writings. (One needs to be very careful, however, about Lukacs's Hegelian idealism.) Lukacs argues, in *History and Class Consciousness*, that bourgeois thought is by its very constitution detotalized and detotalizing: it is a fragmentary mode of knowing. This fragmentary consciousness he calls "false consciousness." Our point here is not to critique the way Lukacs theorizes false consciousness but rather to focus on what he proposes as the *other* of bourgeois thought: "the relation to society as a whole" (51). Totality is far from being an abstraction that forgets about specific differences—it is a concrete recognition of the diverse relations that produce the social. However as Lukacs insists and, of course, as Marx himself has indicated in his "Introduction" to the *Grundrisse*, the concrete of the totality is not identical with the empirical and the individual; the concrete "is a concentration of many determinations, hence a unity of the diverse" (101). For Lukacs it is only by arriving at knowledge of society as a whole that it "becomes possible to infer the thoughts and feelings which men would have in a particular situation if they were able to assess both it and the interests arising from it in their impact on immediate action and on the whole structure of society" (*History and Class Consciousness* 51).

In theorizing social totality, Red Feminism shows how the particularities of gender and sexuality are specificities of class relations—as are the differences in feminism. The binary of Ludic and Red Feminism is the rearticulation of the class binary, which is itself the outcome of the social relations of production.

11

The Class Logic of *A Beautiful Mind*

TEACHING UN-THINKING

The film *A Beautiful Mind* is a public lesson teaching viewers to mistrust analytical explanations of social life and instead rely on their own unique sensual experiences of the world as the threshold of reality. Experiences, they are taught, are too complex and subtle to be analyzed by the vulgarities of reason and concepts. These post-rational subjects are what the State needs to carry out its pro-capital policies without being questioned. Capitalism itself, of course, relies on such subjects of sensuality to boost consumption of its commodities, which more and more are manufactured not to meet the needs of ordinary people (because of the low profit margins) but to give ecstatic sensual pleasures to the shoppers of desire. The film constructs these anti-analytical subjects of "lived" experience through a series of inversions, all of which derive from the inversion of class into aesthetic desire.

By obstructing conceptual critique—because, as the protagonist John Nash says, it is only in the "mysterious equation of love that any logical reasons can be found"—the film isolates the aesthetic (the "beautiful") from social labor relations and works to produce a working class that "looks upon the requirements" of capitalism "as a self-evident natural law." Nash is an anti-teacher who denounces teaching on the first day of class and tells students that by allowing themselves to be taught what they are taught, they are wasting their time. They should free themselves from pedagogy, which he sees as a means for regulating the creative mind. He teaches by (ostensibly) not teaching so that what is taught feels "experienced" by students as their own inner insights, as knowledge that is immediate and flows from within, and not an abstract mediation imposed from without. Although he denounces pedagogy, he does not leave the classroom. In an a-teacherly mode he a-teaches a patterning of the world—"I am attempting to isolate pattern recurrences"—that represents Communists (who, Nash claims, perniciously encode their sinister messages in the obviousness of the pages of daily papers) as the enemy of the people and capitalism as the spontaneous expression of freedom.

In its excesses of meanings, whether in portraying Nash's obsession with hidden messages in periodicals or his formal theories ("game theory"), the film depicts the meaning of the word as floating signs that cannot be tied to any particular referent. The underlying logic of capital and how it works in daily life are too complex and fluid to be grasped by thinking. The world should thus be experienced sensually in its immediate concreteness, that is, aesthetically. Nash is more specific: his journeys through "the physical, metaphysical, delusional and back" have taught him that what matters is the concrete of the body not the abstract of concept.

In the film the thinker is turned into a charming freak, and thinking itself is exemplified in terms of comical acts and weird affectations that no mature person would want to be associated with. In fact, the film provides a viewing stance for the mature ("ordinary") person from which he can look with amusement at thinking and the antics of the thinker, feel superior to the thinker, and consequently affirm his own non-thinking as a sign of his grown-up judiciousness. Non-thinking becomes a sign not only of normalcy but also of ethical decency, because thinking is represented in the film as a trait of irresponsible fantasies and anti-social arrogance. Only a "sick" person, like John Nash, the mathematician-protagonist of *A Beautiful Mind*, who is certifiably "insane," according to the film, can move beyond the pragmatic particularities of daily life, such as giving his baby a bath, and become engrossed in thick thinking—looking for the structural logic of everything everywhere. Thinking is unsafe, and those who teach thinking are aesthetically suspect: they have lost their sense of humor and have become like the "mad Nash" objects of fun. By making thinking odd and even ridiculous, the film educates viewers into an anti-thinking pragmatism that is mistrustful of anything that goes beyond the common sense. The film, however, is not interested in the viewer as an individual—although individualism is an integral part of its theory of social life—but as the multitude of actual or potential workers. *A Beautiful Mind* is a training film for global capital and recruiting people into a workforce that sees capitalism as part of the natural world.

The importance that *A Beautiful Mind* gives to pragmatism and its emphasis on a mistrust of thinking is oblique and quite subtle, but the film's narrative curve makes this point more overtly. It follows Nash's fall into the abstractions of thinking, which are made to overlap and blend with his "madness" and personal pain, and his subsequent re-emergence into concrete, practical everyday life, which is equated with "sanity" and fulfillment in life. *A Beautiful Mind* is represented as a love story (a point that is reemphasized in Nash's Nobel Prize speech), but it is actually a lesson in the dangers of (abstract) thinking. Love is the immersion in life, thinking is a reduction of it. The film is an attempt to seduce viewers into the pleasures of the sensuous concreteness of details in daily life, such as (not) liking the taste of mayonnaise in a sandwich, which, the film implies, are lost in the larger abstract structures of the social. To put it more directly, *A Beautiful Mind* is not simply a "particular" work of art; it is more a "common" lesson taught by contemporary class politics to obscure the working of global capital and the way it resists human equality and freedom from necessity. Nash's story in *A Beautiful Mind* is ultimately a class story, and class stories are cultural idioms that suspend critique so that the social relations of labor and inequality are constantly validated and secured as aesthetic values in the resulting conceptual vacuum.

The film portrays Nash, the thinker, as miserable for most of his life because he has had "two helpings of brain, but only half a heart." He is abnormal according to the film. Normal, the film assumes, is anchored in a feeling heart. The warning against thinking is particularly necessary for training the viewer as a member of a "normal" labor force: a labor force of the heart, one that is, highly skilled, well educated, and compassionate, but decidedly suspicious of thinking.

To be more precise, capitalism, like any mode of production, produces a workforce that is not just technically skilled but, equally important, regards capitalism as a natural part of the natural world. When capitalism is perceived as natural, its practices, such as the extraction of surplus labor from the workers, are also seen as natural. Exploitation, in other words, is concealed by its naturalness, and capital's hegemony over labor is secured naturally. If naturalizing its practices requires that capitalism train a new labor force by discarding or inventing new feelings and different forms of thinking, then it will do just that by deploying its cultural apparatuses such as film. *A Beautiful Mind* is a film that a-teaches new modes of (non)thinking and tutors the viewer-worker in the lessons of spontaneity.

Thinking and feeling, contrary to the common sense, are not mysterious effects of an even more mysterious human "consciousness." As Marx writes, "it is not the consciousness of men that determines their existence, but their social existence that determines their consciousness" (*A Contribution to the Critique of Political Economy* 21). Thinking and feeling are social, practical skills that humans develop in the material production of their objective world and out of the material need to relate and work with others. Ideas, feelings, concepts, and even consciousness itself are effects of these material activities and are expanded or limited by the social conditions (e.g., class relations) under which they take place. Capitalism—the regime now in power—uses its division of labor to reduce the range of feelings and ideas and limit them to those that are profit-producing. Material practices are controlled—those that respond to human needs outside of commodification are done away with—and with them human freedom is restricted. These limits are, of course, historical and will be broken under socialism which sets humans free from the arbitrary limits (set by profit) placed on their thinking and feelings. Socialism is the zone of freedom from necessity—the end of forced labor.

Pedagogy is the practice of human energy as an end in itself and not as a preparation for entering the workforce of profit. *A Beautiful Mind* deploys an a-pedagogy aimed at training people for the capitalist workforce.

How, under capital, are certain kinds of feelings and modes of thinking made obsolete or represented as outdated and residual?

In its accumulation of profit, capitalism needs a workplace that is free from friction and contestation: a post-union workplace of efficiency and impersonality, in which the personal feelings of workers such as their (class) anger place. In the highly competitive workplace of global capitalism, anger has become an inconvenient emotion. It is, therefore, represented in the cultural turn (as we discussed in our analysis of Gibson-Graham's theories of class affects in chapter one) as a residue of early industrial capitalism (the time of the unions) and as limiting efficiency in the workplace of the "new economy."

Since anger has become a problem for the frictionless production of profit, capitalist cultural apparatuses have developed techniques to eliminate or at least suspend and conceal it. Through cosmetic surgery, for instance, certain facial muscles are paralyzed by injecting them with the neurotoxin that causes botulism, thus preventing those facial movements that are culturally identified as expressions of anger and contentiousness. Working people are taught not to be angry and with Botox are made physically incapable of showing their anger, even if they remain angry. In the capitalist labor force, anger is being abolished from the array of "natural" emotions, and the human is redefined without it. This is, of course, done obliquely—not by declaring that anger has become historically burdensome for managerial tasks, but by presenting its absence as a cutting-edge lifestyle that separates the "old" (and useless) from the "new" potentialities, what Gibson-Graham call the "emotions" of "present possibilities," such as "surprise, pride and satisfaction, daily enjoyment" (Gibson-Graham et al., *Class and Its Others* 15). The requirements of profit are represented as spontaneous affects and aestheticized; the eradication of anger (a work requirement) is subtly marketed as the removal of "ugly" wrinkles (the aesthetic). A new worker physique (and with it a novel subjectivity) is manufactured which is free from lines (anger) and wrinkles. Not only does Botox itself produce a profit for its manufacturer, but it also serves to manufacture the cultural trait that capital needs for a smooth, efficient, and friction-free workplace. Very soon no one in the workplace will be able to look angry because, in the everyday logic of capital, anger is becoming the remnant of an obsolete subjectivity. Those who feel anger (or worse "look" angry) are marginal to the evolving new subjectivities without affective legacies.

It is not only "anger" that is regarded to be a legacy feature of a dead past in the class politics of capitalism. Thinking, too, has become a legacy element of a dated and dysfunctional subjectivity. This is the ideological importance of *A Beautiful Mind* as it attempts to overwrite history with ideology. By thinking we do not mean the commonsensical and pragmatic calculations that are necessary for performing everyday tasks from the manipulation of machines in the workplace to the choice of a diet or raising children. Rather, we mean explanatory, critique-al, and root questioning of social and cultural arrangements and their consequences for daily practices. The new global labor force is not only post-anger it is also post-thinking (Ebert and Zavarzadeh, *Hypohumanities*). Unlike expressions of emotion that can be brutally suspended by paralyzing the physical means of expression, marginalizing thinking is a much more complex process and needs more sustained and sophisticated cultural pedagogies.

THE BARGAINING PROBLEM AND CONSCIOUSNESS SKILLS

For the labor force to do its "job," it not only has to be highly proficient technically but also have a particular set of "consciousness skills," which teach workers how to interpret the world in such a way as to legitimate capitalism. Legitimization is always indirectly through "personal" beliefs that are constructed so as to seem to have come from "within" (for example, belief in hard work, private property, a power hierarchy, love, common sense, the importance of family, and reverence for the military). These consciousness skills are taught with varying degrees of subtlety in the schools, media, church, the family, and other channels of ideology. They are grounded in the dominant philosophy which is itself an expression of the social relations of production. The ultimate ideological goal of these consciousness skills is to position workers—through the innumerable cultural intermediaries of films, novels, music, and sports—in such a relation to the social world that they accept the exchange of their wages for their labor-power as an equal and fair exchange and, in effect, consent to their own exploitation, seeing it as a "natural" part of the exchange. This ideological recognition means, among other things, accepting a high level of joblessness and, with it, lack of health care, lower standards of living, substandard education, poor diet, and lack of pensions. For capital, workers need to be taught how to interpret their own work and to see the higher and higher levels of their own exploitation as positive social improvements. However, what is taught has to be taught so subtly and obliquely it is perceived not as a moralizing harangue from outside but as what one has her-himself actually experienced and felt inside. This cultural repositioning of workers is one of the roles ideology plays in normalizing the way things are, and it is carried out quite effectively in popular culture in the entertaining, witty, and ironic idioms of novels, Internet writings, films, and other media spectacles such as sports and parades.

Film appears to be a direct and sensuous mode of communication, one that does not rely heavily on local languages; it has thus become, more than other cultural products, the active medium for repositioning workers across languages and national borders. It teaches viewers the most essential part of an overall outlook for the workforce: to be highly suspicious of thinking, especially analytical and critical thinking ("abstractions"), and instead to always trust common sense—which is actually not thinking at all but a cultural congealing of feelings. Through these consciousness skills, viewer-workers learn to rationalize the new levels of their own exploitation as the result of natural "productivity" and to see their own increasing lack of access to living wages, education, health care, and pensions as necessary sacrifices in order for businesses to remain competitive in the global market so that they can keep their jobs. Workers, in other words, are persuaded by films and other media events to not perceive a "cause-and-effect" relation between the worsening of their own living conditions and the excessive increases and constant improvement in their bosses' living conditions (the compensation for the average CEO is now over 400 times more than the wages of the average worker). In fact the very logic of "cause and effect," as we have pointed out before, is now routinely ridiculed and represented as a sign of outdated thinking in such popular films as *The Matrix*. Viewers are taught to regard social processes as contingent, noncausal, and ultimately uncertain and indeterminate. These are the "new" maxims of capitalism and its class politics. Contemporary films teach viewers how to look at each case in social life individually (for example, getting laid off) and how to disconnect it from other cases and from the underlying logic that shapes all social cases.

In their writings, Deleuze and Guattari *(A Thousand Plateaus)* and the culture critics who have taken up their views have popularized these ideas with considerable success (e.g., Kennedy, *Deleuze and Cinema: The Aesthetics of Sensation*; Massumi, *Parables for the Virtual*). These "subversive" ideas are now an integral part of the canon of capitalist class politics. Along these lines, *A Beautiful Mind* marginalizes critique (explanation) and represents the affective as a life-energizing response that frees spontaneous experience and overcomes the social rationalities (the anti-aesthetic) blocking desires. Critique-al thinking is dismissed as totalization, as closure, while segregating, fragmentary and case-by-case observations are legitimated as the open and non-closural meditations of social life. Thinking, it is assumed, isolates you from social life and turns you into an anti-social being. A crucial scene in *A Beautiful Mind* makes sure viewers get the point. In this scene Nash is shown engrossed in finding the hidden codes by which the enemies of freedom (Communists) are communicating. A young girl, who turns out to be the niece of his (imaginary) college roommate, approaches him and asks what he is doing. Nash replies, "I am attempting to isolate pattern recurrences within periodicals over time." His reply strikes Marcee as odd: "You talk funny Mr. Nash," and she annotates the oddity by telling Nash that although (according to her uncle) he may be smart, he does not seem to be "very nice." "Niceness"—reconciliation—is the axis of bourgeois life. To be "nice," one has to move beyond argument, critique, and reason and become affective.

These popular views teach workers to be pragmatic in their outlook, to consider issues on a case-by-case basis, and to aggressively oppose generalizations because, they are told, generalizations erase differences, and differences are what make individuals what they are—free to desire and choose. The actual reason both popular culture (*Dead Poet's Society*) and theory (Fish, *The Trouble with Principle*) warn people against "generalization" is that "generalization" connects cases and, in effect, shows that their differences are systematic, not strange or eccentric; it draws conclusions about their underlying logic. Films such as *A Beautiful Mind* teach people to always focus on their own limited self-interest ("keeping my job"), and reject all such considerations as their relations to others—as exemplified in their class collectivity and shared objective interests—as abstract (meaning hollow) "principles." Here too *A Beautiful Mind* acts not as a unique work of art (there is no such thing) but as a banal repetition of capitalist slogans in which cynicism and self-interest are depicted as marks of savviness.

THE PLEASURE OF DETAILS

The mainstream readings of *A Beautiful Mind*—as a serious or even entertaining story about the complicated life of a genius/"mad" mathematician, as an artistic exploration of the shadowy recesses of the human mind, or (as its director has implied) as a probing of "mental illness"—are all subtle and diversionary interpretations that cover up the underlying idea of the film, which is that serious, abstract thinking brings with it a disruption of "normal" life and leads to madness. The film is an ideological tract that represents the life of John Nash as an allegory of the thinking-life in ruins. It frightens viewers away from the kind of root thinking that might enable them to move beyond distracting daily details and help them to grasp the social logic governing their lives, because those who discover the dominant social logic patterning their lives will also become aware that the limits imposed on their lives are not natural and inevitable but arbitrary and thus open to change. *A Beautiful Mind* warns against such changes and emphasizes the comfort of stability, the security of the common sense, and the calming pleasure of feelings that come not from thinking but from affective responsibility (which is the other name for "loyalty" without critique).

Alicia is also an a-pedagogue of affect: she interprets the world as an excess of desire whose "infinity" cannot be measured by objective means, as she describes "love" to Nash. The affective obscures all objective realities such as class in the pulsations of the body without organs, that is, undifferentiated difference (Deleuze and Guattari, *A Thousand Plateaus*). She feels and a-teaches the world as a circling, circulation of "élan vital"—the ineffable creativity and positive energy that animate living (Bergson, *Creative Evolution*). The affective is, for her, the basis of ethics and all obligations as she explains to an old college friend of Nash's while she is pushing the baby carriage during one of her walks. Life, according to her lesson, is a matter of heart.

Interrogative thinking, as Nash's life makes clear, is transgressive. It unpeels the layers of cultural representations and always (at times in spite of itself) unmasks the dominant conventions and marks the objective, whether in mathematics or in tax laws, NAFTA's "chapter 11," "human rights," fashion, or other social, legal, and cultural regimes. Interrogative thinking is not simply a matter of mind but a historical response to developing material tasks; it is always at odds with the existing social relations, which use cultural conventions and habits to normalize the dominant patterns of power and keep people in their place in the economic order of ownership (class). Habits and convention—what Hayek and other proponents of capitalism call "tradition" (*The Fatal Conceit*) and regard to be the source of knowledge and civilization itself—have, of course, always been deployed to marginalize interrogative thinking. Normalizing "what exists" and obscuring "what *could* exist" are acts of ideology, but like all such ideological moves, they are slippery and unstable. In *A Beautiful Mind* shock therapy is used in support of ideology to restore the normal because the normal is constantly in need of cultural reinforcements like *A Beautiful Mind*, not only for re-validation but also to re-absorb the ideological remainder.

The film legitimates social privileges by representing them as innate. For instance, it depicts Nash's privileged status by attributing it to his native intelligence: a natural gift that, according to the film, obviously cannot be modified and, therefore, rightfully creates inequality among people. The film cunningly obscures the fact that his privileged position is in fact social: if his "native" intelligence was not useful in re-producing the existing social relations, Nash would simply be treated as a freak preoccupied with outlandish abstractions—as he is indeed at one period in his life. But Nash's intelligence produces knowledge that is highly useful for protecting the established social relations. His contributions to game theory ("The Bargaining Problem" but especially his "Equilibrium Points in N-Person Games") update the obsolete theories of the market by getting rid of Adam Smith's metaphysics of "the invisible hand," which had associated the workings of the market with divine powers and, therefore, put it under suspicion in the contemporary world. Nash's mathematical arguments renovate the theory of the market, now making its operations worldly and democratic. His theory explains the logic of the free market in scientific, post-theological terms that give fresh credence to the ideology of world equality in the market. Game theory represents the market as the effect of individual interests and personal choices and not as the result of some "invisible" force. Nash, in other words, provides the basis for a theory of the market appropriate for a mature capitalism that justifies injustice by democratic (in)equality. Also by working in the top-secret RAND Institute, he actively contributes to the fight against anti-capitalism and works in opposition to socialist forces during the Cold War. It is not his natural gift of intelligence that makes him privileged, it is the social uses of that intelligence.

Thinking—abstract thinking, not what Marx and Engels call "philosophic charlatanry"—is unsettling because it is always a response to the emerging but still hidden material conditions of production, and therefore its consequences cannot always be managed by ideology. This is what makes (abstract) thinking so threatening to the ruling order. Galileo's thoughts are perhaps the most well-known example: the newly emerging material conditions of production made his thinking possible and necessary, but the existing (feudal) social relations of production, through the ideological apparatuses of church and state, represented his thinking as heresy. The role of ideology is to contain all thinking that cannot be recuperated for governing the dominant economic order; it does so by representing the abstractions of thinking as "apart from real history," as if they were self-produced and autonomous bearers of truth.

Materialist abstract thinking "reflect[s] nature more deeply, truly and completely" (Lenin, *Philosophical Notebooks*) and thus contests the ruling ideas— "the ideal expression of the dominant material relations, the dominant material relations grasped as ideas" (Marx and Engels, *The German Ideology*). The surest way for ideology to contain such critique is to manufacture a cynical culture impatience with interrogative thinking and to represent thinkers as arrogant, weird, and ultimately (socially) immature people who have no understanding of the concrete problems of daily life and "real" people. But ideology itself is fraught with contradictions. In Nash's own case, for example—in spite of his acting, in effect, as an agent of capital at the height of Cold-War nationalism—he actually sympathized with the idea of a world government and also transgressed the strict boundaries of gender binaries and the codes of family and marriage. The worrying unpredictability of thinking eventually costs Nash his security clearance. Ideology tries to harness thinking, and when it fails, it discredits the thinker as psychotic and subjects him to shock "therapy."

Thinking, although always done by a person, is actually not personal: one thinks what is historically possible to think because thinking is not a goal in itself but aims at dealing with social tasks. And the task itself, as Marx explains, "arises only when the material conditions for its solution already exist or are at least in the course of formation" (*A Contribution to the Critique of Political Economy* 21). But in order to keep the instituted social relations of production intact, ideological representations depict the emerging forces of history—new tasks—as ephemeral, as a vogue, as passing trends and aberrations of the normal, and/or, paradoxically, as outdated and thus irrelevant. Consequently, the thinkers who think the new tasks, depending on how radical their conclusions, are marked as either a part of a lunatic fringe or, if their ideas are not too uprooting but simply disturbing, as charming, weird persons whom one should humor but not take seriously. Even though ideology is highly resourceful, it always fails, in the long run because the historical conditions producing thinkable thoughts are formed not by chance but out of necessity. They will surface eventually and challenge the dominant institutions obstructing progress toward universal equal access to resources.

A Beautiful Mind seduces the viewer by substituting sensuous photography for complex analysis. The film bypasses any critique of the issues and normalizes the governing ideology in an orgy of sentimentality focused on Nash's relationship to Alicia, who is represented as pure spirituality and love. Although the film's ostensible subject is John Nash's life—his schizophrenia, genius, love, and involvement in postwar science-state relations—its importance is in the way it acts, reflexively, as a documentary on the way people have been so deeply alienated from thinking and radically isolated from thinkers. In a manner similar to Fish's *The Trouble with Principle*, the film valorizes this alienation as part of a no-nonsense approach to life, as characteristic of authenticity and the common person's good sense, which are part of being a regular, pragmatic American with two feet firmly on the ground ("You talk funny Mr. Nash"). This ground is the ground of ideology. By locating viewers in an imaginary common sense and practicality, the film distances them from a critique-al examination of social institutions and cultural assumptions about property, love, work, wages, equality, and privilege. The viewer is positioned to identify with Marcee, who is after all an imaginary "reality"—more a code of verisimilitude and simulation.

The film does so by portraying thinking as creepy and scary. In the period of his intense preoccupation with codes, Nash becomes so chillingly frightening that Alicia asks him whether he is going to hurt her. His answer is terrifying because he says he is not sure whether he is safe to be with. Life, real ("ordinary") life, is depicted in *A Beautiful Mind* as a dense and complicated web of details, and surprising, joyful, unrepeatable little events, whose complexities and unpredictability do not yield themselves to solutions or even to explanations. Explanations are produced through thinking, which is by its nature abstract and generalizing and thus a violation of the differences in the concrete. Local complexities, according to the film, constitute the real life of real people and will have to be approached pragmatically. Pragmatism always wins: the "realities" of life finally beat Nash and his arrogant thinking, forcing him to beg for a teaching job to support himself. The film offers a funny but damning parody of the way abstract logic deals with details and events. In an early scene in the film Nash is shown in a bar, an ordinary social situation, where he tries to do an ordinary social act—to talk to a woman in whom he seems interested. But the language of his "conversation" is so out of place that he comes across not just as an awkward man but as a pathetic person. The abstractions of thinking have made him unfit for social life. Everyday decisions, the film implies, have to be made on a case-by-case basis not by reference to some theoretical "principle" or abstract logic that is said to govern them. Details, according to *A Beautiful Mind,* are everything.

In contemporary cultural discussions, the writings of such authors as Fish, Rorty, and others fetishize details in the name of "real life" and block understanding of the world historical relations through which details actually become details and the particular is made particular. Principles are thus seen as ungroundable acts of desire, as simply rhetoric wrapped up as rational conclusions. In *A Beautiful Mind*, principles are portrayed as simplifications and acts of intellectual violence that avoid the local complications of daily details. Abstractions—the outcome of thinking when it moves beyond details and examines their underlying logic—are viewed as negations of the layered, knotty, and complicated "real" life. Details are seen not only as sites where real life is lived, but also as ethical moments that are points of resistance against "totality" (the code word in contemporary bourgeois theory for "totalitarianism"). The slogan that ties together these various anti-thinking strands in recent cultural debates is, of course, Lyotard's "Let us wage a war on totality; let us be witness to the unrepresentable; let us activate the differences and save the honor of the name" (*The Postmodern Condition* 82). The "name" is the singular, the particular; it diverts critical attention away from the abstract logic of the relations that make the particular concrete possible, because the singular is always "a rich totality of many determinations and relations" (Marx, *Grundrisse* 100). In *A Beautiful Mind*, the concrete, the detail, the singular, is independent of all relations. Relating the singular detail to other details, making connections that will help unearth the structure of totality is represented as robbing life of its normal, naturally beautiful spontaneity.

Chapter 11

ONLY IN THE MYSTERIOUS EQUATION OF LOVE

The film teaches that the good life is a decent life, and defines a decent life as "normal"—namely, a life that is based on the practical and the particular. Life is small, local stories (feeding the baby, playing in the park, doing the laundry, teaching a class, closing a deal) and not a grand narrative (freedom from necessity). Grand narratives such as mathematical patterning or a theory of human freedom are abstractions, and abstractions are represented as unethical: they render the singular as determined by the general (totality). Such an analytical move is itself seen as nothing short of totalitarianism. The decent person should, therefore, be quite suspicious of any disregard for concrete experience and the practicalities of life (giving a baby a bath), because any such indifference will inevitably lead to weirdness and, more terrifyingly, to personal disasters and unhappiness as John Nash's experiences clearly show.

The deep alienation of people from thinking—moving beyond the details—and their amused distancing of themselves from the thinker are the consequences of contemporary labor relations, which are legitimated by education. It is quite telling, therefore, that in the film a group of Ivy League (Princeton University) students are seen mocking and teasing Nash as weird. Thinking requires concentration and focusing, and it inevitably leads one to root questioning. Contemporary pedagogy in America is not about root questioning or even preparing people for fairly thoughtful living. Instead it has become a packaging of people, training them in profit-bearing skills so that they can negotiate their labor in the competitive workplace. This is one reason why Nash's life of total focus is made to look so bizarre. Most people live a diffused life, and the culture of capital affirms that diffusion by treating it as a sign of authenticity and openness, generosity of interests, and nuanced complexity. A good life under capitalism is a life of culturally cultivated distractions, and this is another way of saying that most people live their lives from the outside. They watch themselves going through the motions, making decisions and getting things done, but have no clue why they are doing what they are doing, other than they have to do what they do in order to go on. "Living" is not itself a subject of critical analysis, it is just "done." Nash's (imaginary) old roommate at Princeton tells him that he is "at Harvard now" but still teaching D. H. Lawrence's books. Nash's comment is that he should get himself "new books."

A Beautiful Mind teaches that (abstract) "thinking" is for "them" not "us." The film tutors "us" on how to accept our place in the contemporary social divisions of labor and the existing social class structure. It does this through a rather complicated story in which viewers learn to regard their own estrangement from thinking as normal and desirable. Only "they," who are different from "us," can afford to "think" and sidestep the details, because "we" are busy living "real" lives.

Normalization of the class differences between "them" and "us" is one of the major themes of the film. Nash is represented as living in a world quite separate from the one in which "we" live. It is a world free from mundane daily worries. The photography of the film reinforces the enclosed sense and security of the world in which Nash lives. Princeton is depicted as a sheltered place through recurring images of arches and arcades that give it a womb-like feeling of protection.

And yet, as in all ideological lessons, there is a remainder here too—something that slips the clutches of ideology. *A Beautiful Mind*, in spite of its stern warnings, cannot completely repress the deep yearning of people to get beyond the passing details of their lives into a core of purpose. In other words, the film bears inside itself a strong yearning for thinking that is at odds with the film's overt claims about spontaneity, non-thinking, and the priority of "event" and experience over "structure" and concept.

This ideological fissure is most visible in the film when after many years of torment, caused by what the film represents as his almost psychotic thinking about numbers, John Nash finally re-emerges from his psychosis/ madness/ genius. He becomes normal. His return to normalcy, however, creates an ideological crisis in the film. On the one hand, *A Beautiful Mind* affirms the naturalness and the decency of the normal, but the now normal Nash is reduced to a non-entity: an unremarkable, dull person; a boring and quite ordinary ("bad") pedagogue of beginning students, in charge of basic knowledge. He is now commonsensical, decent, mired in details and free from his obsession with numbers, patterns, structures, and other abstractions. Viewers may like the normal John and be reassured by his new banality, but they secretly yearn for the abnormal and transgressive thinker, Nash, the root knower.

The urge for the extraordinary—in a world made ordinary and homogenized by the demands of profit and all the mid-writings and middling practices repressing the bold and the irregular—is not an eccentric desire for the sublime, a utopian dreaming, or a mere cultural adventurism for "difference." It is simply the need to have a broad understanding of one's life. The ordinary is the effect of flattening the daily—the subjugation of this need for understanding and connection because it conflicts with the fragmented life produced and privileged by capitalism as authenticity and spontaneity. To have an inclusive understanding of one's life requires thinking and finding a relationship among everyday details. But in ideology this is considered to be putting "analysis" ("theory") ahead of "living"; it is a move that is seen as injurious to the joy of life and a sign of cold, calculating reason. *A Beautiful Mind* equates reason with arrogance and represents it as the cause of human unhappiness. It represents itself as biography, which is valorized in bourgeois ideology as the authentic genre of writing "life without theory." Theory—thinking abstractly and beyond the plethora of details—consequently is assumed to be totalitarian because of its interest in underlying patterns.

Far from being natural, however, the ordinary is manufactured ideologically. It is thus a symptom of the deep estrangement of people from the differences making up their life: the ordinary imposes the structure that is necessary for capital on people's life and results in the suppression of their unlikeliness.

The ordinary is alienation made normal and marketed as friendliness, graciousness, and decency itself.

The ordinary is an inversion of difference in an inverted world. It is the logic of getting along in this world, but, like religion, as Marx argues, it is also a protest against this world which oppresses the urge to think beyond the routine. No ordinary person wants to be ordinary. Yet, each one remains ordinary in order to survive under capitalism, whose main strategy for maximizing profit is the merging of people, fusing of cultures, and hybridizing all that is different and at odds with its work protocols, while at the same time formally advocating difference and singularity. In the world repressed by the ordinary, capital manufactures "difference" and advertises it (through its philosophers, cultural writers, and theologians) as a resistance to in-difference. This formulaic difference, which is now the ground of anti-materialist social movements that displace "class" with sexuality, race, gender, and lifestyle, is a cultural move to highlight "details" ("identity") and obscure structure (labor). It is a homogenization camouflaged as heterogeneity. The demand for abolition of the ordinary, as the illusory common ground among people, is a demand for the recognition of the real common ground—the *transgressive,* which, as Marx argues in *Critique of the Gotha Programme,* can go beyond the rule of capital and point to a new social order. *A Beautiful Mind* is the apotheosis of the ordinary, of alienated alterity.

But in a class society, singularity and difference are permitted only for the privileged. In her biography of Nash, Sylvia Nassar writes that elite scientists and mathematicians provide a special place for eccentricity and outrageousness. Nash was among the most outrageous and eccentric; he acted with an almost total disregard for what keeps ordinary people in their place—social graces and self-effacement. The more outrageous Nash became, the more space was given to him. This is the space denied to workers who are confined in the ordinary.

This ideological incoherence is reproduced in *A Beautiful Mind.* In a compromise with this cultural longing for transgressive thinking and getting, at least, a glimpse of a core of meaning in social life, the film offers common sense as serious thinking. Between non-thinking and hyper-thinking, the film opens a middle space for common sense. But common sense has nothing to do with thinking. It is a lump of sentimentality and congealed banalities for safe living. In *A Beautiful Mind* this is represented as deep thinking.

In order to show the silliness of root thinking and affirm the validity of the common sense, the film deliberately confuses thinking with positivism and then satirizes it as shallow living. In a discourse on love, Nash, who has arrived late for his date with Alicia and is in a hurry to find out about her emotions toward himself, wonders whether love can be proven. Instead of a "vulgar" direct response, Alicia asks him how big the universe is. Nash's response is routine: the universe is infinite.

> Alicia: "How do you know for sure?"
> Nash: "I don't, I just believe it."
> Alicia: "It is the same with love, I guess."

The thinker is reduced to a believer, and by implication all thoughts are represented as a species of faith—a form of desire, a writing.

Common sense is the cultural accumulation of practical conclusions from experience. It is a staged transparency and a mediated immediacy. What makes common sense so culturally valuable for capitalism is that it naturalizes the displacement of any analysis of the structures of daily life in favor of anecdotes, that is, examples and testimonies of the behavior of individuals, for these are supposed to negate the systematicity of social life and its institutions. But without such structural knowledge, it will never be clear who actually benefits from the pervasive practices of class inequality.

To make common sense the real ground of (non)thinking for the viewer and discourage the desire for more interrogative thinking, *A Beautiful Mind* uses a set of very powerful rhetorical strategies. It identifies common sense with Alicia (Nash's wife). Alicia's stunning beauty, her selflessness (which foregrounds the thinker's selfishness), and her emotional exuberance (in contrast with Nash's cold rationality) seduce the audience into this "mid-thinking"—common sense—that is the object of mid-writing in bourgeois cultural politics. Jennifer Connelly's agile, warm, and layered performance is in sharp contrast with Russell Crowe's acting, which follows a culturally prescribed semiotics of genius: facial tics, accents, awkward gestures, and walking funny. This contrast enhances the visual rhetoric of the film in which the thinker is always "off," at a distance from real life. Alicia is represented as elemental while Nash is depicted as accidental. Alicia lives; Nash thinks about patterns of living. "Mid-thinking"—common sense—represents life as a series of singular, individual events and practical decisions. Alicia, unlike Nash, has a firm grasp of practicalities and particularities; she is a grown-up, while Nash, until his return to the normal, behaves like an adolescent.

The most important role of capitalist cultural politics is the valorization in different class discourses of the *affective* (the other of class consciousness) from the sentimental to the empathic, and at times, even self-reflexive irony. *A Beautiful Mind* does not leave anything to chance when it comes to conveying its fundamental point. It therefore ends, somewhat awkwardly, with Nash's emotional delivery of his Nobel Prize speech.

In the speech he renounces the abstract and announces his acceptance of cultural affectivities (symbolized by "love") as the greatest discovery of his life. The scientist as critique-al thinker is thus humiliated by acting out the pop-culture scenarios of sentimentality.

He begins his speech by stating that he had always believed in logic and reason: "But after a lifetime of such pursuit, my quest has taken me to the physical, metaphysical, delusional and back." The result of this demanding journey is the acknowledgment of the banal cultural maxim that "there is only in the mysterious equation of love that any logical reasons can be found."

All knowledge, according to the "new" Nash, is desire—a form of writing whose meaning is always in deferment because, like love, it is a mystery. The mystery of love, however, unlike that of knowledge, is not abstract but a spontaneous affect—its mystery is tangible and "real." Nash, the monster ("thinker"), becomes human by wallowing in the sentimental ("common sense").

Binaries

Part 3

Class Ecstasies of the Culture of Capital

12

A "Potlatch of Signs"—Burning, Consuming, Wasting

THE POST AS CULTURAL TRICKSTERING

In the affluent North, it is commonly believed that we are in a "post" society (as in the post production culture of consumption) in which "there are no rules only choices....Everyone can be anyone" by desiring commodities that symbolize one's identity (Ewen and Ewen, *Channels of Desire* 250).

The "post" is the most recent name for this space of longing—a cultural space in which capitalism constantly makes itself new and offers an improved version of itself by appealing to the desire of consumers. "New-ing" strategies, like the post, are essential to capital because they allow capitalism to represent its structural contradictions as cutting-edge reality. The post is both a theory of history and a rhetoric for consumption. One main purpose in claiming that this is a new stage of history is to persuade people to acquire new commodities (e.g., computers, iPhones, etc.) which we are all told are necessary to fully live in the new times and not be left behind. As a theory of history, the post frees capitalism from its past—which is marked by exploitation, racism, colonialism, and homophobia—and allows it to represent itself as a new enlightened capitalism.

This self-representation of capital is legitimated through cultural institutions that are themselves extensions of the existing social relations. Contrary to the common view of the cultural turn as subversive, it has been an especially effective means of legitimating capital. Cultural theory regards itself to be a progressive practice focused on cultural justice and the plurality and freedom of meanings. As we discussed in chapter one, it has used the radical languages of the Left to provide concepts such as the post and interpretive strategies such as deconstruction, but the net effect of these discourses has been to "new" very old-style capitalist exploitation as new forms of liberation (Hall, "The Meaning of New Times"). The cultural turn, in short, has helped capital represent as cutting-edge reality the very practices it needs to continue its exploitation of labor and increase its rate of profit. For instance, if it needs the freedom to transfer capital across national boundaries without any resistance from local states, cultural theory provides the language, rhetoric, and analytical strategies in which capital's needs are represented as the end of the nation-state and the emergence of a new transnational form of co-existence (Hardt and Negri, *Empire*).

The concept of the post as the activity of "new-ing" has been remarkably effective over the last several decades even though the term *postmodern* is no longer in force in cultural vocabularies. Although the term has been historically exhausted and now is being replaced by newer concepts such as globalization (Thomas Friedman, *The World Is Flat*), the underlying assumptions of postmodernism—for example, that we live in a society that is post class, post ideological, post queer, post colonial, and above all post production and therefore consumptionist—still structure the arguments and analyses of dominant cultural theory (as is demonstrated by the work of such diverse theorists as Baudrillard, *La Société de consommation*, translated in part as "Consumer Society"; Cohen and Rutsky, eds., *Consumption in an Age of Information*; Drucker, *Post-Capitalist Society*; Zizek, *The Sublime Object of Ideology*; Pakulski and Waters, *The Death of Class*).

The post is an integral part of capitalist cultural politics because it uses a forward-looking rhetoric to characterize capitalism's material contradictions (which arise out of the production processes) as "old" and translate them into a "new" cultural progress. For example, the inequality of the exchange of labor-power for wages is the source of surplus labor and takes place under the "silent compulsion of economic relations" that set "the seal of the domination of the capitalist over the worker" (Marx, *Capital* I, 899). But this exploitation is obscured by such post concepts as "immaterial labor," which blurs the line between productive and unproductive labor, while the invention of the "multitude," to take another example, suspends class relations altogether (Hardt and Negri, *Labor of Dionysus; Multitude*). Capitalism's coercive practices, which deny humans their basic freedom, are instead represented as an ultimate form of liberty and freedom in a progressive, open democracy that is radically different from all other forms of society in human history.

The contradictions of capitalism, however, cannot be easily solved in the post or any other cultural discourse because these antagonisms are produced through production practices and thus elude cultural solutions. Instead, these contradictions are reflected in the construction of any "new" cultural concepts, particularly those that aim at explaining (away) capitalism's conflicts.

In order to boost its rate of profit by increasing consumption, capital needs a radically new cultural reality to seduce consumers into purchasing the latest commodities as a way of "new-ing" their identities. At the same time, it needs to maintain the old material logic that actually legitimates wage-labor. It needs, in other words, a new culture of consumption but the old logic of private property and what it is tied to, namely, hard work, family, democracy, and obedience to the State. The effectivity of the post is that it covers over these contradictions by constructing a middle-space that is neither new nor old but is somewhere in-between and represents this middle in-between-ness as the place of liberty, openness, and subtle complexities that cannot be understood by a simple linearity or the usual temporality. The old, therefore, is constructed as connected to the new not in the material sense that history is always historical and therefore part of the on going class struggles, but in the sense that new and old are a difference in which one is not distinct from the other. This difference is not *between* them (as in any old-fashioned differentiation) but *within* them, and this is the twist by which the material contradictions are obscured and represented as new cultural subtleties as we discussed in chapter two. The "difference within" is seen as so destabilizing that one cannot find a stable identity to be referred to as new and another as old. The "difference between" (the difference produced by the material relations of labor) is "flattened" (in the sense that Friedman uses the term in his *The World Is Flat*), and displaced by the cultural differences within.

The post, in the contemporary cultural turn, is both beyond and within history: it is not a simple "after" that linearly succeeds the "before" as a chronological effect but a flat event that is not "a state of things, something that could serve as a referent for a proposition" (Foucault, *Language, Counter-Memory, Practice* 173). It is the proof that "the forces operating in history are not controlled by destiny or regulative mechanisms" (154). In other words, history is seen as the flat movement of the "singular randomness of events" (154), and as such, it is autonomous, for example, from the laws of motion of the capitalist system as a whole. The post is thus an instance of the "singularity of events outside of any monotonous finality" (139). It is to be understood in its own exceptional terms.

Another way of putting this is to say that the logic of the post is the logic of "textuality"—as Derrida says, "There is nothing outside of the text" (*Of Grammatology* 158). The post is a re-inscription by which the "difference within" the old and the new are activated (Derrida, *Margins of Philosophy* 3-27). Difference within (what Derrida calls *différance*) breaks the boundaries of identities (the difference *between* two fixed identities such as old and new) and renders any distinction between the two impossible. The old is different within itself, and its self-difference makes it impossible for it to be differentiated from other identities such as the new, which is equally at odds with itself and, therefore, more different from itself than from any entity outside itself. History, too, is self-fractured and not self-identical. It thus cannot be new or old but is always a version of its own self-difference, which Jean-François Lyotard calls "re-writing" ("Rewriting Modernity"). Postmodernity, in this view, is simply a re-writing of modernity not its opposite. This is another way of saying the new is not the binary opposite of the old, rather the two are in a permanent in-between-ness. By removing "difference between," the post discredits all binary opposites: "There is no binary…opposition between rulers and ruled at the root of power relations" (Foucault, *The History of Sexuality* I, 94). In a post history there are no differences between the oppressed and oppressors because their differences within put them at odds with themselves and do not allow them to have a self-same identity that places them in opposition to any other identity. The history produced by the post is a history that makes human agency (class struggles based on the binaries of the workers and owners) outdated. It replaces *agency*—the purposeful activity of class struggle—with *desire*—the pleasure-full performativities of consumption (Harris, *From Class Struggle to the Politics of Pleasure*). Consumption is the master concept in contemporary cultural theory.

The post notion of *différance* is said to have supplanted "class" as the dynamics of history (Marx and Engels, *Manifesto of the Communist Party* 40). In institutional cultural theory, therefore, it is self-evident that the "cultural turn" has activated the self-difference within capitalism as a result of which its practices have shifted from Fordism to post-Fordism (Hall, "The Meaning of New Times"). This change, to use some of Hall's words in describing the "cultural turn," is not "a total rupture" caused by class struggles or other changes in labor relations ("The Centrality of Culture: Notes on the Cultural Revolutions of Our Time"). Rather, it is a "reconfiguration" of the elements within the system from "production" to "consumption" brought about by their own self-difference. The regulated (production) society of modernity is displaced by the de-regulated (consumption) society of the post. In the society of difference, to repeat, "there are no rules only choices" and consequently "everyone can be anyone" (Ewen and Ewen, 250).

The cultural turn fetishizes the differences of Fordism and post-Fordism. In the Fordist (modernist) regime, consumption is almost always purely functional—it is a practice aimed at meeting needs. In post-Fordism (postmodernism), consumption loses its pure functionality and becomes a matter of affect, feeling, desire, and longing. Consumption, in other words, becomes a matter of wants not needs; it acts as a symbolic communication of the identity of the consumer, who by choosing a commodity chooses a lifestyle that provides an identity.

In the post society, consumption is believed to have become the "final frontier" of "identity and subjectivity" (Hall, "The Centrality of Culture" 217-220) because capitalism is thought to change through self-difference and to no longer be a purely economic organization but a cultural articulation of post subjectivities (identities). In post capitalism, culture becomes central to everything, or as the former CEO of IBM, Lou Gerstner, puts it, taking a position identical with Hall, "'culture' isn't just one aspect of the game—it is the game" (*The Fast Company Weblog,* July 2005, http://blog.fastcompany.com/archives/2005/07/27/leading_ideas_culture_drives_success.html). Consumption in post capitalism is no longer a functional and passive reception of mass-produced commodities manufactured on the assembly line but an active, self-fashioning performativity. Through the creative pleasure of goods—particularly, the affective sensuality of objects of desire—the subject experiences its distinctiveness and acquires its autonomy (i.e., free individuality) from the order of economics and becomes a post class cultural agent.

The cultural turn's idea of identity achieved through consumption is at odds with the modernist notion of identity obtained through production. Unlike the modernist identity which is said to have been fixed by class relations (as if class is ahistorical and not dialectical relations), the post identity is represented as contingent, fluid, and nomadic. It is said to shift with new choices of commodities of consumption and therefore is not stable in the way that modernist identity is said to be. It is important to note here that the post identity is not shaped from outside, namely by purchasing commodities. Such a view would locate the source of identity in the commodity and thus outside the subject, becoming a new mode of determinism—determinism by objects. The ideological goal of post identity is to turn the modernist subject—which it regards to have been misrecognized as the subject of class and thus determined from its outside—into a self-determining subject of the body, whose immanent desires shape the trajectory of its actions.

In his "I Shop Therefore I Know that I Am: The Metaphysical Basis of Modern Consumerism," Colin Campbell rejects the theory of the subject that argues "People are what they purchase" (Ritzer et al., "Theories of Consumption" 413). Instead, he contends that "the real location of our identity is to be found in our reaction to products, not in the products themselves" (32). In other words, identity is produced by the affective response of the subject to the commodity. This response derives from the subject's immanent desires and not from the outside object. The subject is, thus, seen as autonomous from the object and as pure subjectivity. Campbell, following such thinkers as Foucault (*History of Sexuality*), Luce Irigaray (*This Sex Which Is Not One*) and Lacan (*Ecrits*), situates this pure subjectivity in the sensual pleasures of the subject. In doing so, he reproduces a post subject that is different from the Cartesian subject of the mind but, nevertheless, like the Cartesian subject, is also a subject whose subjectivity is formed by forces within and not outside it. In support of his argument, Campbell analyzes "personal ads" sections of newspapers and magazines and concludes that:

> Now what I find especially interesting about these ads is that the individuals concerned appear to be defining themselves—that is specifying what they see as their essential identity—almost exclusively in terms of their *tastes*. That is to say in terms of their distinctive profile of wants and desires. ("I Shop" 31)

In this post story, what inscribes the singularity of a person is the affective experience of the aesthetic: an individual's "tastes in music, literature, the arts, food and drink" (31). Campbell argues this is so because taste (i.e., the sensual concrete) defines "us more clearly than anything else." When it comes to the "crucial issue of our 'real' identity," we think we are most authentically defined by "our desires" (31). The "real me," therefore, is to be found in "our special mix or combination of tastes. This is where we are most likely to feel that our uniqueness as individuals—our individuality—actually resides" (31).

The driving force of the subject of taste is pleasure, which in cultural theory is represented as a transgressive act. By consuming commodities, the post subject of desire is seen as going against the social norms that inhibit joy and urge work, encourage seriousness and oppose bliss. In doing so, the subject is viewed as breaking social regulations and enacting its own cultural autonomy. Acts of pleasures are thought to be blows striking at the capitalist cultural conventions that naturalize the social order by restricting the desires of individuals. The pleasures of consumption, therefore, are said to be "guilty pleasures"—"guilty" because they go against social regulations—and when practiced will break the norms of work, thus transforming capitalism into a culture of freedom, joy, and justice.

Through a notion of pleasure that enables the subject to go beyond social rules, cultural theory produces a spontaneous subject whose practices are propelled by its own immanent desires and who is skeptical of reason, history, and conceptual explanation. Instead of explaining the world (which presupposes causality and rationality), the post subject merely interprets the world affectively and relates to it through its own desires. Spontaneity, with its aroma of naturalness, is a necessary feature of the subject for capital because without spontaneity the subject might question the rationality of its desires and be persuaded against impulsively acting on desires through shopping. To produce a spontaneous subject of consumption, post theory returns the subject to experience even though, in its formal discourses, post theory deconstructs experience as part of an outdated metaphysics. Through taste, the post in the cultural turn reproduces the subject of experience who acts affectively and spontaneously and thus rebels against the calculative logic of the administrative reason of capital. The post subject, to put it differently, revives experience through taste (the aesthetic) but posits the aesthetic itself as a resistance against capital (Berube, ed., *The Aesthetics of Cultural Studies*), which it constructs as the grim regime of work (Hardt and Negri, *Multitude*).

In spite of the innumerable differences in the details of the various post stories, identity is always represented as the effect of the sensual, the body, taste, and the practical. These stories, in other words, are stories valorizing the concrete and marginalizing the abstract, which they mark as remote, unreliable, and elitist. By equating the concrete with the real and the real with lived experience (individual taste), post theory gives free rein to ideology because: "This 'lived' experience is not *given*, given by a pure 'reality,' but the spontaneous 'lived experience' of ideology in its particular relation to the real" (Althusser, *Lenin and Philosophy* 223).

To block such a demystification of experience, the cultural turn teaches that "There is no ideology and never has been" (Deleuze and Guattari, *A Thousand Plateaus* 4). The theory of the end of ideology is itself an ideology whose goal is training a new labor force for capital. It is a labor force that is blissfully caught up in the ecstasies of tastes and the sensualities of commodities and their local details; it is thus diverted away from understanding the logic of history that actually shapes these ecstatic details. Narratives of consuming identities are the central lesson of a general cultural pedagogy that teaches working people not to trust the abstract and to rely for their understanding of reality only on the concrete, which is itself ultimately the trope of commodities. Consequently, the post labor force is becoming a labor force that cannot see beyond the densities of concrete commodities and is, therefore, unable to understand the abstract structures of history. The mistrust of the abstract (structure) limits the conceptual knowledge that people need to grasp the logic of history in order to change it. Concrete anecdotes of consumption supplant a world-historical comprehension and obscure the "silent compulsion of economic relations" that actually "sets the seal on the domination of the capitalist over the worker" (Marx, *Capital* I, 899).

Post production identity masks the coercive relations of capital with labor behind the stories of sensuality, body, and the voluptuous joys of consumption. It argues that class difference no longer determines consumption but instead "class difference is constructed through consumption" (MacKay, ed., *Consumption and Everyday Life* 5).

FLÂNEUR IN THE SHOPPING MALL

The "body without organs" (Deleuze and Guattari, *Anti-Oedipus: Capitalism and Schizophrenia* 9-16; *A Thousand Plateaus* 149-166) is one of the many names by which the spontaneous subject is fetishized in the contemporary cultural turn. The discourse of the "body without organs" posits the subject as the subject of absolute intensities of desire before these intensities are distributed and thus diminished in various organs. It understands the subject as the site of the glorious flow of pleasures without distinctions—difference without being differentiated. "The body without organs," like the idea of consumption as a channel of desire, is essentially a mystical conception whose origins are in the writings of Henri Bergson (*Creative Evolution*) and his idea of "*élan vital*" (life force). This numinous view of the subject is popularized through desire theories of consumption in which shopping, as April Lane Benson puts it, is not "about buying, it is about *being*" (*I Shop Therefore I Am*, 502).

In producing a spontaneous subject whose desires (not class conditions) form its identity and practices, the cultural turn generates both a theory of subjectivity and also an epistemology of the spontaneous that extends the logic of acquiring individual identity and meaning through (consuming) desire to be access to "truth" itself. Truth, like individual identity, is represented as being an effect of the desire of the spontaneous subject who is not only the one who knows what it "wants" but also the only judge of what is true. Like its desires, its truth is singular and different from the truths of others because its wants are different from other desiring subjects. Shopping is not only a way of being but also a way of knowing.

In his essay, "I Shop Therefore I Know That I am," Collin Campbell argues that shopping is the basis of a (reassuring) individual identity. He regards what we have called the epistemology of desire to be a consumerist epistemology (33-34) and argues that it is simply an adjunct of a consumerist ontology that he describes as "emanationist or idealist ontology, or theory of reality" and believes that such an ontology "provides the foundation for modern consumerism" (37). Campbell perceives the consumerist ontology to be an "emotional ontology" (35) and writes that in such an ontology the real is itself "equated with intensity of experience" (35). An "emotional ontology," according to Campbell, is an ontology in which "the true judge of whether something is real or not is taken to be its power to arouse an emotional response" in the subject (35). The real is like a commodity: the more intense our emotional response to it the more real it seems. Since our identity is produced by our response to the commodity, the stronger our response to the commodity, the more real it makes our being ("identity") and the firmer our grip on reality becomes.

For the spontaneous subject, the real is intense, new experience, and, therefore, subjective (sensory and sensual) reactions and not objective (material and historical) relations are the means by which we know the world. In such an ontology, reason and conceptuality, which provide an analytics of the objective, are treated as an outdated legacy of the Enlightenment. Reality itself is thought to be a pragmatic matter constructed by what Lyotard calls "language games" (*Just Gaming*) or "phrases" (*The Differend*) that are contingent and nomadic. In this ontology the world is assumed to be an affect that we cannot speak and can only experience: "one cannot find the words" (13). The theory of the real as an unrepresentable experience-affect (88-91) is closely affiliated with an equally affective epistemology in which the subject is always the absolute authority of truth. Truth, in other words, is not what is learned—through reason and by means of conceptual analysis—about the objective world and its practices. Instead, to quote Campbell again, "it is established in the same manner as the existence of wants; that is through a scrutiny of one's internal emotional states" (34). In consumerist theory "truth" is always treated with suspiciousness (Derrida, *The Ear of the Other* 3-38). There is always a "greater desire to experience the real than to know the true" (Campbell 35), and the real is itself "equated with intensity of experience" (36).

Campbell's interpretation of the relation of commodities, consumption and reality is basically an idealist one; he seems to assume that theory produces reality (38-39). His view of a "fundamentally idealist and emanationist ontology" (38) underlying modern consumerism obscures rather than explains reality. This "foundational" ontology, we argue, is itself constructed through the social division of labor; it is a way of legitimating on the cultural level what are the actual objective and material labor relations. The consumptionist view of identity and meaning is not the effect of a consumer onto-epistemology but, is instead, a theory of reality needed by capital to justify its exploitative relation with labor.

Consumptionist ontology is constructed to legitimate an objective class interest. Capitalist cultural politics "represent consumption as a site of identity and meaning" (Stuart Hall, "The Centrality of Culture") in order to normalize an idealist view of identity. This valorizing of consumption over production in such idealist theories leads to an interiorist and spiritualist view of reality—one that depicts the world itself as an effect of the consciousness and desires of the consumer. Consuming subjects are lead to believe that they not only (re-)create themselves and change their personal realities by acquiring ever new identities through shopping, but that they can also change the world through the intense experiences of consumption that make them obtain some commodities and disregard others. After all, the world, according to consumerist ontology, is made of the objects and experiences desired by consumers. Thus consumers are seen as creating new realities and changing the world through their desires. This notion that consuming desires (not class struggles) transform the world is part of the popular and activist common sense of the Left in which culture (not labor) is believed to be the arena of social change and consumption is its dynamics (Canclini, *Consumers and Citizens*). In the consumptionist ontology, culture is everything. The economic is simply a meaning created by the subject's cultural practices of consumption: production is dead and labor is displaced by pleasure. However, what is actually produced in response to the demanding desires of consumers is itself part of class relations and the logic of profit. The demands of the desiring poor ("needs") are never fulfilled because their fulfillment does not offer the same return on investments. The desires that are fulfilled and are said to be transformative of the world are the desires of the class in command, and the new realities brought about by these desires are also the realities of this class.

This confluence of consumptionist ideas—in which consumers transform the world; reality is the effect of the play of differences of desires and thus autonomous from the historical social relations of production; capital is an activating of self-difference that transforms it from a mode of production to a mode of consumption; and the subject is refashioned, shifting from a producer of commodities to a *flaneur* in the shopping mall (Benjamin, *The Arcades Project*)—is exemplary of the ways in which the contemporary cultural turn has provided a diversity of subtle concepts and interpretive strategies to legitimate the unsubtle practices of capital. To say, as Baudrillard, Hall, Deleuze, Lyotard, and others have said, that the desires of the subject of consumption construct its identity and, furthermore, that these desires are autonomous from the material conditions of class and social conditions of labor is to construct an epistemo-ontology that fulfills the economic needs of capital. Post capitalism increases its profits through a pleasurable and, thus, ceaseless consumption of commodities, services, and experiences by consumers. At the same time that the cultural turn represents the subject of the pleasures of consumption as a free cultural agent, it depicts history not as the place where people make their collective destiny but as "a number of errors and fantasies" (Nietzsche, *Human, All Too Human,* 16, 24) that move haphazardly and by chance. In other words, according to a consumptionist epistemology, there is no use in the autonomous cultural agent attempting to understand and change history because history's truth is the truth of chance-full desire, and any attempt to grasp chance gives rise to the risk of an even greater chance. The post subject of pleasure is free only to re-narrate small anecdotes about its own pleasures. It cannot make history, so it is told, because the grand narratives of history have disappeared in the complexities of the *alea*—chance. The subject of desire is free, but its freedom is vacuous.

These consumption theories of identity and similar post stories are constitutive of the contemporary cultural turn which has been a particularly effective ally of capital. Unlike the mainstream neoliberal backing of capitalism, which has become routine and its class bias evident, the cultural turn defends capitalism from the Left. It uses a progressive rhetoric to criticize some of the specific practices of capitalism, such as racism and sexism, but leaves intact the structure of labor relations—the extraction of surplus labor. Under the guise of criticizing and opposing capitalism, as we discussed in chapter one, it actually offers a "progressive" Left reformist program that in the end legitimates capitalism as the only system of economic and social organization of human societies.

Cultural theory justifies its reformist support of capitalism by claiming that in order to change the social world, one must focus on specific aspects of everyday life—for instance education, health care, the environment—and offer specific solutions to problems. The goal of reformism, in Marx's words, is to obscure the fact that exploitation under capitalism is universal and systemic. The cultural turn thus lists "particular wrongs" that can be addressed by "particular rights" (Marx, "A Contribution to the Critique of Hegel's Philosophy of Right. Introduction" 256). In the language of the Left, cultural theory depicts the "all-sided" material social contradictions of capitalism as isolated "particular wrongs" (e.g., racism) of an otherwise democratic system of equality, liberty, and openness, thereby legitimating the system of wage labor.

As part of this reformist project, cultural theory represents practices that actually strengthen capital as if they were transformative practices to change it. For example, it portrays acts of consumption as acts of resistance—obscuring how these practices actually help maintain capitalism and its production relations, which underlie all its institutions, from prisons to racism (Yudice, *The Expediency of Culture*, Regan, *The Politics of Pleasure: Aesthetics and Cultural Theory*; Probyn, *Carnal Appetites: FoodSexIdentities*; McRobbie, *In the Culture Society: Art, Fashion and Popular Music*).

NOT MAKING BUT "MAKING DO"

In starting with distribution and consumption, the cultural turn begins with what Lindsey German calls the "outcome of an unequal class society" (*A Question of Class* 14). Inequalities are developed at the point of production through the social division of labor and cannot be overcome in the places of distribution. Consumption is always consuming what is already produced—which is another way of saying that consumption is always the effect of social relations of production. The cultural turn is a fatalistic, regressive, and clearly anti-egalitarian theory in which people are turned into active agents against their own objective class interests. But it rewrites itself as a grand narrative of redemption in which, "consumption is no longer victimization by the culture or irrational conformity to mass society but is a play of heterogeneity, a disruptive intervention in the smooth operation of the system" (Poster, "The Question of Agency: Michel de Certeau and the History of Consumerism" 103). This inverting representation, which converts the economic into the cultural and portrays the regressive as progressive, is itself a cultural effect of the material social relations of capital against worker.

The theory of consumption as an art of agency and resistance is in actuality a pedagogy of quietism teaching people to accept the existing social relations and live within the limits imposed by capital. It is, to use de Certeau's favorite term, the practice of "making do" (*The Practice of Everyday Life* 29), which is one reason it so fatalistic: it puts up with the "constraining order" (30) brought about by wage-labor and tries to survive within it. It is a theory of agency in which the agent is no longer a maker of history but a cultural trickster who uses a variety of devices to maneuver his way through exploitative conditions and legitimize his accommodating practices as resistance. But this is a fake agency and a fake resistance because it takes the existing social "constraints" as given—almost like natural phenomena—and its main beneficiary is the system which it ostensibly resists.

The ruling ideas about consumption, which are the ideas of the ruling classes, are turned into a truth that goes without saying. De Certeau's highly popular salvational metanarrative of everyday life, for example, portrays consumption as a "different kind of production" (de Certeau, *The Practice of Everyday Life* 31). This faith-based narrative, which is saturated in mystical overtones (de Certeau, *The Mystic Fable*), is renarrated by de Certeau's annotators and other recent writers who have developed its various subplots, such as the story that the consumer is an activist citizen whose consumption behavior changes the state and social relations of production (notably Canclini, *Consumers and Citizens*, as well as Mackay, ed., *Consumption and Everyday Life,* and Yudice, *The Expediency of Culture: Uses of Culture in the Global Era*).

In this grand narrative, consumption and shopping are treated as creative and magical readerly-writerly activities that produce cultural meanings and individual identities (Chartier, "Laborers and Voyagers: From the Text to the Reader"; Falk and Campbell, ed., *The Shopping Experience*). It becomes a textware whose "speech potential is not affected by economics" (Fiske, *Understanding Popular Culture* 34) and is a "festive energizing of the body" (Baudrillard, *The Mirror of Production* 44). Consumption theory and the cultural turn that popularizes it have increasingly become sites for mapping these festivals of the body (Elizabeth Grosz, *Volatile Bodies*; Angela McRobbie, *Postmodernism and Popular Culture*; bell hooks, "Power to the Pussy"). To prove its progressiveness, the cultural turn devotes most of its analytical energies to demonstrating how "every act of consumption is an act of cultural production, for consumption is always the production of meaning" (Fiske, *Understanding Popular Culture* 35). However, these readings produce "new" cultural meanings by suppressing the political economy of production in favor of a *poetics* of consumption or what de Certeau calls *poiesis*—"invention"—which in post theory is the life force of a faith-based individualism freed from class and the social division of labor by the sheer intensity of spontaneous desire.

De Certeau's theory of consumption as *poiesis* is, like Heidegger's theory of technology ("The Question Concerning Technology"), a faith-based theory that erases material production (in which capital reproduces itself) and instead represents consumption as a spiritual act (mind-made invention) for acquiring individuality (identity) in resistance to capitalism. He does so by making a distinction between "strategies" and "tactics" (*The Practice of Everyday Life* 34-

39). The capitalist city, according to him, consists of "places" (shopping malls, for instance) from which the agents of power (such as businesses) control the "other" (consumers) through various "strategies." For de Certeau, "strategy" is the

> calculation (or manipulation) of power relationships that become possible as soon as a subject with will and power (a business, an army, a city, a scientific institution) can be isolated. It postulates a *place* that can be delimited as its *own* and serve as the base from which relations with an *exteriority* composed of targets or threats (customers or competitors, enemies, the country surrounding the city, objectives and objects of research, etc.) can be managed. (36)

Consumers, on the other hand, do not have a "place" of their own. They are itinerants, nomads, wanderers who walk between places. Using the inventive "art of being in between" (30) and making up "tactics"—tricks and subterfuges—they introduce heterogeneity into the homogeneous city and resist its power. "Tactics" are the "tricks" that consumers use against "strategies" of power. "A *tactic*," de Certeau writes, "is a calculated action determined by the absence of a proper locus....The space of a tactic is the space of the other. Thus it must play on and with a terrain imposed on it and organized by the law of a foreign power.... a tactic is an art of the weak" (37).

The trope of the "weak" is the grounding notion of power in faith-based consumptionist theory. It is essentially a post version of mystico-religious quietism ("Blessed are the meek: for they shall inherit the earth" Matthew 5:5) that instructs the weak (the consumer) to accept the existing material relations and use the spiritual power of the mind to invent ways of surviving within these relations for now because later "his seed shall inherit the earth" (Psalms 25:13). The "later," of course, never comes. The power of the consumer ("the meek")—which is the basis for the "new times" notion that production has ended and we have entered the era of a new post capitalism of consumption—turns out to not be a transformative power but rather the tolerance of power through compliance, passivity, and a patient, meek, and timid submissiveness that guarantees the continuation of the dominant relations of labor and capital. Since this passive acceptance is done through active consumption, the submission to power is represented as a resistance to it. This reversal, which is rooted in the inversion of the relation of the material and the cultural in "new times" (Lyotard, "On the Strength of the Weak" 204-212), is at the core of a faith-based cultural politics of consumption.

"Progressive" writers have deployed it as a marker of difference between the culture of Fordism and that of post-Fordism and as a new paradigm of social transformation. Quoting "Soft and weak overcome hard and strong" from the *Tao Te Ching*, for example, Geoff Mulgan uses the engineering tropes of "strong power" and "weak power" (references to the large and small quantities of energy relative to the processes they control) to associate "hard power" with manual labor and "weak power" with mental work. He uses his tropes as the basis of a typology for (post)modern technologies: machineries of the Fordist regime use "strong power" while those of post-Fordism use "weak power." The "weak" has displaced the "strong" in the post-al moment in the cultural turn. "A parallel transformation," he maintains, is taking place in the organization of the social which is causing a "deep structural change" in capitalism ("The Power of the Weak" 347). The passage from the *Tao Te Ching* also implies that the "path" (*tao*) taken by the cultural turn is the way the universe functions—the natural path.

In the Foucauldian theory that underlies various consumptionist claims on the power of the weak/consumer, power is assumed to be autonomous from the relations of production and property. Therefore, power is theorized as a diffuse practice that is post class and as such equally available in all sites of the social to everyone: "power is everywhere...because it comes from everywhere" (*History of Sexuality* I, 93). But power, contrary to Foucault's logic, is an extension of property which is the congealed alienated labor appropriated by capital. The source of power, in short, is labor. Under capitalism where labor is appropriated by capital, power resides with the property owners who control the means of production. Power, contrary to Foucault's culturalist theories, is always an effect of labor (in the form of property). In capitalist societies where material relations (of property) divide people into unequal opposites (binaries) of owners and workers, Foucault's idea of power performs the ideological task of obscuring this class division and instead produces the fantasy of equality: people are equal because "power is everywhere." The material inequality—produced at the point of production—is covered up by cultural equality: the power of purchasing in the shopping malls of consumption. The structural inequalities of wage-labor are diffused in consumption because shopping disguises the fact that the person who pays for a silk shirt with one hour of work is not equal to the one who purchases the same shirt with five hours of labor. But Foucault is adamant: "there is no binary and all-encompassing opposition between rulers and ruled at the root of power relations" (94).

In this post labor, post property society, the weak is not negatively affected by power and is in fact enabled by it because power that is "everywhere" and is "exercised from innumerable points, in the interplay of nonegalitarian and mobile relations" (94), turns the weak into a resistance agent-subject: "Where there is power, there is resistance" (95). This resistance to power, however, is also part of the algorithm of power itself and is therefore immanent to it and, Foucault argues, "is never in a position of exteriority in relation to power" (95). In other words, there is no "outside" (such as revolution) from which power can be overthrown. Equality of power is achieved within the inequalities of wage-labor. This is another way of saying that Foucault and other theorists of the power of the weak accept the existence of capitalism—their resistance is merely cultural. It is aimed at making the atrocities of capital more tolerable through, for example, the cultural narratives of consumption in which the weak becomes powerful not by material means but by the power of the mind—the wit and tactics of "making do." The "power of the weak" is a story told to normalize existing class realities and to substitute quietism for militancy.

The ideological effect of these narratives about the power of the weak, iin other words, is to shift the focus of social practices and their understanding from the material to the cultural, from labor to pleasure, and from "production" to the "producerly," in which consumption itself is seen as an act of production (Fiske, *Reading the Popular* 107).

These tactics allow the consumer to turn consumption into a practice of "poaching" (de Certeau, *The Practice of Everyday Life* 31). Consumers are like the "indigenous Indians" who, de Certeau argues, diverted the "spectacular victory of Spanish colonization" by the "uses" they made of it "even when they were subjected" (32). They can subvert the system of production and power "from within" and "divert" it "without leaving it" (32). "Lacking its own place...a tactic is determined by the *absence of power*" (38). One instance of the "absence of power" that resists power and thus subverts production from within is shoplifting. Shoplifting, like all "tactics," relies on temporality (since resistant consumers do not have a place of their own, they use existing places temporarily) and "a clever *utilization of time*" (38-39). Elaborating on de Certeau, John Fiske argues that "Shoplifting is not a guerilla raid just upon the store owners themselves, but upon the power-bloc in general" (Fiske, *Understanding Popular Culture* 39). Like all forms of consumption, shoplifting is a part of the "clever tricks of the 'weak' within the order established by the 'strong,' an art of putting one over on the adversary on his own turf" (de Certeau, 40). For de Certeau the radical structural change in capitalism has resulted in the emergence of a post community that he calls the "cybernetic society" and which is the "scene of the Brownian movements of invisible and innumerable tactics" (40). What Baudrillard calls "consumer society" (*"Consumer Society"* 29-56) thus is not oppressive (as modernist thinkers have argued) but instead is seen as full of possibilities for self-agency. The regime of wage-labor, accordingly, is undermined by the cybernetic society of agent-consumers because this post society is viewed as the site of the "proliferation of aleatory and indeterminable manipulations within an immense framework of constraints" (de Certeau 40).

Like shoplifting, "moving the price tag from a lower- to a higher-priced item before taking it to the cashier" (Fiske, *Understanding Popular Culture* 39) is a tactic of resistance to capitalism as is the practice of

> two secretaries spending their lunch hour browsing through stores with no intention to buy. They try on clothes, consume their stolen images in the store mirror and in each other's eyes, turn the place of the boutique into their lunchtime space, and make tactical raids upon its strategically placed racks of clothes, shoes, accessories. (39)

These are all said to be acts of consumption-as-production because consumers do not receive products passively but instead intervene through their wits in the status and uses of commodities. However, the repertoire of resistance is not exhausted by such local acts of transgression. Another more radically "inventive" form of consuming-as-producing is believed to be breaking into the very mode of existence of commodities. If "whole" jeans are said to be "connoted" with ruling powers, then "disfiguring" them within these codes of resistance, becomes an active struggle against these powers (4).

The shift from production to consumption is a shift then from labor to pleasure as the shaping force of post history. Producerly consumption in the cultural turn is taken as the sign of the agency of the subject who resists the oppressive system of production (Negri, *The Politics of Subversion*; *Insurgencies*). In actuality, however, it is an excuse to divert the subject away from "making" and taking control of the means of making toward what de Certeau posits as the ultimate form of post resistance, namely "making do" (29-42)—working within the system and with what the system provides rather than attempting to transform it. It is an ethics of adjustment to the social relations as they exist.

SOLARITY OF THE GIFT

All post al theories of consumption are founded on the conservative views of Georges Bataille—either directly (Baudrillard) or through various systems of theoretical relay (Foucault, de Certeau)—especially Bataille's concepts of "expenditure," "waste," "prodigality," "sacrifice," and, most importantly, "sovereignty," all of which are brought together in his theory of "general economy" as opposed to what he calls "restricted economy," by which he specifically means the political economy of production. Bataille's views not only form the basis of ludic social theory but also underlie the ideas of "difference," "supplementarity" and "writing" that have been the grounding concepts of the cultural turn in general (Derrida, "From Restricted to General Economy: A Hegelianism without Reserve" 251-277).

Contemporary theory, as we have discussed, represents desire as the dynamics of culture and marginalizes labor. This reversal is the theoretical foundation of the Left's legitimization of capitalism. It takes one of its most effective forms in the writings of George Bataille, which have become the canonic texts of consumption theories. Bataille condemns capitalism as a regime of rational utility whose exchange relations distort human social life and repress the fundamental character of being human. For Bataille the most effective resistance to capitalist exchange relations is to crush their functional reciprocities through lavish consumption—expenditure without purpose. This will open up a nonpractical social space in which humans acquire sovereignty (from the useful) through laughter (at calculative reason), eroticism (sexuality without goals), and the return to the sacred—by practicing extreme uselessness and waste, such as the "potlatch," intoxication and transgressing literary realism. An orgiastic feast of wasting replaces class struggle, and revolution itself becomes a spectacle of expenditure. For Bataille freedom is liberation from utility, purpose, goal, and practicalities—not emancipation from necessities. The ceaseless play of desire (which can never be satisfied), not the fulfillment of human needs, is the perspective of liberation.

Bataille's theory of resistance to capitalism now dominates institutional theory, but it is actually more an affirmation of capital than an opposition to it. By giving consumption an aura of the sacred and representing it as a condition for sovereignty of the subject, he provides consumers for capitalism. Far from overthrowing capitalism, their expenditures actually fuel its markets. Although he tries to separate the conspicuous consumption of the rich, which is aimed at obtaining social prestige, from absolute consumption, which is its own end, Bataille's spiritualizing of consumption without purpose energizes the market to respond to the desire of the wealthy (supplying their demands for luxuries guarantees superprofits) and ignore the needs of the indigent (whose demands are too mundane to produce more than a standard profit). His call for consumption, in short, legitimizes supplying the most profitable over meeting the needs of the people. In other words, his theory of resistance against capital, like all cultural resistance, is a local opposition that affirms capital in its global structure (wage-labor).

Bypassing exchange relations occurs, for Bataille, through a displacement in which the material is turned into the spiritual by the trope of "potlatch"—destroying material (goods) to obtain spiritual sovereignty. For Bataille, the potlatch is a materiality without materialism: a materiality that is outside the history of labor and free from all determinations. This is the materiality of the extreme moment realized by the sacrifice that affirms the radical desire of humans through absolute loss—expenditure without return—and brings about "freedom from 'all selfish calculations' from all reserve" ("Sacrificial Mutilation and the Severed Ear of Vincent Van Gogh" 69). In his materialism, which has a strong aroma of religion, matter is a product of the mind emancipated from causality through gnosis ("Base Materialism and Gnosticism"). In its essential sense then materialism for Bataille is a space of heterogeneity (the radical difference of the singular) in which what he calls "base materialism" (an irreducible concrete) resists the sameness imposed by the homogenizing concept. The homogeneous is the effect of functionalism and the utilitarianism of capitalism in which the concept (the abstract) fixes meaning and stabilizes identities, thereby negating difference (the concrete "base") in lofty and abstract laws. Bataille's materialism is a form of matterism (as in the matter of language, the matter of body, the matter of race, the matter of taste, etc.), which is the ground of what he calls "horizontal knowing": one of the "two axes of terrestrial life" on which the "distribution of the organic existence on the surface of the earth takes place" ("The Pineal Eye" 83). It is the plane of knowing that is concrete, immediate, and experiential. Bataille's "horizontal" materiality is now canonized in recent theory by the notion of the "rhizome" (Deleuze and Guattari, *A Thousand Plateaus* 3-25) as the other of the historical materialism in which materiality is understood as the effect of what Marx calls "social metabolism" (*Capital* I, 198, 290) and therefore not identical with concrete experience. For Marx, the concrete ("horizontal"/"rhizome") is a historical construct: "a concentration of many determinations" (*Grundrisse* 101) and therefore not a spontaneous sensuality. Marxist materialism for Bataille is a form of idealism because it is a strong conceptuality that produces laws of the social and turns dialectics into a science. For Bataille dialectics is negativity without return—absolute loss—and therefore is at odds with Marxist dialectics which he regards to be a vertical knowledge: "head" knowledge that is a lofty, abstract and arrogant attempt at mastery of the contingent. Communism for Bataille is not freedom from necessity—contingency can never be mastered—but a space of sacrifice. Like Communism in the writings of Negri and Hardt, it is a form of religious ethics. Negri and Hardt model their Communism after Saint Francis of Assisi (*Empire* 413), while Bataille's Communism is a form of spiritual communal unity brought about by sacrifice which is "the convulsive communication of what is ordinarily stifled" ("The Sacred" 242). Materialism, in this view, is not the ground of freedom from necessity but cultural freedom from fixed and functional meanings; it is access to the nomadic meanings repressed by the functional semantics of capitalism. Communism, for Bataille, is communication (of the sacred)—the semiotic carousing of unruly material *words* freed from the abstract regulations of capitalist utilitarian linguistics. This is a materialism of "raw phenomena, and not a system" ("Materialism" 16). Its "representation of matter," Bataille argues, should be taken "from Freud" and not Marx ("Materialism" 15-16). His materialism, it turns out, is in the end psychological—the heterogeneity of dreams and fantasies that give the subject its radical singularity and nomadic identity.

What Bataille represents as materialism and uses to state the priority of consumption over production and argue for "nonproductive expenditure" ("The Notion of Expenditure" 117) is a new spiritualism of commodities. Through a network of metaphors—the "horizontal," the "vertical," "expenditure," "loss," "sacrifice"—Bataille spiritualizes the material and turns it into a mystical medium that enables him to transform the objective, historical class relations shaping people's actual lives into sacred intensities. The horizontal (Deleuze and Guattari's "rhizome") as a resistance against the vertical (Deleuze and Guattari's "arborescent"), for example, is represented by Bataille as a defense of radical heterogeneity against the homogenizing practicalities of efficient capitalism—as a means of resistance to repressive power. In actuality, however, his story of the horizontal and the vertical is a parable persuading the lowly and the humble to submit to the lofty and the powerful by teaching them to interpret their acquiescence—crawling on the ground—as a rebellion against the triumphalist authoritarian power rising above the world. His narrative of the horizontal is a pedagogy of submission. It teaches embracing the corporeal and the subterranean— the "old mole" *revolution* that "hollows out chambers in a decomposed soil repugnant to the delicate nose of utopians" ("The 'Old Mole' and the Prefix *Sur*" 35)—and suspicion of the Icarian *revolution* and soaring imperial eagle. Bataille's "old mole" is, of course, an allusion to and an appropriation of Marx's "old mole" (*The Eighteenth Brumaire*) which is based on a Shakespearean trope (*Hamlet* I.5). However, in Marx's texts the "old mole" is a symbol of active historical struggles and the way revolutions encounter reversals and setbacks and go underground to understand their mistakes—by analysis and not through orgiastic expenditure—and do their "preparatory work" (*The Eighteenth Brumaire*

185) so that they can "leap from" their "seat" in exultation (185) and with a more robust transformative theory. Bataille opposes "revolutionary theory" (Lenin, *What Is to Be Done?* 369) as a soaring, vertical, and utilitarian discourse ("The Use Value of D. A. F. de Sade" 100) and uses the "old mole" to repeat the ideological psalm that solaces the poor and the powerless by reassuring them that their poverty is a form of richness and their weakness is itself power. This, as we have already seen, is the same lesson that Lyotard teaches ("On the Strength of the Weak"). The "old mole" for Marx is not the trope of a mystical life force or a code for the power of the weak. For him, the "old mole" is the emblem of a thoroughgoing revolution that "does its work methodically" (*The Eighteenth Brumaire* 185).

Working with a sensualist formula that severs the local from its global conditions of possibility, Bataille reduces materialism to the materiality of the concrete expenditure without return—it is the means by which one can be freed from capitalist exchange relations without overthrowing the structural relations of production that produce commodities and the system of exchange. Bataille's materialism is an ecstatic feast of sacrifice and sensualites. He finds philosophical questions and arguments about materialism and the material structures of the social to be boring high abstractions. For Bataille, in other words, only orgiastic acts of absolute loss, which he sees as resisting the functionalism of capitalism, count as materiality. However, as even he himself acknowledges, such contraconceptuality—anti-intellectual spontaneities, and violent lunging into consumption, waste, and sacrifice (which mark his various projects from Contre-Attaque to Acephale and Collège de Sociologie)—contain a certain "paradoxical fascist tendency" (*Oeuvres completes* VII, 461, quoted in Allan Stoekl, "Introduction" xviii). His materialism is the materiality of this tendency.

Bataille's idea of materialism as expenditure without return—absolute negativity—is now the framing understanding of materiality in contemporary cultural theory. The Hegelian notion of the "negative" as self-differencing, especially the version re-written by Derrida as "différance" (*Margins of Philosophy* 3-27), not only underlies contemporary theories of consumption—as the negative that destabilizes its identity and thus de-centers it from within production—but also informs such offshoots of consumption theories as the new aestheticism, which is grounded in a performativity of meaning without meaningfulness (Andrzej Warminsky, "'As the Poets Do It': On the Material Sublime"). Derrida uses Bataille's concrete material—"potlatch"—to argue that culture itself is a "potlatch of signs that burns, consumes, and wastes words in a gay affirmation of death: a sacrifice and a challenge" ("From Restricted to General Economy: A Hegelianism without Reserve" 274). This, in turn, becomes a second-order argument for him to talk about "materiality without materialism" ["Typewriter Ribbon: Limited Ink" (2) ("within such limits") 281].

Bataille's notions of "general economy" and "restricted economy" are rooted in what Baudrillard calls an "aristocratic critique" of capitalism ("When Bataille Attacked the Metaphysical Principle of Economy" 60). The aristocratic critique is based on Bataille's valorization of the "negative" in its Hegelian sense and his contempt for "utility" which, in Baudrillard's words, is the "positive principle" of capitalism: "accumulation, investment, depreciation" and the mercantilist morality that underlies it. Utility is, for Bataille, a bourgeois value and a mark of "powerlessness, an utter inability to expend" and, as such, opposed to the fundamental human principle which is the "solar principle of expenditure" (59). "The sun," Bataille writes, "gives without ever receiving" (*The Accursed Share* 28). Solarity, according to him, is what constitutes "sovereignty." It is the capability of "loss" through lavish consumption which is, in turn, the spirit of aristocracy: the disruption of rational utility by laughter, intoxication, ecstasy, and the erotic. Bataille, like many writers of high modernity (Eliot, Pound, Breton, Proust, etc.) rejects capitalism not because it is exploitative but because it is too bourgeois, utilitarian, and indifferent to post material desires without needs. Capitalism is to be resisted because it violates the solar principle and represses the elemental urge to give, to spend, to dispense with, and to simply waste without reserve and, therefore, to move beyond the trading and pragmatics underlying bourgeois daily life. The goal of resistance to capitalism is not to overthrow wage labor or such other mundane material goals but to revive giving without return: generosity, extravagance, and prodigality.

Bataille's thought, thus, becomes more and more a performativity without concepts; he takes refuge in rituals, ceremonies, and forms of stylized sensualities of offerings that are in radical contrast with bourgeois functionalities, which he sees as rooted in production. His post economic society beyond production is a society of desire in which needs are vulgar residues of a non-aristocratic pragmatism. His cultural radicalism consists of opposition to capital and is aimed not at overthrowing but at bypassing circles of exchange. He is simply rearticulating and legitimating, in the theatrical vocabularies of sensual concrete rituals, the existing abstract system of calculation and trading wages for laborpower by which the exploitation of the many occurs and through which the many provide the aristocratic culture of extravagance, prodigality, and exuberance for the few.

"Potlatch" becomes for Bataille a more and more layered sign for "expenditure" in his "The Notion of Expenditure," which is his "reflexion on the world, and on man in the world" (Jean Piel, "Bataille and the World from 'The Notion of Expenditure' to *The Accursed Share*" 99). His conclusion is that production is "subordinate" to consumption (Bataille, "The Notion of Expenditure" 120), which, as we have already discussed, now constitutes the core of a sensual anticapitalist mysticism underlying the writings of de Certeau and other contemporary cultural anti-capitalists. According to Bataille, potlatch is the proof that "[M]an is the most suited of all living beings to consume intensely, sumptuously" (*The Accursed Share* 37). Bataille's mystical view of "potlatch" is derived from Marcel Mauss's *The Gift: Forms and Functions of Exchange in Archaic Societies*. Mauss—who, like Bataille, is a regressive utopian, what Marx and Engels would ironically call a "true socialist" (*Manifesto of the Communist Party*)—regards the gift, which he calls "a complex phenomenon" (34), as representing an extra economic dimension of life (honor, desire, moral). The gift is a token of a deeper spiritual defiance of commercialism (63-81). Capitalist societies are societies of accumulation, but gift societies are societies of giving and expenditure which, unlike capitalist societies, are devoted to social and ethical obligations and not to profit. As Bataille argues, Mauss rejects the notion that the gift is a form of conventional barter (Bataille, "The Notion of Expenditure" 121) and therefore an elementary means of purely economic bargaining or exchange (Mauss, *The Gift* 35). The theoretical popularity of the gift and its interest for Mauss, Bataille, Derrida, Foucault, and Baudrillard is that it radically changes the relation of production and consumption because the gift suspends the circuit of exchange and establishes obligation. In other words, it transforms the economic into the ethical, renders the material as cultural, and replaces labor with the desires of the subject of the potlatch. The translation of the material into the cultural is the fundamental ideological work of capitalist cultural politics.

There are, according to Mauss, different modalities of gift-giving such as the Melanesian "kula" (19) and the "potlatch" (32), which is practiced among "American Northwest" Native Americans. He writes that "potlatch" is a more "radical and accentuated form" (31) of the festival of intense consumption (32-37). For Mauss both the kula and potlatch are forms of generosity and ethical obligation because, even though the potlatch does not have a literal receiver of goods (goods are destroyed), it is performed in the presence of a rival tribe who in return will set up a potlatch more extravagant, more spectacular and devastating. Bataille, on the other hand, argues that the two are entirely different: kula is still caught in the circle of utility exchange while potlatch is a pure gift, an expression of the desire to consume, which he regards to be elemental. Potlatch is pure consumption-as-waste and an affirmation of autonomy from the material. Potlatch for Bataille is the sublime of consumption: an excess of meaning that overflows all systems of representation—an aristocratic unproductivity that is not comprehensible within the dominant bourgeois capitalist system of representation. "It is the constitution of a positive property of loss—from which springs nobility, honor, and rank in a hierarchy" ("The Notion of Expenditure" 122).

In "potlatch" the goods "amassed with great industry from some of the richest coasts in the world" (*The Gift* 33) are destructed and rendered useless; they are returned to their elemental state. Potlatch is an instance of violence and sacrifice in which one tribe attempts to surpass the other in its competition for destroying goods and disregard for utility. "Relatively recently a Tlingit chief appeared before his rival to slash the throats of some of his own slaves. This destruction was repaid at a given date by the slaughter of a greater number of slaves" ("The Notion of Expenditure" 121). The more the principle of utility is removed, the greater the prestige of the tribe. "Potlatch," according to Bataille, "excludes all bargaining" and is an instance of the "spectacular destruction of wealth" (121) that "goes as far as burning of villages and smashing of flotillas of canoes. Emblazoned copper ingots, a kind of money on which the fictive value of an immense fortune is sometimes placed, are broken or thrown into the sea" (122). And of course the person who is the receiver of potlatch—the rival tribe who is humiliated—must destroy even more to maintain its own nobility and aristocratic honor. The goal is to become unique. Bataille quotes Mauss, "The ideal, would be to give a potlatch and not have it returned" (122) because the rival could not match your wealth and reach a higher level of "consumption." Wealth is not "having" but "expending." "It is only through loss that glory and honor are linked to wealth" ("The Notion of Expenditure" 122).

This notion of expending not only underlies the theories of new capitalism—the transformation of capitalism from a production regime to a consumption order—but is also the framing argument of most of the anti-capitalist writings at the present time. Ostensibly it opposes capital (accumulation and profit). Actually, it is an ally of capital because by privileging honor and prestige, it cultivates the singularity of the subject and individualism. To become singular and unique, it implies, the subject must expend (without return). But it is in the expenditure of the subject of the singular that profit is produced, and capital is accumulated. Anti-utility is the post form of trade in which the subject acquires a passing cultural identity while capital gains profit. Only contingent and aleatory identity is the desired form of post identity with its celebration of self-difference. Expenditure as a means for acquiring a constantly shifting lifestyle (identity) is turned in Bataille's writings into a guarantee of profit for capital. It is doubly effective because it also carries with it the banner of defiance of capitalism.

To be more precise, through prodigality and spectacle–expenditure, the consuming subject acquires the quality of subjectivity most valorized in Bataille: "sovereignty." Sovereignty is the uncontested mark of the aristocrat who has overcome the bourgeois ethics of utility and has put behind him production, work, and bourgeois seriousness. Sovereignty resituates the subject of expenditure in the terrain of play, ecstasy, sheer ludic post utility and prodigious destruction. Sovereignty is the sublime of expenditure, and the spiritual transcendence of the material. It is acquisition of a symbolic wealth (honor, glory, play) that enables the subject to finally recognize that commodities are not objects but meanings, which are not created by production and fixed in the object's use-value but rather are nomadic and producerly—invented by the consumer. Absolute consumption is conclusive sovereignty.

The meaning of commodities, their symbolic value, is what—in the writings of Bataille as well as de Certeau, Fiske, Baudrillard, and Stuart Hall—constitutes the basis for a resistance against capitalism. Traditionally, capitalist semiotics is grounded in fixed meanings and stable identities which derive their authority from reference to equally fixed objects, experiences, and ideas. This is the semiotics of reliable exchange and trading. Potlatch is a performativity by which the object of reference is destroyed and meaning is set free to become autonomous and self-referential. What produces meanings is no longer reference but self-difference which keeps them permanently shifting within themselves and consequently among other meanings which are all self-differential. Consumption, then, is pursuit of difference in its most radical self-differing sense (Derrida, "Différance").

Bataille's performativities are sacraments of destructing (instead of a prudent re-signifying) commodities. The destruction of "proper"-ty is seen as violating the laws of capitalism and its stabilizing semantics which reduce heterogeneity to the homogenous meanings of the bourgeois order of signification (Derrida, "White Mythology: Metaphor in the Text of Philosophy"). The mode of production, which accounts only for commodities, is consequently supplemented by the mode of expenditure, and the "restricted economy" (of commodities) is translated into the "general economy," which includes not only commodities but also their excess and overflow of meanings. Bataille's "general economy" is the inclusive science in which "a human sacrifice, the construction of a church or the gift of a jewel" are "no less interesting than the sale of wheat" (*The Accursed Share* 9). Production is subordinate to expenditure ("The Notion of Expenditure" 120), which is another way of saying that what matters is not what is produced (labor) but the producerly: the meaning that the subject of consumption creates by consuming it.

Sovereignty, for Bataille, is the ability to recognize the "negative" without the Hegelian urge to transcend it and arrive at the positivity of a synthesis through dialectics [Bataille, "The Critique of the Foundations of the Hegelian Dialectics"; Corn, "Unemployed Negativity (Derrida, Bataille, Hegel)"]. Sovereignty is not, therefore, identical with the Hegelian notion of "mastery" (*Phenomenology of Spirit* 111-119). Sovereignty is obtained through festivals of loss. The principle of expenditure in Bataille is a critique of materialist dialectics. True dialectic, for Bataille, is preserving the negative and not ending it. The "negative" is the political agent of a democracy of sovereigns. Through "expenditure" the subject of consumption loses his wealth and material advantage and becomes equal with the other because class (which is an impediment to democracy) is the embodiment of surplus, for Bataille, and if the surplus is expended and wasted as soon as it is available, then class society will never develop. "Class struggle" is, therefore, a "form of social expenditure" ("The Notion of Expenditure" 126).

Socialism (as a material regime and not simply an ethical set of obligations) is an unacceptable form of society for Bataille since it is founded upon production and not playful consumption of the surplus and "loss." Bataille's concept of "loss," in the end, is aimed not at an "aristocratic critique" of capitalism but at the discrediting of socialism. "The very principle of the function of production," he writes, "requires that products be exempt from loss" ("The Notion of Expenditure" 123). Like capitalism, socialism is for him the effect of inhibition against "unproductive expenditure" (*The Accursed Share* 153). Socialism is to be opposed because it is the enemy of solarity. It denies that life acquires exuberance only through uselessness—unproductive expenditure—and, of course, as Blake announces: "Exuberance is beauty" (*The Accursed Share* 5). Bataille's political theory is essentially an aesthetics grounded in the transgression against labor, denial of needs, and suspension of telos. It is a hybrid of capitalism and anarchism in which production loses its coherence and capitalism becomes disorganized (Claus Offe, *Disorganized Capitalism*) and in which money becomes "a kind of free-floating signifier detached from real processes to which it once referred" (Lash and Urry, *The End of Organized Capitalism* 292).

Repressive and containing systems are theorized by Bataille as "restricted economy." "Restricted economy" is an organized closed system based on reciprocation which tries to control all its components including its surplus, and in order to do so effectively, constructs a homogenous totality. However, Bataille argues that all systems give rise to "excesses" and "surpluses," which in the end fracture the homogeneity of the system and resituate it in the "general economy." "Proper"-ty, in short, is always excessive, and "general economy" is the economy of im-proper-ty, the loss of property—an economy, in other words, that is beyond concept and conceptualiztion. It is a form of "writing" (Derrida, "From Restricted to General Economy" 270-273).

Bataille's "general economy" is founded upon the principle of the necessity of loss: "the general principle of an excess of energy to be expended"—the "glorious operation" of "useless consumption" (*The Accursed Share* 25, 23). The body needs to "lose" its excesses (excrement), and only through "loss" of its sexual excesses in sexual ecstasy does the subject obtain true sovereignty. Through its totalitarian control, "restricted economy," according to Bataille, "restricts its object to operations carried out with a view to a limited end, that of economic man. It does not take into consideration a play of energy that no particular end limits: the play of *living matter in general*" (*The Accursed Share* 23, emphasis in the original). What is excluded from "restricted economy" (whether financial system, identity, a philosophical concept, or a political ideology) is "difference," "heterogeneity," the "other." "Difference" is the extraeconomic ("the gift") that fractures the limits of the economic and shows how the economic itself is, in fact, a form of "meaning"—in Derrida's reading a mode of "writing" and "textuality." Consumption, for Bataille, then, is a form of textualization of production—the exercise of a producerly invention.

Bataille's theory of "general economy" in its various interpretations has become the basis for the cultural turn in which production is displaced by consumption, labor is translated into desire, and commodity (hardware) is transcended through meanings (textware). What is called new capitalism, however, is "new" only in its cultural vocabularies (Drucker, *Post-Capitalist Society*; Hall, "The Meaning of New Times"; Poster, "Capitalism's Linguistic Turn"; Schiller, *Digital Capitalism*). It remains the same old capitalism in its structuring of labor relations. To put it differently, consumption theories use an emancipatory idiom to re-legitimate—as Bataille's celebration of "archaic societies" demonstrates— an essentially non-egalitarian social order that valorizes small-scale communities in which like-minded people ostensibly share their cultural interests (Rorty, "Solidarity or Objectivity"). The cultural interest here as everywhere else is a disguise for class interest and its desire for protection from the "other." Bataille's society of honor, glory, and sovereignty, which is represented as a progressive move against capitalism, is a post city without the urban proletariat. It is a reactionary attempt to cling to a retrograde social relations of production idealized as an organic post economic community of gifts freed from the circuits of exchange, which is then said to be a radical critique of modernity and its productionism. This is the frame within which, as we stated at the beginning of this chapter, the post is constructed. In this post space, capitalism constantly "new"s itself and offers an improved version of itself by appealing to the desires of a community of consumers. The structural similarities of the old and the new, improved versions are obscured in the post, which is the object of ludic textuality: a playfulness that blurs the lines of before and after. In blurring a decided linear temporality—the markers of class struggles—the post suspends history by translating the crisis of class relations in the objective world into a crisis "within" writing (of history) and thus becomes a self-difference that can come before and after itself.

Theories of consumption are theories in the interest of the class in command. Using progressive idioms, which are actually anti-progress, they marginalize production, which is the only means for developing social products and thus meeting the material needs of the excluded people. History without progress becomes a post-al hybrid of before and after—a hybrid that has no advancing direction and whose motions are represented as the active play of its signs in interminable self-resignifications. In these narratives, history becomes a meaning-effect and, like all meaning-effects, it is said to be an "event" that has no "regulative mechanism" (Foucault, "Nietzsche, Genealogy, History" 154). It therefore precedes and succeeds itself—it is an unstable scene of reversals or (to use Arthur J. Penty's references) a hypermodernity within medievalism and a medievalism inside hypermodernity—a chain, in other words, of supplementarities, substitutions, and self-difference.

Bataille's de-historicizing of history as events of "sacrifice," "potlatch," and "loss" is a familiar rewriting, or as Marx would say, a farcical return (Marx, *The Eighteenth Brumaire of Louis Bonaparte* 103) of this bourgeois fantasy which sees in the "post" (of post industrial) the return of the medieval village without the urban proletariat. Bataille's desire to return to this post urban village of rituals of expenditure is a replay of Penty's "true socialism." Penty, who was a follower of William Morris and John Ruskin (Bell, *The Coming of Post-Industrial Society* 37), points to the inherit instability of the post and its reversals in the "Preface" to his 1922 work, *Post-Industrialism*: "From one point of view, Post Industrialism connotes Medievalism, from another it could be defined as 'inverted Marxism'" (14). Like Bataille, who regards himself to be a socialist but thinks of socialism as a community of gifts and ethical obligations rather than a society in which the material needs of all people are met, Penty declares his sympathy with "the ideals of the socialists" (14). However, he is opposed to progress toward any historical and material form of socialism and therefore rejects "industrialization." Like other post utopians, who isolate consumption from production, Penty does not seem to recognize that machines are social. Therefore it is not the machine (as a mechanical device) but its social uses (whether it is used to produce profit or meet the needs of people) that has brought about the immense social contradictions that critics hope to escape through post-al stories about organic communities in which they seek the future in the past: "There is no branch of art that in one way or another is not threatened with extinction at the hands of mechanical production" (Penty, *Post-Industrialism* 45). This story, in its post version by Walter Benjamin, is now canonized as the culture of "aura" in contemporary critique ("The Work of Art in the Age of Mechanical Reproduction"). The progress of the mode of production, according to Penty, has caused the collapse of quality "only on the more expensive work, which is rapidly a declining quantity, can he escape from the necessity of using such things [as artificial doors]" (45). In his *The Elements of Domestic Design*, Penty is even more clear about the past on which he wants to model the future: "the clear cut, massive simplicity of Norman work" (2). By suspending time as the self-referring meanings of nomadic events, the post becomes the space in which capital solves its contradictions by advocating a return to sacrifice, loss, the simple, the organic, and the natural. Capital, however, is a structure of profit and cannot move away from its contradictions since even here—as it advocates simplicity (obtained by an expenditure without return), loss, and the organic—it builds an "industry" to commodify and profit from post industrial organicity. The outside to capital's contradictions is not in the post of consumption but in transforming the logic of its production. This is achievable not by the gift, which hides the relations of exchange, but through socialism: meeting the needs of people.

Through the mythologies of gift, sacrifice, loss, and solarity, Bataille constructs a seductive cultural politics of consumption that points to an extra-economic society of gift that is free from exchange relations. By combining cybernetic medievalism and an aristocratic critique of capitalism, Bataillian cultural politics naturalizes the dominant class interests by substituting "symbolic value" (honor, prodigality, sovereignty) for "use value" (the needs of working people).

Consumption theory is a faith-based theory whose main and only lesson is a religious one: higher spirituality requires that people give up their needs (and resign themselves to a life of poverty) in order to obtain redemption, inner peace, and holiness. In their book *Empire*, Michael Hardt and Antonio Negri use this lesson to teach that capitalism has moved beyond the imperialism of production to a new world of consumption (empire), from material labor to immaterial labor (290-294), from collectivity (class struggle) to singularity—the aesthetic—(395-396), and from need to spirituality. The centering figure of the empire is not a revolutionary (Marx) but a Holy Man: Saint Francis of Assisi (413). The world constructed in consumption theories is an inverted world and "Religion is the general theory of this world...it is the fantastic realization of the human being in as much as the human being possesses no true reality...to call to abandon their illusion about their condition is a call to abandon a condition which requires illusions" (Marx, "Contribution to the Critique of Hegel's Philosophy of Right. Introduction").

Bataille's "aristocratic critique" of capitalism is a rigorous reinforcing of that exploitative regime; a critique of utility and arguing for the "need to destroy and to lose" ("The Notion of Expenditure" 121) constructs the prodigal subject necessary for the continued accumulation of capital. The sumptuous consumption that he valorizes as the practice of the generous subject of the gift is, in fact, a historical necessity for capitalism since the subject of expenditure is needed in capitalism to manage the crisis of systemic overproduction.

Overproduction is a systemic crisis that capitalism itself cannot solve by its own immanent resources. Sovereignty, generosity, and the ethics of the gift will all construct subjects who, as a matter of course, consume intensely and, in doing so, provide a reliable and steady pool of consumers to absorb overproduction. More specifically, the commodification of generosity and sovereignty, through "symbolic exchange" (gifts) in the U.S. during the Christmas season, generates most of the retail sales for the entire year. "General economy" provides the rationale and strategies to make gift-giving an all-season practice through instituting "festivals, spectacles, and games" ("The Notion of Expenditure" 123). The "loss" created by the prodigal subject is the "gain" of capital. Bataille's "general economy" is a priestly mystification of the orgy of destruction as a necessary device for contemporary capitalism. The invention of "general economy" occludes the working of the economic by resituating the material in the symbolic and turning labor into meanings—in doing so it translates the objective "social metabolism" of labor into the subjective interpretations of signs.

Consumption theory is not only a guideline for wasting, but also an epistemology for the new cultural discourses and a frame for contemporary cultural critique. The singularity of consumption—each consumer consumes differently—which follows the aleatory movements of desire, as we have already suggested, provides a theory of knowing the world through sensual experience and a marginalization if not a dismissal of all explanatory and abstract analysis. The world that emerges from Bataille's writings and is canonized in the interpretations of de Certeau, Baudrillard, Derrida, and Deleuze is a world without "regulatory mechanism": this world of pure difference is the one promised by capitalist individualism. The singular of consumption is the entrepreneur of the sensual: a "body without organs" whose desire is represented as the non-laws of the empire of the senses, shopping, and ecstasies of expenditure.

Contemporary cultural critique is thus governed by the non-laws of the new order of the sensual which reverses the laws of necessity into contingency and rewrites the relation of culture to its material base as one of indeterminacy and autonomy. The shift from production to consumption not only produces the prodigal subject of shopping but also the ecstatic pleasures of sensual critique— a critique that bypasses the political economy of labor (base) in order to experience the concrete of cultural performatives in themselves. There is perhaps no more clear statement of the logic of the new consumptionist critique than in the writing of yet another "true socialist"—Fredric Jameson. In his *Postmodernism or, the Cultural Logic of Late Capitalism*, he writes that the historical materialist analytics of "base and superstructure" is "not really a model of anything" (409) but a mere "heuristic recommendation." In post production critique, "it is always the superstructure that is determinate" (396). This is the logic of a new faith-based cultural critique in which the spiritual shapes the material and the cultural determines the economic (F. A. Hayek, *The Fatal Concept: The Errors of Socialism* 11-28). Consumption theory is the spiritual halo of capitalism in which class is pronounced dead and agency belongs to the *flâneur* of the shopping mall.

Bibliography

Abbas, M. A., and Ackbar Abbas. *Hong Kong: Culture and the Politics of Disappearance.* Minneapolis: U of Minnesota P, 1997.
A Beautiful Mind. Dir. Ron Howard. Perf. Russell Crowe, Ed Harris, and Jennifer Connelly. Universal Pictures, 2001.
Adorno, Theodor W. *The Culture Industry: Selected Essays on Mass Culture.* London and New York, Routledge, 2001.
Agamben, Giorgio. *The Coming Community.* Minneapolis: U of Minnesota P, 1993.
———. *Means without End: Notes on Politics.* Minneapolis: U of Minnesota P, 2000.
Agatston, Arthur. *The South Beach Diet.* New York: St. Martin's, 2005.
Aglietta, Michael. *A Theory of Capitalist Regulation: The U.S. Experience.* New Ed. London: Verso, 2001.
Ahmad, Aijaz. "Reconciling Derrida: 'Specters of Marx' and Deconstructive Politics." *Ghostly Demarcations: A Symposium on Jacques Derrida's* Specters of Marx. Ed. M. Sprinker. London: Verso, 1999. 88-109.
Alexander, Cynthia. *Digital Democracy.* New York: Oxford UP, 1998.
Althusser, Louis. *For Marx.* LondonL NLB, 1977.
———. *Lenin and Philosophy.* New York: Monthly Review P, 1971.
Alvesson, Mats, and Hugh Willmott, eds. *Critical Management Studies.* London: Sage, 1992.
———. *Studying Management Critically.* London: Sage, 2003.
Ankersmit, F. R. *Aesthetic Politics: Political Philosophy Beyond Fact and Value.* Stanford: Stanford UP, 1996.
Arditi, Benjamin, and Jeremy Valentine. *Polemicization: The Contingency of the Commonplace.* New York: New York UP, 1999.
Arendt, Hannah. "A Classless Society." *Totalitarianism.* New York: Harcourt, 1968. 3-38.
Aristotle. *Metaphysics. The Basic Works of Aristotle.* Ed. R. McKeon. New York: Random House, 1941. 689-926.
Armstrong, Philip, Andrew Glyn, and John Harrison. *Capitalism since 1945.* Oxford: Blackwell, 1991.
Aronowitz, Stanley. *How Class Works: Power and Social Movement.* New Haven: Yale UP, 2003.
Atkins, Robert C. *Dr. Atkins' New Diet Revolution.* Rev. and updated ed. New York: Avon, 1999.
Atlas, James. *My Life in the Middle Ages.* New York: HarperCollins, 2005.
Aune, James Arnt. *Selling the Free Market: The Rhetoric of Economic Correctness.* New York: Guilford, 2001.
Babson, Steve. *The Unfinished Struggle: Turning Points in American Labor, 1877-Present.* Lanham, MD: Rowman & Littlefield, 1999.
Bakhtin, Mikhail. *Essays and Dialogues on His Work.* Ed. Gary Saul Morson. Chicago: U of Chicago P, 1986.
Barthes, Roland. *Mythologies.* New York: Hill and Wang, 1972.
———. *The Pleasure of the Text.* New York: Hill and Wang, 1975.

———. "Reality Effect." *The Rustle of Language*. New York: Hill and Wang, 1986. 141-48.

Bataille, Georges. *The Accursed Share: An Essay on General Economy*. Vol 1. New York: Zone Books, 1988.

———. "Base Materialism and Gnosticism." *Visions of Excess*. 45-52.

———. "The Critique of the Foundations of the Hegelian Dialectics." *Visions of Excess*. 105-115.

———. "Materialism." *Visions of Excess*. 15-16.

———. *Oeuvres complètes* VII. Paris: Gallimard, 1970.

———. "The Notion of Expenditure." *Visions of Excess*. 116-129.

———. "The 'Old Mole' and the Prefix *Sur* in the Words *Surhomme* [Superman] and Surrealist." *Visions of Excess*. 32-44.

———. "The Pineal Eye." *Visions of Excess*. 79-90.

———. "The Sacred." *Visions of Excess*. 240-245.

———. "Sacrificial Mutilation and the Severed Ear of Vincent Van Gogh." *Visions of Excess*. 61-72.

———. "The Use Value of D. A. F. de Sade." *Visions of Excess*. 91-102.

———. *Visions of Excess: Selected Writings, 1927-1939*. Minneapolis: U of Minnesota P, 1985.

Baudrillard, Jean. "Consumer Society" *Jean Baudrillard: Selected Writings*. Ed. Mark Poster. Stanford: Stanford UP, 1988. 29-56.

———. *For a Critique of the Political Economy of the Sign*. St. Louis, MO: Telos P, 1981.

———. *The Mirror of Production*. St. Louis: Telos P, 1975.

———. *Simulacra and Simulation*. Ann Arbor: U of Michigan P, 1994.

———. *La Société de consommation*. Paris: Gallimard, 1970.

———. "When Bataille Attacked the Metaphysical Principle of Economy." *Canadian Journal of Political and Social Theory* 11.3 (1987): 59-62.

Beaud, Michel. *A History of Capitalism 1500-2000*. New ed. New York: Monthly Review P, 2001.

Beck, Ulrich. *Risk Society: Towards a New Modernity*. London: Sage, 1992.

Bell, Daniel. *The Coming of Post-Industrial Society*. New York: Basic Books, 1976.

———. *The End of Ideology*. Rev. ed. New York: Free Press, 1962.

Bellomo, Michael. *The Stem Cell Divide*. New York: AMACOM, 2006.

Benhabib, Seyla. *Another Cosmopolitanism: Hospitality, Sovereignty, and Democratic Iterations*. New York: Oxford University Press, 2006.

Benhabib, Seyla, Judith Butler, Drucilla Cornell, and Nancy Fraser. *Feminist Contentions: A Philosophical Exchange*. New York: Routledge. 1995.

Benjamin, Walter. *The Arcades Project*. Cambridge: Harvard UP, 2002.

———. *Reflections*. New York: Harcourt, 1978.

———. "The Work of Art in the Age of Mechanical Reproduction." *Illuminations*. New York: Schocken, 1969. 217-252.

Bennett, Tony, Lawrence Grossberg, and Meaghan Morris, eds. *New Keywords: A Revised Vocabulary of Culture and Society*. Rev. ed. Oxford: Blackwell, 2005.

Bennett, William J. *Why We Fight: Moral Clarity and the War on Terrorism*. Washington D.C.: Regnery, 2003.

Bennington, Geoffrey. "Derrida and Politics." *Jacques Derrida and the Humanities: A Critical Reader*. Ed. Tom Cohen. Cambridge: Cambridge UP, 2001. 193-212.

———. *Legislations: The Politics of Deconstruction*. London: Verso, 1994.

Benson, April Lane, ed. *I Shop Therefore I Am: Compulsive Buying and the Search for Self.* Northvale, NJ: Jason Aronson, 2000.

Berdayes, Vicente. "Traditional Management Theory as Panoptic Discourse: Language and the Constitution of Somatic Flows." *Culture and Organization* 8.1 (2002): 35-49.

Bergson, Henri. *Creative Evolution.* New York: University Press of America, 1983.

Berlant, Lauren. "Critical Inquiry, Affirmative Culture." *Critical Inquiry* 30.2 (2004): 445-451.

———. *Intimacy.* Chicago: U of Chicago P, 2000.

Bersani, Leo. *Homos.* Cambridge: Harvard UP, 1996.

———. "Is the Rectum a Grave?" *AIDS: Cultural Analysis/ Cultural Activism.* Ed. Douglas Crimp. Cambridge: MIT Press, 1988. 197-222.

Berube, Michael. "Ignorance Is a Luxury We Cannot Afford." *Chronicle of Higher Education,* 5 Oct. 2001: B5.

———, ed. *The Aesthetics of Cultural Studies.* Oxford: Blackwell, 2004.

Beynon, Huw, and Theo Nichols, eds. *Patterns of Work in the Post-Fordist Era: Fordism and Post-Fordism.* 2 vols. Northampton, MA: Edward Elgar, 2006.

Bhabha, Homi K. *The Location of Culture.* New York: Routledge, 1994.

Bittner, Van A. *CIO News,* 27 October 1947.

Boehm, Christopher. *Hierarchy in the Forest: The Evolution of Egalitarian Behavior.* Cambridge: Harvard UP, 1999.

Bonnell, Victoria, and Lynn Hunt, eds. *Beyond the Cultural Turn.* Berkeley: U of California P, 1999.

Bourdieu, Pierre. *Distinction: A Social Critique of the Judgement of Taste.* Cambridge: Harvard UP, 1984.

———. "The Essence of Neoliberalism." *Le Monde Diplomatique* (Dec. 1998).

Brecht, Bertolt. *Brecht on Theatre: The Development of an Aesthetic.* Ed. J. Willett. New York: Hill and Wang, 1964.

Brennan, Timothy. "Resolution." *Critical Inquiry* 31.2 (2005): 406-418.

Brockmann, Suzanne. *Flashpoint.* New York: Ballantine, 2004.

Brody, David. *Workers in Industrial America: Essays on the Twentieth Century Struggle.* New York: Oxford UP, 1980.

Brooks, Cleanth. "The Formalist Critics." *Kenyon Review* 13 (1951): 72-81.

———. *The Well Wrought Urn.* New York: Harcourt, Brace and World, 1947.

Brooks, David. *Bobos in Paradise: The New Upper Class and How They Got There.* New York: Simon and Schuster, 2000.

———. *On Paradise Drive.* New York: Simon and Schuster, 2004.

———. "The Triumph of Hope over Self-Interest." *The New York Times,* 12 Jan. 2003.

Buffington, Nancy, and Clyde Moneyhun. "A Conversation with Gerald Graff and Ira Shor." *JAC* 17.1 (1997): 1-21.

Bukharin, Nikolai. *Imperialism and World Economy.* New York: Monthly Review P, nd.

Bukharin, Nikolai, and Evgeny Preobrazhensky. *The ABC of Communism.* Ann Arbor: U of Michigan P, 1988.

Burrell, Gibson, and Karen Dale. "Building Better Worlds? Architecture and Critical Management Studies." *Studying Management Critically.* Ed. M. Alvesson and H. Willmott. London: Sage, 2003. 177-196.

Burton-Jones, Alan. *Knowledge Capitalism: Business, Work, and Learning in the New Economy.* New York: Oxford UP, 1999.

Bush, George W., et al. "President Urges Readiness and Patience: Remarks by the President, Secretary of State Colin Powell and Attorney General John Ashcroft." Camp

David. 15 September 2001. http://www.whitehouse.gov/news/releases/2001/09/20010915-4.html.
Butler, Judith. *Antigone's Claim: Kinship between Life and Death.* New York: Columbia UP, 2000.
———. *Bodies That Matter: On the Discursive Limits of "Sex."* New York: Routledge, 1993.
———. *Gender Trouble.* 10th anniv. ed. New York: Routledge, 1999.
———. "Merely Cultural." *Social Text* 15.3-4 (1997): 265-277.
———. "On Linguistic Vulnerability." *Excitable Speech.* New York: Routledge, 1997. 1-41.
———. *Precarious Life: The Powers of Mourning and Violence.* New York: Verso, 2004.
———. *Undoing Gender.* New York: Routledge, 2004.
Butler, Judith, Ernesto Laclau, and Slavoj Zizek. *Contingency, Hegemony, Universality.* London: Verso, 2000.
Campbell, Colin. "I Shop Therefore I Know That I Am: The Metaphysical Basis of Modern Consumerism." *Elusive Consumption.* Ed. Karin Ekström and Helene Brembeck. Oxford: Berg, 2004. 27-44.
Campbell, Joseph. *The Hero with a Thousand Faces.* 2nd ed. Princeton: Princeton UP, 1968.
Canclini, Nestor Garcia. *Consumers and Citizens: Globalization and Multicultural Conflicts.* Minneapolis: U of Minnesota P, 2001.
Caruth, Cathy, ed. *Trauma: Explorations in Memory.* Baltimore: Johns Hopkins UP, 1995.
Carver, Raymond. "I Could See the Smallest Things." *What We Talk About When We Talk About Love.* New York: Vintage, 1982. 31-36
———. "Tell the Women We're Going." *What We Talk About When We Talk About Love.* New York: Vintage, 1982. 57-66.
Castells, Manuel. *The Rise of the Network Society.* 2nd ed. Oxford: Blackwell, 2000.
Chambers, Ross. *Loiterature.* Lincoln: U of Nebraska, 1999.
Chaney, David. *The Cultural Turn: Scene-Setting Essays on Contemporary Cultural History.* New York: Routledge, 1994.
———. *Lifestyles.* New York: Routledge, 1996.
Chang, H. J. *Globalization, Economic Development and the Role of the State.* London: Zed Books, 2002.
Chartier, Roger. "Laborers and Voyagers: From the Text to the Reader." *Diacritics* 22.2 (1992): 49-61.
Clark, Terry Nicholas, and Seymour Martin Lipset, ed. *The Breakdown of Class Politics: A Debate on Post-Industrial Stratification.* Baltimore: The Johns Hopkins UP, 2001.
Cochran, Bert. *American Labor in Midpassage.* New York: Monthly Review Press, 1959.
Cohen, Sande, and R. L. Rutsky, eds. *Consumption in an Age of Information.* Oxford: Berg, 2005.
Cohen, Tom, ed. *Jacques Derrida and the Humanities: A Critical Reader.* Cambridge: Cambridge UP, 2001.
Connolly, William E. *Identity/Difference: Democratic Negotiations of Political Paradox.* Expanded ed. Minneapolis: U of Minnesota P, 2002.
Coole, Diana. *Negativity and Politics: Dionysus and Dialectics from Kant to Poststructuralism.* New York: Routledge, 2000.
Corlett, William. *Class Action: Reading Labor, Theory, and Value.* Ithaca: Cornell UP, 1998.

Corn, Tony. "Unemployed Negativity (Derrida, Bataille, Hegel)." *On Bataille: Criticial Essays*. Ed. L. A. Boldt-Irons. Albany: SUNY Press, 1995. 79-94.
Correspondents of the *New York Times*. *Class Matters*. New York: Times Books, 2005.
Coulter, Catherine. *The Target*. 1998. New York: Jove-Berkley, 1999.
Coyle, Diane. *Paradoxes of Prosperity: Why the New Capitalism Benefits All*. New York: Texere, 2001.
Crosland, Antony. *The Future of Socialism*. London: Jonathan Cape, 1956.
Cruz-Malave, Arnaldo, and Martin F. Manalansan, eds. *Queer Globalizations: Citizenship and the Afterlife of Colonialism*. New York: New York UP, 2002.
Cullenberg, Stephen, Jack Amariglio, and David Ruccio, eds. *Postmodernism, Economics and Knowledge*. New York: Routledge, 2001.
Dalkir, Kimiz. *Knowledge Management in Theory and Practice*. New York: Butterworth-Heinemann, 2005.
Dallmayr, Fred. "Farewell to Metaphysics: Nietzsche." *Critical Encounters between Philosophy and Politics*. Notre Dame: U of Notre Dame P, 1987. 13-38.
Danner, Mark. *Torture and Truth: America, Abu Ghraib, and the War on Terror*. New York: New York Review of Books, 2004.
Davis, Karen A. "Dot-Com Bust Creating More Homeless." Associated Press, June 15, 2001.
Day, Gary. *Class*. New York: Routledge, 2001.
Debord, Guy. *Comments on the Society of the Spectacle*. London: Verso, 1990.
———. *Society of the Spectacle*. Detroit: Black and Red, 1983.
de Certeau, Michel. *The Mystic Fable: The Sixteenth and Seventeenth Centuries*. Chicago: U of Chicago P, 1995.
———. *The Practice of Everyday Life*. Berkeley: U of California P, 1984.
Dees, Cindy. *The Medusa Project*. New York: Silhouette Books, 2005.
Deetz, Stanley. "Disciplinary Power, Conflict Suppression and Human Resources Management." *Studying Management Critically*. Ed. M. Alvesson and H. Willmott. London: Sage, 2003. 23-45.
de Lauretis, Teresa. "Statement Due." *Critical Inquiry* 30.2 (2004): 365-368.
Deleuze, Gilles, and Felix Guattari. *Anti-Oedipus: Capitalism and Schizophrenia*. Minneapolis: U of Minnesota P, 1983.
———. *A Thousand Plateaus: Capitalism and Schizophrenia*. Minneapolis: U of Minnesota P, 1987.
de Man, Paul. *Allegories of Reading: Figural Language in Rousseau, Nietzsche, Rilke, and Proust*. New Haven: Yale UP, 1979.
———. *The Resistance to Theory*. Minneapolis: U of Minnesota P, 1986.
Demsetz, Harold. "Towards a Theory of Property Rights." *The American Economic Review* 57.2 (1967): 347-359.
Derrida, Jacques. *Archive Fever*. Chicago: U of Chicago P, 1996.
———. "Cogito and the History of Madness." *Writing and Difference*. Chicago: U of Chicago P, 1978. 31-63.
———. "Countersignature." *Paragraph* 27.2 (2004): 7-42.
———. "Différance." *Margins of Philosophy*. 1-28.
———. *Dissemination*. Chicago: U of Chicago P, 1981.
———. *The Ear of the Other: Otobiography, Transference, Translation*. Lincoln: U of Nebraska P, 1988.
———. "Faith and Knowledge: The Two Sources of 'Religion' at the Limits of Reason Alone." *Religion*. Ed. Jacques Derrida and Gianni Vattimo. Stanford: Stanford UP, 1998. 1-78.

———. "Force of Law: The 'Mystical Foundation of Authority.'" *Deconstruction and the Possibility of Justice*. Ed. Drucilla Cornell, Michael Rosenfeld, and David Gray Carlson. New York: Routledge, 1992. 3-67.

———. "From Restricted to General Economy: A Hegelianism without Reserve." *Writing and Difference*. Chicago: U of Chicago P, 1978. 251-77.

———. *The Gift of Death*. Chicago: U of Chicago P, 1995.

———. *Given Time: I. Counterfeit Money*. Chicago: U of Chicago P, 1992.

———. "Letter to a Japanese Friend." *A Derrida Reader: Between the Blinds*. Ed. Peggy Kamuf. New York: Columbia UP, 1991. 269-276.

———. *Limited Inc.* Evanston: Northwestern UP, 1988.

———. "The Madness of Economic Reason: A Gift without Present." *Given Time: I. Counterfeit Money*. Chicago: U of Chicago P, 1992. 34-70.

———. *Margins of Philosophy*. Chicago: U of Chicago P, 1982.

———. "Marx & Sons." *Ghostly Demarcations: A Symposium on Jacques Derrida's "Specters of Marx."* Ed. Michael Sprinker. London: Verso, 1999. 213-269.

———. *Memoires: For Paul de Man*. Rev. ed. New York: Columbia UP, 1989.

———. *Of Grammatology*. Baltimore: The Johns Hopkins UP, 1976.

———. *Of Hospitality: Anne Dufourmantelle Invites Jacques Derrida to Respond*. Stanford: Stanford UP, 2000.

———. *On the Name*. Stanford: Stanford UP, 1995.

———. *The Other Heading: Reflections on Today's Europe*. Bloomington: Indiana UP, 1992.

———. *Paper Machine*. Stanford: Stanford UP, 2005.

———. "Parergon." *The Truth in Painting*. Chicago: U of Chicago P. 15-148.

———. "Politics and Friendship." *The Althusserian Legacy*. Ed. E. A. Kaplan and M. Sprinker. London: Verso, 1993. 183-231.

———."Politics and Friendship: A Discussion with Jacques Derrida." Geoffrey Bennington. Centre for Modern French Thought. 1 December 1997. http://www.sussex.ac.uk/ Units/frenchthought/derrida.htm.

———. *Politics of Friendship*. London: Verso, 1997.

———. *Positions*. Chicago: U of Chicago P, 1981.

———. *Signéponge/Signsponge*. New York: Columbia UP, 1984.

———. *Specters of Marx*. New York: Routledge, 1994.

———. "Structure, Sign, and Play in the Discourse of the Human Sciences." *Writing and Difference*. Chicago: U of Chicago P, 1978. 278-294.

———. "The Time Is Out of Joint." *Deconstruction Is/In America: A New Sense of the Political*. Ed. A. Haverkamp. New York: New York UP, 1995. 14-38.

———. "Typewriter Ribbon: Limited Ink" (2) ('within such limits')." *Material Events: Paul de Man and the Afterlife of Theory*. Ed. T. Cohen, B. Cohen, J. H. Miller, and A. Warminski. Minneapolis: U of Minnesota P, 2001. 277-360.

———. "White Mythology: Metaphor in the Text of Philosophy." *Margins of Philosophy*. 207-272.

Derrida, Jacques, and Maurizio Ferraris. *A Taste for the Secret*. Cambridge: Polity, 2001.

Derrida, Jacques, Jürgen Habermas and Giovanna Borradori. *Philosophy in a Time of Terror: Dialogues with Jürgen Habermas and Jacques Derrida*. Chicago: U of Chicago P, 2003.

Descartes, René. *Discourse on Method and the Meditations*. Harmondsworth, Middlesex: Penguin, 1968.

de Saussure, Ferdinand. *Course in General Linguistics*. New York: McGraw-Hill, 1966.

Disch, Lisa. "Deconstructing 'Capitalism.'" *Theory and Event* 3.1 (1999).

Dosse, Françoise. *History of Structuralism*. Vol. I. Minneapolis: U of Minnesota P, 1997.
Drucker, Peter F. *Post-Capitalist Society*. New York: HarperCollins, 1994.
Dubofsky, Melvyn, and Foster Rhea Dulles. *Labor in America: A History*. 7th ed. Wheeling, IL: Harlan Davidson, 2004.
Du Gay, Paul, and Michael Pryke, eds. *Cultural Economy*. London: Sage, 2002.
Duggan, Lisa. *The Twilight of Equality?: Neoliberalism, Cultural Politics, and the Attack on Democracy*. Boston: Beacon, 2004.
Dumenil, Gerard, and Dominique Levy. *Capital Resurgent: Roots of the Neoliberal Revolution*. Cambridge: Harvard UP, 2004.
Duncombe, Stephen, ed. *Cultural Resistance Reader*. New York: Verso, 2002.
During, Simon. *Cultural Studies*. New York: Routledge, 2005.
Eagleton, Terry. *After Theory*. New York: Basic Books, 2003.
Ebert, Teresa L. *Cultural Critique (with an attitude)*. Forthcoming.
―――. "Interview with Teresa L. Ebert." *Dialogues on Cultural Studies*. Ed. Shaobo Xie and Fengzhen Wang. Calgary: U of Calgary P, 2002. 47-78.
―――. *Ludic Feminism and After: Postmodernism, Desire and Labor in Late Capitalism*. Ann Arbor: U of Michigan P, 1996.
―――. "Manifesto as Theory and Theory as Material Force: Toward a Red Polemic." *JAC* 23.3 (2003): 553-562.
Ebert, Teresa L., and Mas'ud Zavarzadeh. *Hypohumanities*. Forthcoming.
Edelman, Lee. *No Future: Queer Theory and the Death Drive*. Durham: Duke UP, 2005.
Edgell, Stephen. *Class*. New York: Routledge, 1993.
Ekström, Karin, and Helene Brembeck, eds. *Elusive Consumption*. Oxford: Berg, 2004.
Eliot, T. S. "Hamlet." *Selected Prose of T. S. Eliot*. Ed. Frank Kermode. New York: Harcourt, 1975. 45-49.
―――. "The Metaphysical Poets." *Selected Prose of T. S. Eliot*. Ed. Frank Kermode. New York: Harcourt, 1975. 59-67.
Elliott, Carole. "Representations of the Intellectual: Insights from Gramsci on Management Education." *The Journal for Managerial and Organizational Learning* 34.4 (2003).
Empson, William. *Seven Types of Ambiguity*. 1930. Harmondsworth, Middlesex: Penguin, 1961.
Engels, Friedrich. *Anti-Dühring*. *Collected Works*. Vol. 25. New York: International P, 1987. 5-309.
―――. *The Condition of the Working-Class in England*. *Collected Works*. Vol. 4. New York: International P, 1976. 295-596.
―――. *The Origin of the Family, Private Property, and the State*. *Collected Works*. Vol. 26. New York: International P, 1990. 129-276.
―――. "Outline of a Critique of Political Economy." *Collected Works*. Vol. 3. New York: International P, 1975. 418-443.
―――. "Review of Karl Marx, *A Contribution to the Critique of Political Economy*." *Collected Works*. Vol. 16: New York: International P. 472.
Esping-Andersen, Gosta. *Changing Classes: Stratification and Mobility in Post-Industrial Societies*. London: Sage, 1993.
Evans, Mary. "The Culture Did It: Comments on the 1997 British General Election." *Culture and Economy after the Cultural Turn*. Ed. Larry Ray and Andrew Sayer. London: Sage, 1999. 229-245.
Evans, Philip, and Thomas S. Wurster. *Blown to Bits: How the New Economics of Information Transforms Strategy*. Cambridge: Harvard Business School P, 1999.

Ewen, Stuart, and Elizabeth Ewen. *Channels of Desire: Mass Images and the Shaping of American Consciousness.* 2nd ed. Minneapolis: U of Minnesota P, 1992.

Falk, Pasi, and Colin Campbell, eds. *The Shopping Experience.* London; Sage, 1997.

Featherstone, Mike. *Consumer Culture and Postmodernism.* London: Sage, 1991.

Feehan, Christine. *Deadly Game.* New York: Jove-Berkley, 2007.

———. *Mind Game.* New York: Jove-Berkley, 2004.

———. *Night Game.* New York: Jove-Berkley, 2005.

———. *Shadow Game.* New York: Jove-Berkley, 2003.

Felman, Shoshana. *The Juridical Unconscious: Trials and Traumas in the Twentieth Century.* Harvard UP, 2002.

Felski, Rita. *Doing Time: Feminist Theory and Postmodern Culture.* New York: New York UP, 2000.

———. *Literature after Feminism.* Chicago: U of Chicago P, 2003.

Feyerabend, Paul. *Against Method: Outline of an Anarchistic Theory of Knowledge.* London: Verso, 1978.

Fish, Stanley. "Theory's Hope." *Critical Inquiry* 30.2 (2004): 374-378.

———. *The Trouble with Principle.* Cambridge: Harvard UP, 1999.

Fiske, John. *Reading the Popular.* New York: Routledge, 1989.

———. *Understanding Popular Culture.* Boston; Unwin Hyman, 1989.

Fones-Wolf, Elizabeth A. *Selling Free Enterprise: The Business Assault on Labor and Liberalism: 1945-60.* Urbana: U of Illinois P, 1994.

Foster, John Bellamy. *Marx's Ecology: Materialism and Nature.* New York: Monthly Review P, 2000.

Foucault, Michel. *History of Sexuality.* Vol. 1. New York: Vintage, 1980.

———. "Intellectuals and Power." *Language, Counter Memory, Practice.* Ed. Donald E. Bouchard. Ithaca: Cornell UP, 1977. 205-217.

———. *Language, Counter Memory, Practice.* Ed. Donald E. Bouchard. Ithaca: Cornell UP, 1977.

———. "My Body, This Paper, This Fire." *Aesthetics, Method, and Epistemology.* Ed. James D. Faubion. *Essential Works of Foucault, 1954-1984.* Vol. 2. New York: The New P, 1998. 393-417.

———. "Nietzsche, Genealogy, History." *Language, Counter-Memory, Practice.* Ed. Donald E. Bouchard. Ithaca: Cornell UP, 1977. 139-164.

———. "Polemics, Politics and Problemizations: An Interview with Michel Foucault." *The Foucault Reader.* Ed. Paul Rabinow. New York: Pantheon, 1984. 381-390.

———. "Truth and Power." *Power/Knowledge.* Ed. Colin Gordon. New York: Pantheon, 1980. 109-133.

———. "What Is Enlightenment?" *The Foucault Reader.* Ed. Paul Rabinow. New York: Pantheon, 1984. 32-50.

Frank, Thomas. *One Market under God.* New York: Anchor Books, 2001.

———. *What's the Matter with Kansas?: How Conservatives Won the Heart of America.* New York: Metropolitan Books, 2004.

Fraser, Nancy. *Justice Interruptus: Critical Reflections on the "Postsocialist" Condition.* New York: Routledge, 1997.

Fraser, Nancy, Axel Honneth, Joel Golb, and James Ingram. *Redistribution or Recognition?: A Political-Philosophical Exchange.* London: Verso, 2003.

Friedman, Milton. *Capitalism and Freedom.* 40th anniv. ed. Chicago: U of Chicago P, 2002.

Friedman, Thomas L. *The World Is Flat: A Brief History of the Twenty-First Century.* New York: Farrar, Straus and Giroux, 2005.

Frist, Bill. "Meeting Stem Cell's Promise-Ethically." *The Washington Post*, 18 July 2006: A19.
Frow, John. *Cultural Studies and Cultural Value*. New York: Oxford UP, 1995.
Frye, Northrop. "The Archetypes of Literature." *Fables of Identity*. New York: Harcourt, 1963. 7-20.
Fukuyama, Francis. *The End of History and the Last Man*. New York: Free Press, 1992.
Fussell, Paul. *Class*. New York: Ballantine, 1983.
Gallop, Jane. "The Teacher's Breasts." *Anecdotal Theory*. Durham: Duke UP, 2002.
Game, Ann. *Undoing the Social: Towards a Deconstructive Sociology*. Toronto: U of Toronto P, 1991.
Garber, Marjorie. *Symptoms of Culture*. New York: Routledge, 1998.
Gates, Bill. "Can Your Digital Nervous System Do This?" *Business @ the Speed of Thought*. New York: Warner, 1999. 22-38.
———. "Prepare for the Digital Future." *Business @ the Speed of Thought*. New York: Warner, 1999. 407-415.
———. *The Road Ahead*. Rev. ed. New York: Penguin, 1996.
Geertz, Clifford. *The Interpretation of Cultures*. New York: Basic Books, 1977.
German, Lindsey. *A Question of Class*. London: Bookmarks, 1996.
Gibson-Graham, J. K. *The End of Capitalism (as we knew it): A Feminist Critique of Political Economy*. Minneapolis: U of Minnesota P, 2006.
———. *A Postcapitalist Politics*. Minneapolis: U of Minnesota P, 2006.
Gibson-Graham, J. K., Stephen Resnick, and Richard Wolff, eds. *Class and Its Others*. Minneapolis: U of Minnesota P, 2000.
———. *Re/Presenting Class: Essays in Postmodern Marxism*. Durham: Duke UP, 2001.
———. "Toward a Poststructuralist Political Economy." *Re/Presenting Class: Essays in Postmodern Marxism*. Ed. J. K. Gibson-Graham, Stephen Resnick, and Richard Wolff. Durham: Duke UP, 2001. 1-24.
Giddens, Anthony. *Runaway World: How Globalization Is Reshaping Our Lives*. New York: Routledge, 2000.
Gilder, George. *Microcosm: The Quantum Revolution in Economics and Technology*. New York: Simon and Schuster, 1989.
———. *Recapturing the Spirit of Enterprise*. San Francisco: ICS Press, 1992.
———. "Triumph over Materialism." *Microcosm: The Quantum Revolution in Economics and Technology*. New York: Simon and Schuster, 1989. 371-384.
Gilpin, Robert. *The Challenge of Global Capitalism*. Princeton: Princeton UP, 2000.
Gluckman, Amy. *Homo Economics*. New York: Routledge, 1997.
Gorz, Andre. *Farewell to the Working Class*. Boston: South End P, 1982.
Graff, Gerald. *Clueless in Academe*. New Haven: Yale UP, 2003.
Gramsci, Antonio. *Selections from Cultural Writings*. Ed. David F. Forgacs and G. Nowell-Smith. Cambridge: Harvard UP, 1985.
Graves, Ginny. "Protein Diets: The Real Story." *Fitness*, July 2000: 91-94.
Greenberg, Karen J., and Joshua L. Dratel, ed. *The Torture Papers*. New York: Cambridge UP, 2005.
Grosz, Elizabeth. *Architecture from the Outside: Essays on Virtual and Real Space*. Cambridge: MIT Press, 2001.
———. *Volatile Bodies: Toward a Corporeal Feminism*. Bloomington: Indiana UP, 1994.
Guttersen, Connie. *The Sonoma Diet*. Des Moines: Meredith Books, 2005.
Habib, M. A. R. *A History of Literary Criticism: From Plato to the Present*. Oxford: Blackwell, 2005.

Hall, Gary. "The Politics of Secrecy: Cultural Studies and Derrida in the Age of Empire." *Cultural Studies* 21.1 (2007): 59-81.

Hall, Stuart. "The Centrality of Culture: Notes on the Cultural Revolutions of Our Time." *Media and Cultural Regulation*. Ed. Kenneth Thompson. London: Sage, 1997. 207-238.

———. *Different*. London: Phaidon Press, 2001.

———. "The Meaning of New Times." *New Times*. Ed. Stuart Hall and Martin Jacques. London: Verso, 1990. 116-134.

Haraway, Donna. *Simians, Cyborgs, and Women: The Reinvention of Nature*. New York: Routledge, 1991.

Hardt, Michael, and Antonio Negri. *Empire*. Cambridge: Harvard UP, 2000.

———. *Labor of Dionysus: A Critique of the State-Form*. Minneapolis: U of Minnesota P, 1994.

———. *Multitude: War and Democracy in the Age of Empire*. New York: Penguin, 2004.

Harman, Chris. *Explaining the Crisis*. London: Bookmarks, 1987.

———. "Spontaneity, Strategy and Politics." *International Socialism* 104 (Autumn 2004): 3-48.

Harris, David. *From Class Struggle to the Politics of Pleasure: The Effects of Gramscianism on Cultural Studies*. New York: Routledge, 1992.

Harrison, Lawrence E., and Samuel P. Huntington, eds. *Culture Matters: How Values Shape Human Progress*. New York: Basic Books, 2000.

Harvey, David. *A Brief History of Neoliberalism*. Oxford: Oxford UP, 2005.

Hayek, F. A. *The Fatal Conceit: The Errors of Socialism*. Ed. W. W. Bartley. Chicago: U of Chicago P, 1988.

———. *The Road to Serfdom*. Chicago: U of Chicago P, 1994.

Hayles, N. Katherine. *My Mother Was a Computer: Digital Subjects and Literary Texts*. Chicago: U of Chicago P, 2005.

———. *Writing Machines*. Cambridge: MIT UP, 2002.

Hegel, G. W. F. *Elements of the Philosophy of Right*. Cambridge: Cambridge UP, 1991.

———. *Phenomenology of Spirit*. Oxford: Oxford UP, 1977.

Heidegger, Martin. *The Basic Problems of Phenomenology*. Bloomington: Indiana UP, 1982.

———. *Being and Time*. New York: Harper and Row, 1962.

———. "Letter on Humanism." *Basic Writings*. Ed. David F. Krell. New York: Harper and Row, 1977. 189-242.

———. *Poetry, Language, Thought*. New York: Harper & Row, 1971.

———. "The Question Concerning Technology." *Basic Writings*. Ed. David F. Krell. New York: Harper and Row, 1977. 283-318.

Hine, Thomas. *I Want That! How We All Became Shoppers*. New York: HarperCollins, 2002.

Hobbes, Thomas. *Leviathan*. 1951. Harmondsworth, Middlesex: Penguin, 1981.

Hobsbawm, Eric. *Age of Extremes*. London: Abacus, 1994.

Holloway, John. *Change the World without Taking Power*. New ed. London: Pluto P, 2005.

hooks, bell. "Power to the Pussy: We don't wannabe dicks in drag." *Outlaw Culture: Resisting Representations*. New York: Routledge, 2006. 9-26.

———. *Where We Stand: Class Matters*. New York: Routledge, 2000.

Howard, Linda. *All The Queen's Men*. 1999. New York: Pocket Books, 2000.

———. *Mr. Perfect*. 2000. New York: Pocket Books, 2001.

Howe, Irving, ed. *Literary Modernism.* New York: Fawcett, 1967.
Huntington, Samuel P. *The Clash of Civilizations and the Remaking of the World Order.* New ed. New York: Free P, 2002.
Hutnyk, John. *Bad Marxism: Capitalism and Cultural Studies.* London: Pluto, 2004.
Huws, Ursula. *The Making of a Cybertariat: Virtual Work in a Real World.* New York: Monthly Review P, 2003.
Irigaray, Luce. *This Sex Which Is Not One.* Ithaca, NY: Cornell UP, 1985.
Irons, Peter H. "American Business and the Origins of McCarthyism: The Cold War Crusade of the United States Chamber of Commerce." *The Specter: Original Essays on the Cold War and the Origins of McCarthyism.* Ed. R. Griffith and A. Theoharis. New York: New Viewpoints, 1974. 72-89.
IRS. "Corporation Income Tax Brackets and Rates." <http://www.irs.gov/pub/irs-soi/02corate>.
Ismail, M. Asif, and Christine Morente. "Capital Hill Stem-Cell Backers Received Health Industry Dollars." August 30, 2001. <http://www.publicintegrity.org/report.aspx?aid=296>.
Jacoby, Sanford M. *Modern Manors: Welfare Capitalism since the New Deal.* Princeton: Princeton UP, 1998.
James, William. "What Pragmatism Means." *Pragmatism.* New York: New American Library, 1974. 41-64.
Jameson, Fredric. "The Cultural Logic of Late Capitalism." *Postmodernism or, the Cultural Logic of Late Capitalism.* 1-54.
———. "Culture and Finance Capital." *The Cultural Turn.* 136-163.
———. *The Cultural Turn: Selected Writings on the Postmodern, 1983-1998.* London: Verso, 1998.
———. "First Impressions." Rev. of *The Parallax View* by Slavoj Zizek. *London Review of Books,* 28.17 (7 Sept. 2006).
———. *Late Marxism: Adorno, or, the Persistence of the Dialectic.* London: Verso, 1990.
———. *The Political Unconscious: Narrative as a Socially Symbolic Act.* Ithaca: Cornell UP, 1981.
———. *Postmodernism or, the Cultural Logic of Late Capitalism.* Durham: Duke UP, 1991.
Jammer, Max. *The Conceptual Development of Quantum Mechanics.* New York: McGraw-Hill, 1966.
Janzen, Tara. *Crazy Hot.* New York: Bantam Dell, 2005.
Jenkins, Henry. *Textual Poachers.* New York; Routledge, 1992.
Jenks, Chris. *Culture.* New York: Routledge, 1993.
Johnson, Barbara. "Melville's Fist: The Execution of *Billy Budd.*" *The Critical Difference.* 1980. Baltimore: Johns Hopkins UP, 1985. 79-109.
Johnson, Steven. *Everything Bad Is Good for You.* New York: Riverhead Books, 2005.
Jones, Roger S. *Physics as Metaphor.* New York: New American Library, 1983.
Joughin, John J., and Simon Malpas, eds. *The New Aestheticism.* Manchester: Manchester UP, 2003.
Joyce, Patrick, ed. *Class.* New York: Oxford UP, 1995.
Kant, Immanuel. *Critique of Judgment.* New York: Hafner-Macmillan, 1951.
Kautsky, Karl. "*I*mperialism and the War." 1914. http://marxists.org/archive/kautsky/1914/09/war.htm.
Kennedy, Barbara M. *Deleuze and Cinema: The Aesthetics of Sensation.* Edinburgh: Edinburgh UP, 2003.

Kenyon, Sherrilyn. "'Captivated' by You." *Born to Be BAD*. New York: Pocket Books, 2005. 241-366.
King, Stephen. "On Impact." *New Yorker*, 19-26 June 2000.
King, William McGuire. "The Reform Establishment and the Ambiguities of Influence." *Between the Times: The Travail of the Protestant Establishment in America, 1900-1960*. Ed. W. R. Hutchinson. Cambridge: Cambridge UP, 1989. 123-127.
Knabb, K., ed. *Situationist International Anthology*. Berkeley: Bureau of Public Secrets, 2002.
Kozol, Jonathan. *Savage Inequalities: Children in America's Schools*. New York: Harper, 1992.
Kraus, Chris, and Sylvère Lotringer, eds. *Hatred of Capitalism/A Semiotext(e) Reader*. New York: Semiotext(e), 2001.
Krentz, Jayne A., ed. *Dangerous Men and Adventurous Women: Romance Writers on the Appeal of the Romance*. Philadelphia: U of Pennsylvania P, 1992.
Kumar, Amitava, ed. *World Bank Literature*. Minneapolis: U of Minnesota P, 2003.
Kuhn, Thomas S. *The Structure of Scientific Revolutions*. 2nd ed. Chicago: U of Chicago P, 1970.
Lacan, Jacques. *Ecrits: A Selection*. Trans. Bruce Fink. New York: Norton, 2002.
———. *The Four Fundamental Concepts of Psycho-Analysis*. Ed. J.-A. Miller. New York: Norton, 1981.
LaCapra, Dominick. *Writing History, Writing Trauma*. Baltimore: Johns Hopkins UP, 2000.
Laclau, Ernesto. "Deconstructing Classes." *Contingency, Hegemony, Universality*. J. Butler, E. Laclau and S Zizek. London: Verso, 2000. 296-301.
———. "The Death and Resurrection of the Theory of Ideology." *Modern Language Notes* 112 (1997), 297-321.
———. "The Politics of Rhetoric." *Material Events: Paul de Man and the Afterlife of Theory*. Tom Cohen, B. Cohen, J. H. Miller, A. Warminski, eds. Minneapolis: U of Minnesota P, 2001.
———. "Populist Rupture and Discourse." *Screen Education* 34 (1980): 87-95.
———. *New Reflections on the Revolutions of Our Time*. London: Verso, 1990.
———. "Structure, History and the Political." *Contingency, Hegemony, Universality*. J. Butler, E. Laclau, and S. Zizek. London: Verso, 2000. 182-212.
———. "Why Constructing a People Is the Main Task of Radical Politics." *Critical Inquiry* 32.4 (2006): 646-680.
———. "Why Do Empty Signifiers Matter to Politics?" *Emancipation(s)*. London: Verso. 36-46.
Laclau, Ernesto, and Chantal Mouffe. *Hegemony and Socialist Strategy*. London: Verso, 1985.
Lacoue-Labarthe, Philippe. *Heidegger, Art and Politics: The Fiction of the Political*. Oxford: Blackwell, 1990.
Lacoue-Labarthe, Philippe, and Jean-Luc Nancy. *The Literary Absolute*. Albany: SUNY Press, 1988.
Lang, Anne Adams. "Behind the Prosperity, Working People in Trouble." *The New York Times*, 20 November 2000.
Larrain, Jorge. *Marxism and Ideology*. Atlantic Highlands, NJ: Humanities P, 1983.
Lash, Scott, and John Urry. *Economies of Signs and Space*. London: Sage, 1994.
———. *The End of Organized Capitalism*. Madison: U of Wisconsin P, 1988.
Leacock, Eleanor Burke. "Introduction." *The Origin of the Family, Private Property and the State*. By Frederick Engels. New York: International P, 1972. 7-66.

———. *Myths of Male Dominance: Collected Articles on Women Cross-Culturally.* New York: Monthly Review P, 1981.

———. "Relations of Production in Band Society." *Politics and History in Band Societies.* Ed. E. Leacock and R. Lee. Cambridge: Cambridge UP, 1982. 159-170.

Le Blanc, Paul. *A Short History of the U.S. Working Class.* New ed. Amherst, NY: Humanity Books, 1999.

Lee, Richard Borshay. "Is there a Foraging Mode of Production?" *Canadian Journal of Anthropology* 2.1 (1981): 13-19.

———. *The !Kung San: Men, Women, and Work in a Foraging Society.* Cambridge: Cambridge UP, 1979.

———. "Politics, Sexual and Non-Sexual, in Egalitarian Society." *Politics and History in Band Societies.* Ed. E. Leacock and R. Lee. Cambridge: Cambridge UP, 1982. 37-50.

———. "Reflections on Primitive Communism." *Hunters and Gatherers,* v. 1: *History, Evolution and Social Change.* Ed. T. Ingold, D. Riches, and J. Woodburn. Oxford: Berg, 1988. 252-268.

Lee, Richard, and Irven DeVore, eds. *Man the Hunter.* Chicago: Aldine, 1968.

Lemert, Charles. "General Social Theory, Irony, Postmodernism." *Postmodernism and Social Theory.* Ed. S. Seidman and D. Wagner. Oxford: Blackwell, 1992. 17-46.

———. "What Is Culture? Amid the Flowers, Seeds or Weeds?" *Durkheim's Ghosts: Cultural Logics and Social Things.* Cambridge: Cambridge UP, 2006. 36-58.

Lenin, V. I. "Conspectus of Hegel's Book *The Science of Logic.*" *Collected Works.* Vol. 38. Moscow: Progress, 1976. 85-238.

———. *Imperialism, the Highest Stage of Capitalism. Collected Works.* Vol. 22. Moscow: Progress, 1964. 185-304.

———. *On the Emancipation of Women.* 4th rev. ed. Moscow. Progress, 1974.

———. "On the Question of Dialectics." *Collected Works.* Vol. 38. Moscow: Progress, 1976. 353-361.

———. *Philosophical Notebooks. Collected Works.* Vol. 38. Moscow: Progress, 1976.

———. *What Is to Be Done? Collected Works.* Vol. 5. Moscow: Foreign Languages Publishing, 1961. 347-529.

Levinas, Emmanuel. *Otherwise Than Being: Or Beyond Essence.* Pittsburgh: Duquesne UP, 1998.

Levi-Strauss, Claude. *Introduction to the Work of Marcel Mauss.* New York: Routledge, 1987.

Lewis, Tom. "The Politics of 'Hauntology' in Derrida's *Specters of Marx.*" *Ghostly Demarcations: A Symposium on Jacques Derrida's "Specters of Marx."* Ed. Michael Sprinker. London: Verso, 1999. 134-167.

Lichtenstein, Nelson. *The Most Dangerous Man in Detroit: Walter Reuther and the Fate of American Labor.* New York: Basic Books, 1995.

———. *State of the Union: A Century of American Labor.* Princeton: Princeton UP, 2002.

Limbaugh, Rush. "It's Not About Us; This Is War!" *The Rush Limbaugh Show.* 4 May 2005.

Lipietz, Alain. "From Althusserianism to 'Regulation Theory.'" *The Althusserian Legacy.* Ed. E. Ann Kaplan and M. Sprinker. London: Verso, 1993. 99-138.

Lipietz, Alain, and Malcolm Slater. *Toward a New Economic Order: Post-Fordism, Democracy and Ecology.* Oxford: Blackwell, 1992.

Lipset, Seymour Martin, and Gary Marks. *"It Didn't Happen Here." Why Socialism Failed in the United States.* New York: Norton, 2001.

Locke, Edwin A., ed. *Postmodernism and Management*. Greenwich, CT: JAI Press, 2003.

Lockhart, Charles. *The Roots of American Exceptionalism: Institutions, Culture and Policies*. New York: Palgrave Macmillan, 2003.

Lowell, Elizabeth. *Amber Beach*. 1997. New York: Avon, 1998.

———. *Death Is Forever*. New York: Avon, 2004. Rpt. of Ann Maxwell. *The Diamond Tiger*. 1992, 1999.

———. *Jade Island*. 1998. New York: Avon, 1999.

———. "Love Conquers All: The Warrior Hero and the Affirmation of Love." *Dangerous Men and Adventurous Women*. Ed. Jayne Ann Krentz. Philadelphia: U of Pennsylvania P, 1992. 89-97.

———. *Pearl Cove*. 1999. New York: Avon, 2000.

———. *Tell Me No Lies*. 1986. Rpt. 1992, 1996, 2001, 2006. Don Mills; Ontario: HQN Books, 2006.

Lukacs, Georg. *History and Class Consciousness*. Cambridge: The MIT P, 1983.

———. *Realism in Our Time: Literature and the Class Struggle*. New York: Harper and Row, 1971.

Lyotard, Jean-François. *The Differend*. Minneapolis: U of Minnesota P, 1988.

———. *Just Gaming*. Minneapolis: U of Minnesota P, 1988.

———. "Nanterre, Here, Now." *Political Writings*. Minneapolis: U of Minnesota P, 1993.

———. "On the Strength of the Weak." *Semiotexte* 3.2 (1978): 204-214.

———. *The Postmodern Condition*. Minneapolis: U of Minnesota P, 1984.

———. "Rewriting Modernity." *The Inhuman: Reflections on Time*. Stanford: Stanford UP, 1991. 24-35.

Mackay, Hugh, ed. *Consumption and Everyday Life*. London: Sage, 1997.

Malthus, Thomas Robert. *An Essay on the Principle of Population*. Ed. Philip Appleman. New York: Norton, 1976.

Mandel, Ernest. *An Introduction to Marxist Economic Theory*. New York: Pathfinder P, 1983.

Mann, Patricia S. *Micro-Politics: Agency in a Postfeminist Era*. Minneapolis: U of Minnesota P, 1994.

Marcus, Sharon. "Fighting Bodies, Fighting Words: A Theory and Politics of Rape Prevention." *Feminists Theorize the Political*. Ed. J. Butler and J. Scott. New York: Routledge, 1992. 385-403.

Marcuse, Herbert. *The Aesthetic Dimension: Towards a Critique of Marxist Aesthetics*. Boston: Beacon P, 1978.

———. *Negations: Essays in Cultural Theory*. Boston: Beacon Press, 1968.

Maresca, John J. "DOCUMENT: A New Silk Road: Proposed Petroleum Pipeline in Afghanistan." *Monthly Review* 53.7 (Dec. 2001): 28-35.

Marx, Karl. *Capital*. Vol. 1. Trans. B. Fowkes. Intro. E. Mandel. New York: Penguin, 1976.

———. *Capital*. Vol. 3. Trans. David Fernbach. Intro. E. Mandel. New York: Penguin, 1981.

———. "Contribution to the Critique of Hegel's Philosophy of Law: Introduction." *Collected Works*. Vol. 3. New York: International P, 1974. 173-187.

———. "A Contribution to the Critique of Hegel's Philosophy of Right. Introduction." *Early Writings*. Trans. R. Livingstone and G. Benton. New York: Vintage, 1975. 243-258.

———. *A Contribution to the Critique of Political Economy*. Intro. Maurice Dobb. New York: International P, 1970.

———. "Critical Marginal Notes on the Article 'The King of Prussia and Social Reform. By a Prussian.'" *Collected Works*. Vol. 3. New York: International P, 1975. 189-206.
———. *Critique of the Gotha Programme*. New York: International P, 1966.
———. *Early Writings*. Ed. Lucio Colletti. New York: Vintage, 1975.
———. *Economic and Philosophic Manuscripts of 1844. Collected Works*. Vol. 3. New York: International P, 1975. 229-443.
———. *The Eighteenth Brumaire of Louis Bonaparte*. New York: International P, 1975.
———. *Grundrisse*. London: Penguin, 1973.
———. "Moralising Criticism and Critical Morality." *Collected Works*. Vol. 6. New York: International P, 1976. 312-340.
———. *The Poverty of Philosophy. Collected Works*. Vol. 6. New York: International P, 1976. 105-212.
———. "Preface to the First Edition of *Capital*." *Capital*. Vol. 1. Trans. B. Fowkes. Intro. E. Mandel. New York: Penguin, 1976. 89-93.
———. *Theories of Surplus-Value*. Part II. Moscow: Progress, 1968.
———. *Wage-Labour and Capital and Value, Price and Profit*. New York: International P, 1976.
Marx, Karl, and Frederick Engels. "Address of the Central Authority to the League, March 1850." *Collected Works*. Vol. 10. New York: International P, 1978. 277-287.
———. *The German Ideology. Collected Works*. Vol. 5. New York: International P, 1976. 19-539.
———. *Manifesto of the Communist Party*. Moscow: Progress, 1977.
———. *Selected Correspondence*. 3rd rev. ed. Moscow: Progress, 1975.
Maslow, Abraham. *Eupsychian Management*. Homewood, Ill.: R. D. Irwin, 1965
———. *Maslow on Management*. Rev. ed. Wiley, 1998.
Massumi, Brian. "The Autonomy of Affect." *Parables for the Virtual*. 23-45.
———. *Parables for the Virtual: Movement, Affect, Sensation*. Durham: Duke UP, 2002.
Matthews, Pamela R., and David McWhirter, eds. *Aesthetic Subjects*. Minneapolis: U of Minnesota P, 2003.
Mauss, Marcel. *The Gift: Forms and Functions of Exchange in Archaic Societies*. New York: Norton, 1967.
Maxwell, Ann. *The Ruby*. 1995 rpt. New York: Harper, 1999.
———. *Shadow and Silk*. 1997 rpt. New York: Zebra Books, 2002.
Mayo, Elton. *Social Problems of an Industrial Civilization*. New York: Arno P, 1977.
McCoy, Alfred. *A Question of Torture: CIA Interrogation, from the Cold War to the War on Terror*. New York: Metropolitan Books, 2006.
McKenna, Lindsay. *Heart of the Wolf*. 1993 rpt. *Morgan's Mercenaries: In the Beginning*. New York: Silhouette Books, 2000.
———. *Her Healing Touch*. New York: Silhouette Books, 2003.
———. *An Honorable Woman*. New York: Silhouette Books, 2003.
McRobbie, Angela. *In the Culture Society: Art, Fashion and Popular Music*. New York: Routledge, 2005.
———. "Looking Back at New Times and Its Critics." *Stuart Hall: Critical Dialogues in Cultural Studies*. Ed. D. Morley and K.-H. Chen. New York: Routledge, 1996. 238-261.
———. *Postmodernism and Popular Culture*. New York: Routledge, 1994.
———. *The Uses of Cultural Studies*. London: Sage, 2005.
Meek, Ronald L., ed. *Karl Marx and Frederick Engels on Malthus*. New York: International Publishers, 1954.

Mercer, Kobena. "Black Hair/Style Politics." *Welcome to the Jungle: New Positions in Black Cultural Studies.*" New York: Routledge, 1994. 97-128.
Michaels, Walter Benn. *The Trouble with Diversity: How We Learned to Love Identity and Ignore Inequality.* New York: Metropolitan Books, 2006.
Mies, Maria. *Patriarchy and Accumulation on a World Scale: Women in the International Division of Labor.* London: Zed Books, 1986.
Mies, Maria, and Vandana Shiva. *Ecofeminism.* London: Zed Books, 1993.
Mies, Maria, and Veronica Bennholdt-Thomsen. *The Subsistence Perspective: Beyond the Globalized Economy.* London: Zed Books, 2000.
Miller, J. Hillis. "Catachresis, Prosopopoeia, and the Pathetic Fallacy: The Rhetoric of Ruskin." *Poetry and Epistemology.* Ed. R. Hagenbuchle and L. Skandera. Regensburg: F. Pustet, 1986.
———. "What Is a Kiss? Isabel's Moments of Decision." *Critical Inquiry* 31.3 (Spring 2005): 722-746.
Miller, Toby, and Geoffrey Lawrence. "Globalization and Culture." *A Companion to Cultural Studies.* Ed. Toby Miller. Oxford: Blackwell, 2006.
Milner, Andrew. *Class.* London: Sage, 1999.
Mir, Ali, and Raza Mir. "Producing the Governable Employee: The Strategic Deployment of Workplace Empowerment." *Cultural Dynamics* 17.1 (2005): 51-72.
Mohr, John, and Roger Friedland, eds. *Matters of Culture.* New York: Cambridge UP, 2004.
Morgan, Lewis Henry. *Ancient Society.* Gloucester, MA: Peter Smith, 1974.
Mort, Frank. "The Politics of Consumption." *New Times.* Ed. Stuart Hall and Martin Jacques. London: Verso, 1990, 160-172.
Mulgan, Geoff. "The Power of the Weak." *New Times.* Ed. Stuart Hall and Martin Jacques. London: Verso, 1990. 347-363.
Negri, Antonio. *Insurgencies: Constituent Power and the Modern State.* Minneapolis: U of Minnesota P, 1999.
———. *Marx Beyond Marx: Lessons on the* Grundrisse. South Hadley, MA: Bergin & Garvey, 1984.
———. *The Politics of Subversion.* Cambridge: Polity, 2005.
———. "The Specter's Smile." *Ghostly Demarcations: A Symposium on Jacques Derrida's* Specters of Marx. Ed. M. Sprinker. London: Verso, 1999. 5-16.
———. "Twenty Theses on Marx: Interpretation of the Class Situation Today." *Marxism Beyond Marxism.* Ed. S. Makdisi, C. Casarino, and E. Karl. New York: Routledge, 1996: 149-180.
Nelson, Cary. *Manifesto of a Tenured Radical.* New York: New York UP, 1997.
Nietzsche, Friedrich. *The Anti-Christ.* Tucson: See Sharp Press, 1999.
———. *Beyond Good and Evil.* Harmondsworth, Middlesex: Penguin, 1973.
———. *Human, All Too Human.* Lincoln: U of Nebraska P, 1984.
———. *On the Genealogy of Morals.* New York: Vintage, 1969.
———. *The Will to Power.* New York: Vintage, 1967.
Norris, Pippa, ed. *Digital Divide: Civic Engagement, Information Poverty, and the Internet Worldwide.* New York: Cambridge UP, 2001.
Offe, Claus. *Disorganized Capitalism.* Cambridge: MIT Press, 1985.
Ollman, Bertell, ed. *Market Socialism: The Debate among Socialists.* New York: Routledge, 1998.
O'Neill, John. "Economy, Equality and Recognition." *Culture and Economy after the Cultural Turn.* Ed. L. Ray and A. Sayer. London: Sage, 1999.

———. "Oh, My Others, There Is No Other! Civic Recognition and Hegelian Other-Wiseness." *Theory, Culture, Society* 18 (2001): 77-90.
Ornish, Dean. *Eat More, Weigh Less.* New York: HarperCollins, 1993.
Owen, Robert. *The Development of Socialism. Selected Works.* Vol. 2. London: W. Pickering, 1993.
Pakulski, Jan, and Malcolm Waters. *The Death of Class.* London: Sage, 1996.
Palmer, Diana. "Let Me Tell You about My Readers." *Dangerous Men and Adventurous Women.* Ed. Jayne A. Krentz. Philadelphia: U of Pennsylvania P, 1992. 155-158.
Parker, Martin. "Business, Ethics and Business Ethics: Critical Theory and Negative Dialectics." *Studying Management Critically.* Ed. M. Alvesson and H. Willmott. London: Sage, 2003. 197-219.
Penty, Arthur J. *The Elements of Domestic Design.* Westminster: Architectural P, 1930.
———. *Old Worlds for New: A Study of the Post-Industrial State.* London: Allen and Unwin, 1917.
———. *Post-Industrialism.* London: Allen and Unwin, 1922.
Pepper, Thomas. *Singularities: Extremes of Theory in the Twentieth Century.* Cambridge: Cambridge UP, 1997.
Perlo, Victor. *Super Profits and Crisis: Modern U.S. Capitalism.* New York: International P, 1988.
Peters, Tom. *Liberation Management.* New York: A. A. Knopf, 1992.
———. *The Pursuit of WOW!* New York: Vintage, 1994.
———. *Thriving on Chaos: Handbook for a Management Revolution.* New York: HarperCollins, 1988.
Petras, James. "The CIA and the Cultural Cold War Revisited." *Monthly Review* 51 (Nov. 1999).
Phillips, Susan Elizabeth. "Romance and the Empowerment of Women." *Dangerous Men and Adventurous Women.* Ed. Jayne A. Krentz. Philadelphia: U of Pennsylvania P, 1992. 53-59.
Piel, Jean. "Bataille and the World from 'The Notion of Expenditure' to *The Accursed Share.*" *On Bataille: Critical Essays.* Ed. L. A. Boldt-Irons. Albany: SUNY Press, 1995. 95-106.
Piore, Michael J., and Charles F. Sabel. *The Second Industrial Divide: Possibilities for Prosperity.* New York: Basic Books, 1986.
Plotnitsky, Arkady. *Reconfigurations: Critical Theory and General Economy.* Gainesville: UP of Florida, 1993.
Pollack, Andrew. "Stem Cell Bill Seen as a Qualified Boon for Research." *The New York Times,* 19 July 2006.
Porter, Michael E. "Attitudes, Values, Beliefs, and the Microeconomics of Prosperity." *Culture Matters: How Values Shape Human Progress.* Ed. L. E. Harrison and S. P. Huntington. New York: Basic Books, 2000. 14-28.
Poster, Mark. "Capitalism's Linguistic Turn." *What's the Matter with the Internet?* Minneapolis: U of Minnesota P, 39-59.
———. "The Question of Agency: Michel de Certeau and the History of Consumerism." *Diacritics* 22.2 (1992): 94-107.
"Post-modernism Is the New Black." *The Economist,* 19 December 2006.
Postrel, Virginia. *Substance of Style: How the Rise of Aesthetic Value Is Remaking Commerce, Culture and Consciousness.* New York: HarperCollins, 2003.
Poulet, Georges. "Phenomenology of Reading." *New Literary History* 1.1 (1969): 53-68.
Probyn, Elspeth. *Blush: Faces of Shame.* Minneapolis: U of Minnesota P, 2005.
———. *Carnal Appetites: FoodSexIdentities.* New York: Routledge, 2000.

Putney, Mary Jo. *Dancing on the Wind*. New York: Topaz-Penguin, 1994.
Pryor, Frederick L. "What Does It Mean to Be Human? A Comparison of Primate Economies." *Journal of Bioeconomics* 5.2-3 (2003): 97-145.
Ray, Larry, and Andrew Sayer, eds. *Culture and Economy after the Cultural Turn*. London: Sage, 1999.
Ray, Michael, and Alan Rinzler, eds. *The New Paradigm in Business*. New York: Putnam, 1993.
Rayback, Joseph G. *A History of American Labor*. Expanded and updated. New York: Free P, 1966.
Readings, Bill. *The University in Ruins*. Cambridge: Harvard UP, 1996.
Reed, Naomi C. "The Specter of Wall Street: 'Bartleby, the Scrivener' and the Language of Commodities." *American Literature* 76.2 (2004): 247-273.
Regan, Stephen. *The Politics of Pleasure: Aesthetics and Cultural Theory*. London: Open University P, 1992.
Reich, Robert. *The Work of Nations*. New York: Vintage, 1992.
Resnick, Stephen A., and Richard D. Wolff. *Knowledge and Class: A Marxian Critique of Political Economy*. Chicago: U of Chicago P, 1987.
Rifkin, Jeremy. *The Age of Access*. New York: Penguin-Putnam, 2000.
Ritzer, George. *The Globalization of Nothing*. London: Sage, 2004.
Ritzer, George, Douglas Goodman, and Wendy Wiedenhoft. "Theories of Consumption." *The Handbook of Social Theory*. Ed. G. Ritzer and B. Smart. London: Sage, 2002. 119-134.
Robbins, Bruce. "Just Doing Your Job: Some Lessons of the Sokal Affair." *The Yale Journal of Criticism* 10.2 (1997): 467-474.
Roberts, Nora. *Three Fates*. 2002. New York: Jove-Berkley, 2003.
"Romance Writers of America's 2005 Market Research Study on Romance Readers." https://www.rwanational.org/eweb/docs/05MarketResearch.pdf.
Ronell, Avital. *Stupidity*. Urbana: U of Illinois P, 2002.
———. *The Telephone Book*. Lincoln: U of Nebraska P, 1989.
Roosevelt, Frank, and David Belkin, eds. *Why Market Socialism? Voices from Dissent*. New York: M. E. Sharpe, 1994.
Rorty, Richard. *Achieving Our Country: Leftist Thought in Twentieth-Century America*. Cambridge: Harvard UP, 1998.
———. *Contingency, Irony, and Solidarity*. Cambridge: Cambridge UP, 1989.
———. "Solidarity or Objectivity?" *Objectivity, Relativism, and Truth*. Cambridge: Cambridge UP, 1991. 21-34.
Rose, Margaret A. *The Post-Modern and the Post-Industrial*. Cambridge: Cambridge UP, 1991.
Ross, Andrew. *Fast Boat to China: Corporate Flight and the Consequences of Free Trade*. New York: Pantheon, 2006.
Rossi-Landi, Ferruccio. *Language as Work and Trade: A Semiotic Homology for Linguistics and Economics*. South Hadley, MA: Bergin and Garvey, 1983.
———. *Linguistics and Economics*. The Hague: Mouton, 1975.
Rudoren, Jodi. "Stem Cell Work Gets States' Aid after Bush Veto." *The New York Times*, 25 July 2006.
Ruse, Michael, and Christopher Pynes, eds. *The Stem Cell Controversy: Debating the Issues*. Amherst, NY: Prometheus Books, 2003.
Sahadi, Jeanne. "CEO Pay: Sky High Gets Even Higher." *CNNMoney.com*, 30 August 2005 <http://money.cnn.com/2005/08/26/news/economy/ceo_pay>.

Sahlins, Marshall. "Notes on the Original Affluent Society." *Man the Hunter*. Ed. R. Lee and I. DeVore. Chicago: Aldine, 1968. 85-92.

———. *Stone Age Economics*. 1972. New York: Routledge, 2003.

Said, Edward W. "The Pen and the Sword: Culture and Imperialism." Interview with David Barsamian. *Z Magazine* July/August 1993: 62-71.

Saler, Michael. "Adorno on Mars." Rev. of *Archaeologies of the Future* by Fredric Jameson. *TLS*, 16 June 2006, 31.

Sartre, Jean-Paul. *The Ghost of Stalin*. New York: George Braziller, 1968.

———. *Search for a Method*. New York:Vintage, 1968.

Saunders, Frances Stonor. *The Cultural Cold War: The CIA and the World of Arts and Letters*. New York: New P, 2001.

Schiffrin, Andre. *The Business of Books: How International Conglomerates Took Over Publishing and Changed the Way We Read*. London: Verso, 2000.

Schiller, Dan. *Digital Capitalism: Networking the Global Market System*. Cambridge: MIT Press, 2000.

Schor, Naomi. *Reading in Detail: Aesthetics and the Feminine*. New York: Methuen, 1987.

Scott, Christopher. *Stem Cell Now: From the Experiment That Shook the World to the New Politics of Life*. Upper Saddle River, NJ: Pi P, 2005.

Scruton, Roger. *An Intelligent Person's Guide to Modern Culture*. South Bend, IN: St. Augustine's P, 2000.

Sears, Barry. *A Week in the Zone*. New York: HarperCollins, 2000.

Sedgwick, Eve Kosofsky. *Touching Feeling: Affect, Pedagogy, Performativity*. Durham: Duke UP, 2003.

Shohat, Ella. *Taboo Memories, Diasporic Voices*. Durham: Duke UP, 2006.

Shumway, David. "Cultural Studies and Questions of Pleasure and Value." *The Aesthetics of Cultural Studies*. Ed. M. Berube. Oxford: Blackwell, 2005. 103-116.

Skeggs, Beverley. *Class, Self, Culture*. London: Routledge, 2003.

Skinner, Kiron K., Annelise Anderson, and Martin Anderson, eds. *Reagan, In His Own Hand: The Writings of Ronald Reagan That Reveal His Revolutionary Vision for America*. New York: Free P, 2001.

Skye, Christina. *Code Name: Baby*. Don Mills, Ontario: HQN Books, 2005.

———. *Code Name: Blondie*. Don Mills, Ontario: HQN Books, 2006.

Sloterdijk, Peter. *Critique of Cynical Reason*. Minneapolis: U of Minnesota P, 1988.

Smith, Adam. *The Wealth of Nations*. Chicago: U of Chicago P, 1976.

Smith, Paul. "Looking Backwards and Forwards at Cultural Studies." *A Companion to Cultural Studies*. Ed. Toby Miller. Oxford: Blackwell, 2001. 331-340.

Spivak, Gayatri Chakravorty. *A Critique of Postcolonial Reason*. Cambridge: Harvard UP, 1999.

———. *In Other Worlds: Essays in Cultural Politics*. New York: Routledge, 2006.

———. *Outside in the Teaching Machine*. New York: Routledge, 1993.

Spivak, Gayatri Chakravorty, and David Plotke. "A Dialogue on Democracy." *Socialist Review* 94 (1994): 1-22.

———. "Speculations on Reading Marx: After Reading Derrida." *Post-structuralism and the Question of History*. Ed. D. Attridge, G. Bennington and R. Young. Cambridge: Cambridge UP, 1987. 30-64.

Steinhauer, Jennifer. "When the Joneses Wear Jeans." *Class Matters*. Correspondents of the *New York Times*. New York: Times Books, 2005. 134-145.

Sterne, Jonathan. "The Burden of Culture." *The Aesthetics of Cultural Studies*. Ed. M. Berube. Oxford: Blackwell, 2005. 80-102.

Stolberg, Sheryl Gay. "First Bush Veto Maintains Limits on Stem Cell Use." *The New York Times*, 20 July 2006.
Stoekl, Allan. "Introduction." *Visions of Excess*. By G. Bataille. Minneapolis: U of Minnesota P, 1985. ix-xxv.
Strangelove, Michael. *The Empire of Mind: Digital Piracy and the Anti-Capitalist Movement*. Toronto: U of Toronto P, 2005.
Sutton, Francis X., et al. *The American Business Creed*. Cambridge: Harvard UP, 1956.
Swados, Harvey. "The Myth of the Happy Worker." *The American Labor Movement*. Ed. Leon Litwack. Englewood Cliffs, NJ: Prentice-Hall, 1962. 169-172.
Szeman, Imre. *Zones of Instability: Literature, Postcolonialism, and the Nation*. Baltimore: Johns Hopkins UP, 2004.
Taussig, Michael T. *The Devil and Commodity Fetishism in South America*. Chapel Hill: U of North Carolina P, 1980.
Taylor-Corbett, Shaun. "Embryo Research: Profit vs Ethics?" 24 August 2000. http://www.publicintegrity.org/genetics/report.aspix?aid=325.
Thatcher, Margaret. "Interview." *Women's Own*, 31 October 1987.
Thompson, E. P. "The Long Revolution." *New Left Review* I (1961): 24-39.
Thompson, Paul. "Foundation and Empire: A Critique of Hardt and Negri." *Capital and Class* 86 (Summer 2005): 99-134.
Treuer, David. *Native American Fiction: A User's Manual*. Saint Paul, MN: Graywolf P, 2006.
Trippi, Joe. *The Revolution Will Not Be Televised: Democracy, the Internet, and the Overthrow of Everything*. New York: Regan Books, 2004.
Trotsky, Leon. *The Permanent Revolution and Results and Prospects*. 1931. New York: Pathfinder Press, 1969.
———. *Their Morals and Ours*. New York: Pathfinder, 1973.
Tucker, R., ed. *The Marx-Engels Reader*, 2nd ed. New York: Norton, 1978.
Urry, John "The End of Organized Capitalism." *New Times*. Ed. Stuart Hall and Martin Jacques. London: Verso, 1990. 94-102.
Voloshinov, V. N. *Marxism and the Philosophy of Language*. Trans. L. Matejka and I. Titunik. Cambridge: Harvard UP, 1973.
Wallace, Max. *The American Axis: Henry Ford, Charles Lindbergh, and the Rise of the Third Reich*. New York: St. Martin's, 2003.
Warde, Alan, and Stephen Edgell, eds. *Consumption Matters: The Production and Experience of Consumption*. Oxford: Blackwell, 1997.
Warminski, Andrzej. "'As the Poets Do It': On the Material Sublime." *Material Events: Paul de Man and the Afterlife of Theory*. Ed. T. Cohen, B. Cohen, J. H. Miller, and A. Warminski. Minneapolis: U of Minnesota P, 2001. 3-31.
Warner, Michael. "Uncritical Reading." *Polemic: Critical or Uncritical*. Ed. Jane Gallop. New York: Routledge, 2004. 13-38.
Warren, Elizabeth, and Amelia Warren Tyagi. *The Two-Income Trap*. New York: Basic Books, 2003.
Watt, Ian. *The Rise of the Novel: Studies in Defore, Richardson and Fielding*. 1957. Berkeley: U of California P, 2001.
Webber, Michael, and David L. Rigby. *The Golden Age Illusion: Rethinking Postwar Capitalism*. New York: Guilford, 1996.
Weber, Max. "Class, Status Party." *From Max Weber: Essays in Sociology*. Ed. H. H. Gerth and C. Wright Mills. New York: Oxford UP, 1946. 180-195.
———. *The Protestant Ethic and the "Spirit" of Capitalism*. New York: Routledge, 1992.

Weinberg, Steven. "Two Cheers for Reductionism." *Dreams of a Final Theory*. New York: Pantheon, 1992. 51-64.
Wellek, Rene. *Concepts of Criticism*. New Haven: Yale UP, 1963.
West, Cornel. *Democracy Matters: Winning the Fight against Imperialism*. New York: Penguin, 2004.
———. *Race Matters*. 2nd ed. New York: Vintage, 2001.
White, Hayden. *Metahistory*. Baltimore: John Hopkins UP, 1973.
Williams, Raymond. *Problems in Materialism and Culture*. London: Verso, 1980.
Williams, Whiting. "The Public Is Fed Up with the Union Mess." *Factory Management and Maintenance* 104 (January 1946): 97.
Wimsatt, W. K. *Hateful Contraries: Studies in Literature and Criticism*. Lexington: U of Kentucky P, 1965.
Wolf, Kenneth Baxter. *The Poverty of Riches: St. Francis of Assisi Reconsidered*. New York: Oxford UP, 2005.
Wolf, Naomi. *Fire with Fire: The New Female Power and How to Use It*. New York: Fawcett, 1993.
Wolf, Robert Paul. *Moneybags Must Be So Lucky: On the Literary Structure of Capital*. Amherst: U of Massachusetts P, 1988.
Woodiwiss, Anthony. "Deconstructing Class." *Social Theory after Postmodernism*. London: Pluto P, 1990. 151-184.
Woodward, Richard B. "Reading in the Dark." *Village Voice Literary Supplement*, October 1999.
Wordsworth, William, and Samuel Coleridge. "Preface." *Lyrical Ballads, 1798-1805*. London: Methuen, 1961.
Wright, Erik Olin. *Class Counts: Comparative Studies in Class Analysis*. New York: Cambridge UP, 1997.
———. *Classes*. London: Verso, 1985.
Xie, Shaobo, and Fengzhen Wang, eds. *Dialogues on Cultural Studies: Interviews with Contemporary Critics*. Calgary: U of Calgary P, 2002.
Yudice, George. "Civil Society, Consumption, and Governmentality in an Age of Global Restructuring: An Introduction." *Social Text* 45.5 (Winter 1995): 1-25.
———. *The Expediency of Culture: Uses of Culture in the Global Era*. Durham: Duke UP, 2003.
Zavarzadeh, Mas'ud. "The Pedagogy of Totality." *Journal of Advanced Composition Theory* 23.1 (2003): 1-54.
———. "Postality: The (Dis)Simulations of Cybercapitalism." *Post-Ality: Marxism and Postmodernism*. Ed. M. Zavarzadeh, T. L. Ebert, and D. Morton. Washington, DC: Maisonneuve P, 1995. 1-75.
———. *The Totality and Post*. Forthcoming.
Zizek, Slavoj. "Class Struggle or Postmodernism? Yes, please!" *Contingency, Hegemony, Universality*. Judith Butler, Ernesto Laclau, and Slavoj Zizek. London: Verso, 2000. 90-135.
———. *Did Somebody Say Totalitarianism?* London: Verso, 2001.
———. *The Sublime Object of Ideology*. London: Verso, 1989.
———. *The Ticklish Subject: The Absent Center of Political Ontology*. London: Verso, 2000.

Index

Adorno, T., 37, 61
Agamben, G., 14, 20, 28, 37, 46
Aglietta, M., 10, 65
Ahmad, A., 79
Althusser, L., xciii, 10, 61, 123
Arendt, H., 5
Armand, I., 147
Atkins, R., 110, 111, 112, 113
Atlas, J., 112

Badiou, A., 46
Bakhtin, M., 48
Barthes, R., 20, 121
Bataille, G., 115, 181–192
Baudelaire, C., 39, 70
Baudrillard, J., 7, 37, 58, 115, 144
Beck, U., 70–71
Beckett, S., 30, 58
Bell, D., 54, 64
Benjamin, W., xix, 62, 70
Bennett, W., 105
Bennington, G., 53
Berkeley, G., 41
Berlant, L., 6
Berube, M., 104–106 109
Bhabha, H., 75
Blackmur, R. P., 46
Bloch, J., 11
Boehm, C., 82
Bonnell, V., 28
Bourdieu, P., 19, 72, 110
Brecht, B., xix
Brennan, T., xv
Brockmann, S., 100, 101
Brooks, C., 28, 46
Brooks, D., 93, 109
Bukharin, N., 130
Butler, J., xvii, 7, 37, 41, 46, 50, 56, 75, 123, 139–140

Campbell, C., 171–74
Canclini, N. G., 45, 108
Castells, M., xviii, 65

Chambers, R., 61
Cochran, B., 46
Cocroft, E., 59
Coleridge, S., 29, 55
Conley, D., 90
Cornell, D., 140
Coulter, C., 100
Crosland, A., 64
Cullenberg, S., 13

Danner, M., 103
de Certeau, M., 45, 61, 177–78, 180–81, 185
Dees, C., 98
Deleuze, G., 28, 37, 46, 71, 75, 172
de Man, P., 30, 46, 49, 55, 56, 92, 127
Demsetz, H., 85
Derrida, J., xii–xiii, xviii, 4–5, 8–10, 12, 15–16, 19–21, 27, 29, 36–37, 39–43, 46–57, 60, 72, 75–78, 80, 92, 115, 127–128, 169, 184
de Saussure, F., 56, 58
Descartes, R., 47
Dickens, C., 55
Disch, L., 136
Drucker, P., 90
Du Gay, P., 48

Ebert, T. L., xvi, xix, 38, 121, 138
Edelman, L., 46
Eliot, G., 55
Eliot, T. S., 30, 46, 58
Engels, F., xiv, xvi, xx, 11, 13, 30, 66, 113, 115, 122–25, 131
Esping-Andersen, G., xv
Ewen, E., 167
Ewen, S., 167

Faulkner, W., 30, 37, 58, 92
Felman, S., 104
Felski, R., 141
Feyerabend, P., xvii
Fish, S., 46, 48, 123

Fiske, J., 45, 61,177,180
Fones-Wolf, E., 22–36
Foster, J. B., 123–24
Foucault, M., 20, 46–48, 75, 130, 146, 169, 79
Freud, S., 49
Friedman, M., 42, 73
Frist, B., 117
Frow, J., 123
Frye, N., 46
Fussell, P., xv, 92

Gallop, J., 109, 139
Garber, M., 108
Gates, B., 71, 126–129
Gautier, T., 30
Geertz, C., 28
Gibson-Graham, J. K., 4, 5, 11, 14, 16–19, 37, 52, 58, 68–69, 135–37, 153
Giddens, A., 70
Gilder, G., 40
Gonzales, A., 101
Gorz, A., 68
Gramsci, A., 146
Guattari, F., 28, 46, 75, 172

Hall, S., 7, 9, 10, 11, 29, 37–38, 46, 48
Hardt, M., xii, 7, 14–16, 28, 38, 53–54, 75–78
Harvey, D., 14–15, 136
Hatch, O., 117
Hayek, F. A., 27, 39, 156
Hayles, N. K., 46, 126, 192
Hegel, G. W. F., 49, 97
Heidegger, M., 27–28, 49, 58–59, 62–64, 75–76
Hobbes, T., 83–84
Hobsbawm, E., 64
Hook, S., 36, 46
hooks, b., 6
Horkheimer, M., 61
Howard, L., 100, 102
Hunt, L., 28
Huntington, S., 106
Hutnyk, J., 13, 14

James, W., 148
Jameson, F., xviii, 4, 5, 10, 20, 28, 37, 39, 65, 140
Jenks, C., 48, 58

Jevons, W. S., 73
Joyce, J., 30, 58

Kant, I., 62
Kenyon, S., 100
King, S., 111
Kozol, J., 130
Kristof, N. D., 36, 136

Lacan, J., 37, 46, 57, 75
LaCapra, D., 104
Laclau, E., 7, 11, 14, 36, 46, 56, 67–68, 92, 144
Lacoue–Labarthe, P., 46
Lash, S., 69–70
Leacock, E. B., 81–83
Lee, R., 83–85
Lenin, V. I., xviii, 21, 96, 109, 141, 147, 157
Levinas, E., 76
Levi-Strauss, C., 46
Lewis, J. L., 23
Lewis, T., 79
Lipietz, A., 10, 68
Locke, J., 83
Lowell, E., 98, 101
Lukacs, G., 146, 148–49
Lyotard, J.–F., 19, 20, 29, 36–37, 46, 75, 104, 108, 148, 159, 169

MacDonald, D., 46
Mallarme, S., 30
Malthus, T. R., 122
Mandel, E., 93, 143
Marcus, S., 135
Marcuse, H., xx, 98, 114
Maresca, J. L., 107
Marshall, A., 73
Marx, K. x, xi, xii, xiv, xvi, xx, 1, 3–4, 11–15, 17–18, 21, 32, 35, 38, 39–40, 53, 56, 64–66, 71–73, 79, 82–83, 89, 97, 109, 112–113, 115, 123–124, 130–132, 135, 140, 145, 149, 157, 159, 162, 176, 183, 190
Maslow, A., 32
Massumi, B., 6
Mauss, M., 185–186
Maxwell, A., 96, 98, 100
Mayo, E., 32
McRobbie, A., xvi

Michaels, W. B., 15
Mies, M., 138
Miller, J. H., xvi
Morgan. L., H. 82
Mouffe, C., 11, 67–68, 144
Murphy, P., 24

Negri, A., xii, xx, 7, 9, 10, 14–15, 28, 53–54, 75, 78
Nelson, C., 6
Nietzsche, F., 11, 47, 49, 74

O'Neill, J., 18
Ornish, D., 110–113

Pakulski, J., xiii, 7, 92, 109
Palmer, D., 97
Pater, W., 30
Peters, T., 79
Podhoretz, N., 46
Poe, E. A., 30, 57
Pound, E., 46
Preobrazhensky, E., 130
Probyn, E., 46
Pryke, M., 48
Putney, M. J., 97, 100

Rahv, P., 46
Ransom, J. C., 46
Ray, L., 28
Readings, B., 60
Reagan, R., 36, 45
Resnick, S., 5, 14, 16, 69
Reuther, W., 22–23, 26, 31
Rifkin, J., 18, 52
Robbins, B., xviii
Ronell, A., 37
Roosevelt, D. D., 23
Rorty, R., 46, 109, 131, 140, 148,
Ross, A., xviii
Rossi-Landi, F., 56
Rousseau, J.-J., 83
Ruskin, J., 29

Sahlins, M. 84
Said, E., xv
Sartre, J.-P., 37, 49
Saunders, F. S., 59
Sayer, A., 28
Schmitt, C., 5

Sedgwick, E. K., 28, 108
Shiva, V., 138
Shohat, E., 46
Simmel, G., 70
Skeggs, B., xvii
Slichter, S. H., 26
Sloterdijk, P., 105
Smith, A., 39, 71,73
Smith, G., 117
Spivak, G. C., 14, 75,137,139
Stein, G., 30, 58
Sterne, J., 61
Sterne, L., 57
Strangelove, M., 37

Tate, A., 46
Taussing, M., 131
Thatcher, M., 12, 19, 74
Thompson, P., 38
Thurmond, S., 117
Trilling, L., 46
Trotsky, L., 7
Tyagi, A. W., 91

Ulmer, G., xvi
Urry, J., 69–70

Wanniski, J., 73
Warren, E., 91
Waters, M., xiii, 7, 93, 109
Weber, M., 93
Weinberg, S., 99
White, H., 28
Wilde, O., 30
Winters, Y., 46
Wolff, R., 5, 14, 16–17, 69
Woolf, V., 30, 58
Wordsworth, W., 29, 55

Zavarzadeh, M., xvi, xix, 82
Zizek, S. xxi, 37, 46, 75, 108, 123

About the Authors

Teresa L. Ebert writes on cultural and critical theory. Her books include *Ludic Feminism and After* and *Cultural Critique (with an attitude)*, which will be published next year.

Mas'ud Zavarzadeh has written *Seeing Film Politically* and several other books. His new book, *Totality and the Post,* will be published next fall.